NEW FORMATIONS

PRODUCTION CO-ORDINATION AND ADVERTISEMENTS:
For enquiries/bookings contact Vanna Derosas, Lawrence & Wishart.

SUBSCRIPTIONS:
UK: Institutions £145.00, Individuals £40.
Rest of world: Institutions £145.00; Individuals £40.
Single copies: £14.99 plus £2 post and packing.
Back issues: £14.99 plus £2 post and packing for individuals;
£45 plus £2 post and packing for institutions.
Payments can be made by credit/debit card (no American Express).

CONTRIBUTIONS AND CORRESPONDENCE:
Send to either: The Editor, Jeremy Gilbert, School of Social Sci-
ences, Media and Cultural Studies, University of East London, 4-6
University Way, London E16 2RD, UK, J.Gilbert@uel.ac.uk; or
The Editor, Wendy Wheeler, Faculty of Humanities, Arts, Languages
and Education, London Metropolitan University, 166-220 Holloway
Road, London N7 8DB, UK, w.wheeler@londonmet.ac.uk

BOOKS FOR REVIEW:
Send to: Ben Highmore, Reviews Editor, *new formations*,
EDB University of Sussex, Falmer, Brighton BN1 9RG
B.Highmore@sussex.ac.uk

new formations publishes themed issues, themed sections and discrete
articles. Contributors are encouraged to contact the editors to discuss
their ideas and to obtain a copy of our style sheet, which can also be
obtained on our website at http://www.newformations.co.uk

Manuscripts should be sent in triplicate; experts in the relevant field
will referee them anonymously. The manuscripts will not be returned
unless a stamped, self-addressed envelope is enclosed. Contributors
should note that the editorial board cannot take responsibility for
any manuscript submitted to *new formations*.

ISSN   0 950 237 8
ISBN   9781 907103 124

Printed by MPG Books Group in the UK.

new formations is published three times a year by
Lawrence & Wishart, 99a Wallis Road, London E9 5LN
Tel: 020-8533 2506 Fax: 020-8533 7369
Website: www.lwbooks.co.uk/journals/newformations

Orders and Subscription payments to:
Lawrence and Wishart, PO Box 7701
Latchington, Chelmsford CH3 6WL
landw@btinternet.com

Notes on Contributors

Éric Alliez is Professor of Contemporary French Philosophy at the Centre for Research in Modern European Philosophy, Middlesex University, London. His works include: *Capital Times* (1997); *The Signature of the World: What is Deleuze and Guattari's Philosophy* (2005); *De l'impossibilité de la phénoménologie. Sur la philosophie française contemporaine* (1995); (as editor) *Gilles Deleuze. Une Vie philosophique* (1998); (with J.-Cl. Bonne) *La Pensée-Matisse* (2005); (in collaboration with Jean-Clet Martin) *L'Œil-Cerveau. Nouvelles Histoires de la peinture moderne* (2007). He has been the general editor of the works of Gabriel Tarde, and is a founding member of the journal *Multitudes*, and is currently working on *Défaire l'Image*, the last volume of his 'aesthetic' research programme.

Véronique Bergen is a Belgian philosopher, poet and novelist, the author of many critically-acclaimed works. Her philosophical and critical publications include *Jean Genet entre mythe et réalité* (1993), *L'Ontologie de Gilles Deleuze* (2001) and *Résistances Philosophiques* (2009).

Rosi Braidotti is Distinguished Professor in the Humanities at Utrecht University in the Netherlands, and founding director of the Centre for the Humanities (UU). Her books include: *Patterns of Dissonance* (Polity Press, 1991); *Nomadic Subjects: Embodiment and Sexual Difference in Contemporary Feminist Theory* (Columbia University Press, 1994); *Metamorphoses: Towards a Materialist Theory of Becoming* (Polity Press, 2002); and *Transpositions: On Nomadic Ethics* (Polity Press, 2006).

Jorge Camacho is currently completing a PhD at the School of Humanities and Social Sciences, University of East London. He teaches at the Department of Communication, Universidad Iberoamericana, Ciudad de México, and his current research interests are situated in the crossroads between political philosophy and philosophy of technology, specifically around issues of social power related to the diffusion of new technologies and new media.

Claire Colebrook is Edwin Earl Sparks Professor of Literature at Penn State University. She has published on Gilles Deleuze, feminist theory and literary theory. Her two most recent publications are *Milton Evil and Literary History* (Continuum 2008), and *Deleuze and the Meaning of Life* (Continuum Studies in Continental Philosophy, 2009).

Jeremy Gilbert teaches Cultural Studies at the University of East London. His most recent book is *Anticapitalism and Culture: Radical theory and popular politics* (2008).

Peter Hallward teaches at the Centre for Research in Modern European Philosophy at Middlesex University, and is the author of *Damming the Flood: Haiti and the Politics of Containment* (2007); *Out of this World: Deleuze and the Philosophy of Creation* (2006); *Badiou: A Subject to Truth* (2003); and *Absolutely Postcolonial* (2001). He is currently working on a project entitled 'The Will of the People'.

Patricia MacCormack is Reader in Communication and Film at Anglia Ruskin University, Cambridge. She has published numerous journal articles and chapters on Continental Philosophy, perversion and queer theory, teratology, body modification and horror film. She is the author of *Cinesexuality* (2008); and co-editor of *The Schizoanalysis of Cinema* (2009).

Chrysanthi Nigianni holds a PhD from the University of East London, and has recently joined the thinking-machine of a neo-materialist feminism. Educated in the social sciences - she has a sociology degree from Panteion University (Athens), and an MSc in Sociology from the London School of Economics (LSE) - she then took the turn to philosophy and feminism with the focus being on queer theory, theories of sexuality and continental philosophy. She has taught at the University of East London (London) and at Anglia Ruskin University (UK). She is co-editor of *Deleuze and Queer Theory* (2009).

Katrina Schlunke teaches Cultural Studies at the University of Technology Sydney within the Communications Programme. She is the author of *Bluff Rock: Autobiography of a Massacre*; co-author of *Cultural Theory in Everyday Practice*; and an editor of *Cultural Studies Review*.

Nicholas Thoburn is a lecturer in Sociology at the University of Manchester. He is the author of *Deleuze, Marx and Politics* (Routledge, 2003) and co-editor of *Deleuze and Politics* (Edinburgh University Press, 2008).

new formations is indexed in British Humanities Index, ProQuest CSA, EBSCOhost, Literature Online database (ProQuest CSA), eLibrary database (ProQuest CSA), MLA bibliography, Swetswise, InfoTrac (Thomson Gale), First Search (OCLC)

CONTENTS
NUMBER 68

Deleuzian politics?

EDITORIAL

Jeremy Gilbert and Chrysanthi Nigianni

This issue of *new formations* arises from the extraordinary growth of interest in the work of Gilles Deleuze (in particular, but not exclusively, his work with Félix Guattari) in the English-speaking world in recent years; an explosion which has generated enough heat and light to have attracted the attention even of the notoriously Anglo-indifferent French philosophical scene. In truth, like any event, this 'turn to Deleuze' is not the sudden emergence that it might appear to be, but is the cumulative effect of a long and often piecemeal process of translation, interpretation, appropriation and accommodation. From the earliest translations of fragments of Deleuze & Guattari's work in the 1980s, through the pioneering major translations by scholars such as Brian Massumi and Paul Patton and the experimental take-up of schizoanalysis by groups of researchers in the UK, USA and most notably Australia in the late 1980s and into the 1990s, to the recent establishment of a dedicated English-language journal of Deleuze Studies, the consolidation of a body of interpretation and application of Deleuzian ideas in English has in truth taken several decades, even if it is only recently that this work has become central to the corpus of Anglophone cultural theory.

Given the historic concerns of cultural studies and cultural theorists in the English-speaking world - not least those best represented in the pages of *new formations* - it is perhaps strange that this should have taken so long. Their projects to delineate a fully materialist ontology and a fully social and political theory of the psychic, their attempts to give expression to a politics which is at once libertarian and radically collectivist in its orientation, the radical and militant interdisciplinarity which characterises their work, would all seem to mark out Deleuze & Guattari as natural resources and allies for work in the tradition of cultural studies; much more so than many better-known theoretical sources (Lacan, Althusser, Derrida, even Foucault). The question of why their take-up has been so slow, despite the early advocacy of influential figures such as Lawrence Grossberg, deserves a study in its own right, but that is not our topic here. Rather, we hope to present a range of work which both demonstrates and, occasionally, questions, the usefulness of Deleuzian ideas for addressing key cultural theoretical questions in novel and politically productive ways.

The vast range of subjects upon which Deleuze wrote, and the number of disparate fields within which his ideas have proved influential, would make it quite impossible for any one volume to offer a fully representative picture, so our focus here is primarily on the relevance of Deleuzian ideas for the key motivating concern of *new formations* throughout its history: namely, the

DOI:10.3898/NEWF.68.EDITORIAL.2009

question of the political uses and implications of cultural theory. We do not present Deleuzian politics as a given fact, but rather seek to pose the question of its productive possibility in the current intellectual and political conjuncture. A particular concern of several of our papers is the possible radical implications of Deleuze's thought for a reformulation of sexual politics, and these papers were mostly presented in an initial form at the 'Deleuzian Lines, Queer Flights' conference at the University of East London, October 2005. We suggest that while this is by no means the only political usage of Deleuzian ideas as we enter the second decade of the twenty-first century, sexual politics at this time clearly presents a set of problems and questions which are in desperate need of reformulation and re-radicalisation. The normalisation of liberal feminism seems to mesh every-more tightly today with a neoliberal culture of individualisation, neurotic self-management, unmitigated consumerism, celebrity-fixation and restrictive over-sexualisation; and this is especially, if not exclusively, true for those girls and young women, who seem to have had the range of publicly-desirable modes of being available to them squeezed dramatically in recent times. Where the decades following the emergence of second-wave feminism saw a vast expansion of the freedoms and opportunities available to them, we seem to find ourselves today in a world in which pink princess dresses and celebrity-endorsed glamour define the parameters of normative femininity for girls and young women respectively. At the same time, the deterritorialisation of the twentieth-century family model has in the vast majority of cases only exposed parents and children to different forms of the regulation of desire, as parents work longer hours, while children are exposed to historic levels of advertising (explicit and disguised), and schools are pressured to serve exclusively the needs of the competitive labour market. If a radical and collectivist politics of desire, becoming, and sexual multiplicity were ever needed badly, then they are needed now.

Jeremy Gilbert's introductory contribution sets the scene for the rest of the volume. This piece attempts both to identify the key problematic issues involved in investigating the question of 'Deleuzian politics' and to identify some of the differences and similarities between Deleuzian thought and other traditions which have centrally informed Anglophone cultural theory.

Véronique Bergen's essay explores the most fundamental questions concerning the role of politics in Deleuze's thought, with particular reference to his elaboration of a vitalist ontology. For Bergen, this vitalism both motivates the normative direction of Deleuze's thought and informs its analytical and pragmatic approaches to questions of power, desire and agency.

Rosi Braidotti's article pursues this theme further, addressing a paradox: how to engage in affirmative politics, which entails the production of social horizons of hope, while at the same time doing critical theory, which means resisting the present. Drawing on the neo-vitalism of Deleuze, with reference to Nietzsche and Spinoza, the article argues in favour of an affirmative ethics, defined as a radical ethics of transformation.

Claire Colebrook starts from Deleuze's and Guattari's distinction between passive and active vitalism as set out in their last book, *What is Philosophy?* Her article posits the possibility of a new conceptualisation of political bodies outside notions of individual will, intent and agency: mobilising forces of change from within the act of encountering.

Jorge Camacho explores and evaluates the philosophical and political divergence between Deleuze and Guattari and their recently-influential friend, Antonio Negri: assessing this divergence in the light of the period of revolts and radical political experimentation that broke out in Argentina since 2001. Siding with Deleuze, philosophically and politically, it concludes that the positive outcome of such 'tragic' perspective is a constant concern for launching and re-launching instances of concrete political experimentation.

Patricia MacCormack's essay examines the ways in which Irigaray, Deleuze and Guattari each posit a challenge to phallologocentric paradigms via reconfigurations of enfleshed subjectivity and the deployment of concepts such as multiplicity, fluidity and connectivity. As an experiment in extending and exploring these concepts, while simultaneously attempting to create a fold between the theories, this article offers the idea of 'becoming-vulva'.

Chrysanthi Nigianni's essay begins from the argument that Deleuze's method of 'transcendental empiricism' requires a shift in the way we conceptualise both 'ethics' and 'politics'. This shift is examined in relation to the cinematic thinking of the film *Breaking the Waves*, since the latter problematises established ideas of what an ethics of (sexual) difference might be, as well as received political values tied to modern individualism, such as freedom, autonomy, and reason.

Nicholas Thoburn's paper is a critique of the political figure of the militant. In particular it seeks to understand the ways militancy effectuates processes of political passion and a certain unworking or deterritorialisation of the self in relation to political organisations and the wider social environment within which militants would enact change.

Finally, our round-table presents a discussion between four leading commentators on 'Deleuzian politics'. Éric Alliez, one of the world's leading exponents of Deleuze's and Guattari's work, and the author of such major works as *Capital Times: Tales from the conquest of time* and *The Signature of the World: What is Deleuze and Guattari's philosophy?* joins Peter Hallward - Deleuze's most prominent critic in the English-speaking world and author of *Out of this World: Deleuze and the philosophy of creation* - and our contributors Claire Colebrook and Nicholas Thoburn, for a riveting discussion of the philosophical, ethical and political issues at stake in any elaboration or critique of Deleuze's thought.

DELEUZIAN POLITICS?
A SURVEY AND SOME SUGGESTIONS

Jeremy Gilbert

1. Gilles Deleuze, *Negotiations*, Martin Joughin (trans.), New York, Columbia University Press, 1995, p171.

2. Gilles Deleuze and Félix Guattari, *Anti-Oedipus*, Robert Hurley, Mark Seem and Robert R. Lane (trans.), Minneapolis, University of Minnesota Press, 1983, p380.

3. As Claire Colebrook points out in the round-table included in this issue, even Deleuze's early interest in David Hume has political implications; on the other hand, even the last book signed by both Deleuze and Guattari - *What is Philosophy*, Graham Burchell and Hugh Tomlinson (trans.), London, Verso - is at best ambivalent about the very possibility of politics, with its praise for 'artistocratic' writers and its express contempt for democracy (p108) and its appeal to a vitalism which is explicitly 'passive' in character (p213).

4. Peter Hallward, *Out of this World: Deleuze and the Philosophy of Creation*, London, Verso, 2006; Phillipe Mengue, *Deleuze et la question de la democratie* [Deleuze and the Question of Democracy], Paris, L'Harmattan, 2003.

5. Ibid., p72.

DELEUZIAN POLITICS?

Gilles Deleuze famously described his work with Félix Guattari as 'political philosophy'.[1] And yet, the first and most explicitly revolutionary volume of their jointly-authored ouevre also insists that 'no political programme will be elaborated within the framework of schizoanalysis'.[2] From the outset, then, even the most apparently 'political' element of Deleuze's work contains an apparent ambiguity: is this is a political project or not? Could there be a 'Deleuzian politics' at all?

Any thorough engagement with the totality of Deleuze's work is only likely to leave the inquirer more perplexed than ever as to how to answer this question, as both political and dramatically anti-political gestures proliferate throughout that work from beginning to end.[3] At least two major studies of Deleuze's work - one in English, the other in French - have, within the past five years, concluded that the answer to these questions is simply 'no': Deleuze is a mystic, a nostalgist for elitist modes of avant-gardism which have no purchase on the present, at best an implicit conservative whose romanticism leaves no scope for rational calculation or collective action.[4]

If they are to remain credible, it is important that such studies refrain from placing simplistic and inappropriate demands on any given philosophical system. After all, why should such a system generate a singular and determinate 'politics'? Even Marx and Engels' work did not do so, as is attested by the disparate range of political theories to which their historical, philosophical, social and economic analyses gave rise, from Lenin to Bernstein to Luxemburg to Gramsci to Mao and beyond. So another way of posing the question of 'Deleuzian politics' might be to ask whether there is any form of political action or expression which could not find some justification in the broad metaphysical and analytical framework elaborated by Deleuze (with and without Guattari). Does this 'system' set any limits at all to its possible forms of political expression? Part of the value of the studies by Peter Hallward and Phillipe Mengue is that they try to address this question, although their conclusions are different and in both cases contentious. For Mengue, Deleuze's anti-populist distaste for democracy, debate and the free play of opinions proves an irreducible obstacle to the realisation of the radical/liberal democratic position that he sees as the only logical implication of Deleuze's most fundamental ethical and aesthetic priorities:[5] so Deleuze cannot embrace

DOI:10.3898/NEWF.68.01.2009

democracy, with its pluralistic production of what Mengue calls 'the doxic plane of immanence'[6] - the domain of the endless creation, contestation, emergence and dissipation of opinion - even though his philosophical points of reference ought to lead him towards a radical liberal embrace of just this phenomenon. For Hallward, Deleuze's emphasis on the value of the singular and the virtual - of becoming and 'creatings' over being and 'creatures' - ultimately forecloses the possibility of any thought of relationality, and as such of any thought of politics at all.[7] From this perspective, what is excluded from Deleuze's system is the possibility of any determinate political decision whatsoever.[8]

However, despite the persuasiveness and scholarship which characterises both of these books, they do both tend to deploy a rather narrow understanding of what 'Deleuzian politics' might mean in order to criticise this hypothetical entity. In addressing themselves to Deleuze's work rather as if it could be expected to deliver up a coherent system of values, consequent aims, and appropriate strategies - and in emphasising the distinctive normative preferences expressed in Deleuze's writing - they both tend to downplay the aspect of Deleuze's thought which has most excited those commentators who have seen in it a rich source of analytical concepts for twenty-first century political theory. For such commentators, it has been Deleuze's capacity to shed new light on contemporary relations of power - irrespective of any inferences that can be made about his own political perspectives - which is of the greatest importance. So neither Hallward nor Mengue really gives any attention to the question of whether the analytical resources offered by Deleuze's work - especially, but not exclusively, that written with Guattari - might be deployed from a range of political perspectives not necessarily limited to those which would seem to receive some explicit endorsement within it. This is not to say that either Hallward or Mengue themselves necessarily ought to have attended to this issue, but it does raise it as an interesting question for us to consider.

Distinguishing between the normative and descriptive elements of any theory is never easy, because implicit norms will always govern descriptions, while the presumed accuracy of implicit descriptions of the world will always inform the delineation of norms. It is not my intention here to propose any final separability of Deleuze's normative positions from his descriptive ones, but it is certainly worthy of note that, particularly in Capitalism and Schizophrenia,[9] there is a degree of tension and ambiguity, even some marked shifts at times, around the categorical status of some of Deleuze's key terms. Within the first few pages of A Thousand Plateaus, for example, 'rhizome' and 'rhizomatic' go from being positively marked terms of approbation for all types of networked, lateral, polyvalent, polycentric relation[10] to being descriptive terms for a particular aspect of given sets of relations: rather than distinguishing beloved 'rhizomes' from hated 'trees', as Deleuze and Guattari are often assumed to, this essay actually posits a rhizomatic and an arborescent dimension to all sets of relations.[11] This move is quite typical, and it only makes the ultimate assessment

6. Ibid., p52.

7. Hallward, op. cit., p152.

8. Ibid., p136-9.

9. *Anti-Oedipus* and *A Thousand Plateaus* were conceived by Deleuze and Guattari as two volumes of a single work of which this is the title.

10. Gilles Deleuze and Félix Guattari, *A Thousand Plateaus*, Brian Massumi (trans.), London, Athlone, 1988, pp3-12.

11. Ibid., p20.

of the political valency of Deleuze's work all the more difficult, appearing as it does to leave open the question of whether it might be possible to find the rhizome/tree distinction analytically useful, without being committed to the implicit anarchism of the initial exposition of the concept.

Perhaps this is a false conundrum. Like Derrida, Deleuze often emphasises the value and importance of aspects of existence - fluidity, horizontality, complexity, etc - which the philosophical tradition has tended to marginalise, but this need not be understood as an exclusive valorisation of those aspects in all possible contexts. John Protevi has proposed that the normative orientation of all of Deleuze's philosophy should be understood in terms of its preference for whatever promotes 'joyous affect' at any conceivable level of existence, and it is hard to find any evidence in the entire Deleuzian corpus with which to refute this very helpful formulation. This hypothesis leaves us, for example, with a relatively straightforward answer to the question of whether or not to prefer 'rhizomes' to 'trees'. From this perspective, the answer would be that rhizomes are only preferable to trees to the extent that they are more likely than trees to promote joyous affect. Of course, this leaves open the question of how one knows joyous affect when one sees it, and the very strong assumptions which Deleuze tends to make in implicitly answering it.

Protevi defines joyous affect as that which increases the potential power of bodies, enabling them 'to form new and potentially empowering encounters'.[12] Véronique Bergen's recent *Résistances Philosophiques* [*Philosophical Resistances*][13] (an intriguing and rigorous interrogation of the concepts of political resistance generated by the philosophies of Sartre, Badiou and Deleuze respectively) offers a useful summary with which to fill out Protevi's formulation when she argues that 'understanding being and thought in terms of flux, in terms of forces rather than names, Deleuze's vitalist ontology posits resistance as the position which an assemblage adopts in order to defend and augment its powers of life'.[14] For Deleuze, joy is that which enhances the 'powers of life', and as such is always understood in terms of becoming: mutability, movement and change, while any analytical assumptions as to the fixity of given categories or identity must always be overcome in the pursuit of it. If there is one clear set of emphases in Deleuze's work which express identifiable and consistent normative preferences while also generating distinctively new descriptive concepts, it surely lies in Deleuze's persistent interest in the mutable, the multiple, the changeable, the mobile; and his consonant effort to overcome any overvaluation of the static, the enduring and the fixed. In fact, this theme in Deleuze's work is precisely that drawn out in important contributions to this collection by two leading Deleuze scholar Claire Colebrook and Rosi Braidotti.

VERSIONS OF ANTI-ESSENTIALISM: DELEUZE, DELANDA AND LACLAU

This emphasis on the value of mutability will hardly sound like a radical or unfamiliar trope to readers familiar with the milieu and recent history of

12. John Protevi, *Political Affect: Connecting the Social and the Somatic*, Minneapolis, University of Minnesota Press, 2009, p51.

13. Paris, Presse Universitaire de France, 2009.

14. Ibid., p72.

Anglophone cultural theory. The general assumption as to the social and historical contingency of forms of social being (or 'identity') is surely the key conceptual reference point for an entire area of thought and discussion which includes much of postcolonial studies, studies in gender, sexuality and ethnicity, cultural studies and cultural theory more broadly. This assumption is given various names by both critics and defenders: 'social constructionism', 'historicism' and 'anti-essentialism' being perhaps the most common. It is frustrating but important for any attempt to map this terrain to realise that every one of these terms has quite different usages in different historical moments and intellectual contexts, and that critics and supporters of the hypothetical positions which they designate tend to make assumptions about what they imply for others which are not always accurate. Even while some of its most prominent exponents set out some time ago to problematise the implications of any simplistically voluntaristic or individualist 'anti-essentialism',[15] even while its most commercially successful representative has historically defined himself in opposition to 'historicism',[16] some version of this perspective remains arguably the definitive characteristic of almost all cultural theory. So does Deleuze offer anything new to this already noisy and long-running set of debates?

This question can only be posed in such a way from the perspective of a certain Anglophone history of ideas. Though there has been considerable catch-up of late, the relative paucity of texts dedicated to Deleuze - in comparison to, say, Derrida[17] - in English to date is indicative of the lateness with which he has been taken up widely by an English-reading audience; but there is little question that it was Deleuze who was one of they key figures to inaugurate the entire phase of French philosophy within which this emphasis on change, self-difference and instability would come to be seen as hallmarks of almost all contemporary thought.[18] Nonetheless, the present context is one in which approaches derived from deconstruction and 'post-structuralism' more broadly are still more familiar to most scholars, and have been established for far longer, than approaches derived from Deleuze, so it is legitimate to consider the latter with reference to the former in order to draw out what is distinctive to them. One way of doing this is to consider precisely one of the terms mentioned above as it has been deployed in certain key texts of both post-structuralist and Anglophone Deleuzian theory: 'anti-essentialism'.

Although the terms 'essentialism' and 'anti-essentialism' have come to be used most frequently to designate ways of understanding the relative contingency of social identities, particularly after the debates around 'identity politics' in the second half of the 1980s,[19] the terms were used in an immediately prior moment to refer more specifically to ideas concerning the relative contingency of the relationships obtaining between different elements of a social formation. The classic discussion of the relationship between these slightly different understandings of essentialism is to be found in Laclau and Mouffe's *Hegemony and Socialist Strategy*,[20] which developed an

15. See, for example, Paul Gilroy, *The Black Atlantic*, London, Verso, 1993; Gayatri Spivak, *In Other Worlds*, New York, Routledge, 1987.

16. Slavok Zizek, *The Sublime Object of Ideology*, London, Verso, 1989.

17. As of December 2009, Amazon.com and Amazon.co.uk each feature approximately twice as many titles on or about Derrida as Deleuze. By contrast, the figures for Francophone books, on Amazon.fr, are very nearly equal for the two philosophers, with slightly more on or about Deleuze than Derrida.

18. See Vincent Descombes, *Modern French Philosophy*, Cambridge, University of Cambridge Press, 1980.

19. See, for example, Judith Butler, *Gender Trouble*, New York, Routledge, 1990; Kobena Mercer, *Welcome to the Jungle*, London, Routledge, 1994.

20. London, Verso, 1985.

influential approach motivated by a commitment to the radically contingent, non-necessary and relational character of social and political identities, a commitment subtended by a similar understanding of all social formations as similarly contingent and historically specific.

Over the years this position has been charged with idealism, with ignoring historical constraints (especially economic constraints) on the formation and behaviour of political subjects and institutions, and even with denying the existence of mind-independent reality.[21] The tone of these criticisms is probably motivated less by Laclau and Mouffe's insistence on the radical contingency of social relations and identities, than by the conceptual and methodological innovation which they propose for the mapping of such radically contingent formations. Broadly speaking, this move involves explicitly abandoning any distinction between immaterial 'thought' and material 'reality', as the consequence of a rejection of any distinction between discursive and non-discursive practices.[22] Laclau and Mouffe justify this move through a meticulous argument which draws primarily on Derrida's early claim that in the absence of any final principle of meaning or identity outside of a field of contingent relations which can guarantee the consistency, order, finitude and finality of that field - in other words, in the absence of a 'transcendental signified'[23] - the general field of relationality for which 'discourse' is one name cannot be easily delimited. This is a complex manoeuvre in both Derrida and Laclau and Mouffe, and in both cases it has generated a great deal of misunderstanding on the part of readers who have understood their statements to amount to an insistence that there is no other reality than language; in fact, they would be better understood as claims that there is no social practice that is not caught up in a network of unpredictable relations which destabilises its effects and significance, much as the effect and significance of linguistic signs is always destabilised by their irreducible relationality.

This partial misreading of Laclau and Mouffe is given some further impetus by their claim that the most important immediate consequence of abandoning the distinction between discourse and the extra-discursive is that this move legitimates the deployment of linguistic and rhetorical categories as categories of socio-political analysis. From this point of view, for example, 'Synonymy, metonymy, metaphor are not forms of thought that add a second sense to a primary, constitutive literality of social relations, instead they are part of the primary terrain itself in which the social is constituted'.[24] Discourse analysis, of a certain kind, therefore becomes a model for social and political analysis in general. It is worth keeping in mind that this move is fully consonant with Laclau and Mouffe's other fundamental operation, that of modelling the relationality of social relations directly on the relationality obtaining between linguistic signs in Saussure's schema.[25] Logics which were previously confined to the analysis of linguistic phenomena are now understood to be appropriate to the analysis of social phenomena more broadly. It is very important to understand, however, that this argument does

21. See, for example, Jonathan Joseph, *Hegemony: A Realist Analysis*, London, Routledge, 2002, pp111-3.

22. Laclau and Mouffe, op. cit., pp107-10.

23. Jacques Derrida, *Of Grammatology*, Gayatri Spivak (trans.), Baltimore, John Hopkins University Press, 1974, p49.

24. Laclau and Mouffe, op. cit., p110.

25. See Ferdinand de Saussure, *Course in General Linguistics*, Roy Harris (trans.), London, Duckworth, 1983.

not proceed from any refutation of the materiality of those social phenomena. In fact, the reverse is true: Laclau and Mouffe predicate their argument on the presumed materiality of all phenomena, including language.[26] Indeed, we might say that the ultimate claim made by Laclau and Mouffe here is that materiality itself can be understood to operate according to logics previously thought to be only operable in the domain of language (this is certainly the conclusion drawn by Judith Butler at the moment of her greatest intellectual proximity to Laclau and Mouffe[27]).

It is interesting then to contrast Laclau and Mouffe's 'anti-essentialism' with that of a leading Anglophone Deleuzian, who explicitly situates his work in opposition to the perceived trends towards 'idealism' of which Laclau and Mouffe are often thought typical. Manuel DeLanda has set out his position in a number of recent works: most concisely in his contribution to Buchanan and Thoburn's important edited collection, *Deleuze and Politics*.[28] Maintaining a rigorously 'realist' insistence on the separation between both thought and reality and between the discursive and the extra-discursive, DeLanda makes the usual 'realist' elision between refusing these distinctions and assuming that 'the world is a product of our minds'.[29] The latter is certainly not a claim that either Derrida or Laclau and Mouffe would make, and does not necessarily follow from a refusal of the distinction between the discursive and the extra-discursive or of the legitimacy of transcendental signifieds.

Nevertheless DeLanda offers a perspective which contrasts and overlaps in interesting ways with that of Laclau and Mouffe. In his most extensive elaboration of this perspective, DeLanda identifies the consonance between Deleuze's metaphysics and recent innovations in non-linear science, and understands the latter as itself inimical to any form of 'essentialism'.[30] 'Essentialism' is here understood in terms of its classical origins in Platonic and related schools of philosophy, which understand all individuated entities as the expression of an unchanging and ahistorical 'essence'. What DeLanda derives from Deleuze and from complexity science is an understanding of even the most mundane physical objects as never really in a state of absolute stasis, or exemplars of an unchanging, pre-existing pattern, but as the outcome of complex, contingent and often unpredictable processes of individuation. The model of such individuating processes which might be familiar to most readers would be the evolution of species by natural selection. Where pre-Darwinian systems of zoological classification tended to understand species as unchanging, and individual creatures as variants of an identifiable norm, evolutionary theory understands populations to be in a state of constant variation, each individual the outcome of a complex set of interactions between multiple variables. It is from this kind of scientific understanding of individuation and variability that DeLanda's 'anti-essentialism' derives, rather than from an account of the relationality of identities at any given moment; these are not necessarily incompatible approaches, as we will see, but the general emphasis is quite different.

DeLanda's recent work has been at pains to identify those processes

26. Ernesto Laclau, *New Reflections on the Revolution of Our Time*, London, Verso, 1990, pp105-7.

27. Judith Butler, *Bodies that Matter*, New York, Verso, 1993.

28. Manuel DeLanda, 'Deleuze Materialism and Politics' in Ian Buchanan and Nicholas Thoburn (eds), *Deleuze and Politics*, Edinburgh, Edinburgh University Press, 2008.

29. Ibid., p160.

30. Manuel DeLanda, *Intensive Science and Virtual Philosophy*, London, Continuum, 2002, pp9-41.

31. Manuel
DeLanda, *A New
Philosophy of
Society: Assemblage
Theory and Social
Complexity*, London,
Continuum, 2006.

32. Gilles Deleuze,
Dialogues, Hugh
Tomlinson (trans.),
New York, Columbia
University Press,
1987, p25.

33. Deleuze
and Guattari, *A
Thousand Plateaus*,
op. cit., pp39-74;
DeLanda 'Deleuze,
Materialism and
Politics', op. cit.

34. See, for example,
A Thousand Plateaus,
op. cit., p4.

35. Jacques Derrida,
'White Mythology:
metaphor in the text
of philosophy', in
Margins of Philosophy,
Hemel Hempstead,
Harvester
Wheatsheaf, 1982.

36. DeLanda, op. cit.

37. Foucault
deploys the concept
of 'discursive
formation' rather
differently from
Laclau and
Mouffe, with
explicit reference
to the existence
of discursive and
non-discursive
forces; but his
initial deployment
of the terms in
*The Archaeology of
Knowledge* was clearly
aimed at finding
a non-essentialist
language with
which to discuss
the history of ideas,
which he could not
find in pre-existing
vocabularies derived
from Marxism,
structuralism or
psychoanalysis.

which can be clearly identified as at work in the emergence, formation and persistence of social entities,[31] and in this we might see an expression of his own rigorous 'realism'. DeLanda's own interpretations and revisions of Deleuze and Guattari have all tended to reduce the role played by those terms and concepts which seem to have largely metaphorical or analogical value as descriptions of social phenomena. Deleuze and Guattari, by contrast, while claiming that their concepts were not 'metaphors',[32] borrowed terminologies and ideas from a range of scientific sources, transposing them into the field of social relations in a manner which is clearly as metaphorical (or non-metaphorical) as Laclau's transposition of terms from rhetoric and linguistics. The example which DeLanda himself cites most recently is the complex language of sedimentation, stratification and 'double articulation' which they borrow from geology and elevate into a language for the description of almost any aspect of social or physical reality.[33] Certainly this move has great descriptive potential, enabling the analyst to understand a whole range of interconnected social, economic, cultural and environmental phenomena in terms of a similar set of categories (degrees of rigidity and fluidity, levels and degrees of stratification). It is not clear that it has any greater claim to realism than does Laclau and Mouffe's expansion of the categories of rhetoric, however. The point here is that the persistent claims made by Deleuzian advocates that their approach is more 'realist' or 'materialist' than those 'post-structuralist' approaches of which Laclau and Mouffe are typical are not well-founded, even while DeLanda may well have some such claim for his own interpretations of Deleuze. In fact, in *Intensive Science and Virtual Philosophy*, DeLanda explicitly aims to work against the acknowledged metaphoricity of key Deleuzian concepts. Neither DeLanda nor any other commentator that I know of has properly explored the implications for Deleuze's own explicit rejection of notions of metaphor and 'signification'[34] *tout court* of Derrida's complex problematisation of metaphoricity as such.[35]

Leaving this question aside, DeLanda's work does seem to be motivated by a strikingly similar set of objectives to Laclau and Mouffe's. In his most recent book, he explicitly mobilises the Deleuzo-Guattarian concept of 'assemblages' 'against essences'.[36] In effect, the work that DeLanda sees this concept as doing is very similar to the work done by the concept of 'social formation' or 'discursive formation' for writers such as Laclau and Mouffe and Foucault;[37] it is also the outcome of a similar intellectual trajectory to that which Laclau and Mouffe see as enabling the concept of hegemony to emerge within the Marxist lexicon of the early twentieth century.[38] In all cases, a language is sought (or is seen as being sought) which can capture adequately the historically contingent, non-necessary and ultimately mutable nature of the precise configurations of relationships making up existing social entities. This is the basis for Laclau and Mouffe's deconstruction of that class essentialism which understands social classes as the inevitable and only collective agents of historical change.[39] It is interesting to compare and contrast this terminology with DeLanda's when he sets himself against the 'social essentialism' which he believes 'social constructivism' to be guilty of when it asserts that 'only the contents of experience really exist'.[40] As we have already seen, at least in the case of Laclau and Mouffe, it is a chimera to attribute any such hypothesis to them. Far more central to their arguments, ironically, has been the assertion - entirely consonant with DeLanda's approach - that 'society' does not exist in the sense of a clearly bounded and knowable totality.[41]

For Laclau and Mouffe, as for DeLanda, it is the heterogeneity, multiplicity and relatively incoherent nature of social formations which must always be stressed, because it is only on the basis of such an understanding that effective strategies can be enacted for democratic social change.

It is also only on the basis of such an understanding of the precariousness and fluidity of social relations that the crucial roles played by those elements which do succeed in temporarily stabilising social formations can be fully appreciated. Here these two sets of positions would tend to diverge. Whether Laclau and Mouffe's conception of hegemony is potentially compatible with a schizoanalytic framework is an open question (although I have argued that it is[42]), but it is certainly true that other elements of Laclau and Mouffe's model of the social run in quite different directions from anything derived from Deleuze. This is true particularly insofar as Laclau and Mouffe rely on a set of Lacanian terms, concepts and presuppositions which understand social formations to be temporarily held in place by identifications with 'empty signifiers' which necessarily stand in for an unfulfillable desire for the 'absent fullness' which is said to haunt all social formations.[43] A Deleuzian perspective would certainly acknowledge that some social formations operate according to such a logic, but arguably the entire project of Capitalism and Schizophrenia is to demonstrate that not all do or must. This observation might be the basis for a Deleuzian departure from Laclau and Mouffe, which would understand their conception of the mechanics by which social formations are constituted as simply too limited to encompass the full range of human (and non-human) experience; or it might be the basis for a creative engagement between these different sets of positions. This is not a point for us to resolve here, but it still is striking to note just how resonant these two sets of approaches are, each keen to distinguish itself from its Marxist antecedents in remarkably similar ways.

ABSTRACT SEX AND THE VISCOSITY OF RACE

These points of difference as well as similarity between Deleuzian and post-structuralist approaches become more marked when we move from the terrain of general political and social theory to that of specific debates in cultural theory. In particular, some notable contributions of recent years have broken new ground in the theorisation of gender and race respectively.

Anglophone feminist theory has been entering into productive relationships with the thought of Deleuze and Guattari, at least since the early 1990s,[44] when Rosi Braidotti began her influential exploration of the feminist potential of 'nomadology'[45] and Elizabeth Grosz's *Volatile Bodies* posited Deleuze and

38. *Hegemony and Socialist Strategy*, op. cit., pp47-91.

39. Ibid., p190.

40. DeLanda, *A New Philosophy of Society*, op. cit., pp45-6.

41. *Hegemony and Socialist Strategy*, op. cit., pp93-145.

42. Jeremy Gilbert, *Anticapitalism and Culture*, Oxford, Berg, 2008.

43. See, for example, Ernesto Laclau, *Emancipations*, London, Verso, 1996, p42; Chantal Mouffe, *The Democratic Paradox*, London, Verso, 2000.

44. For an even earlier commentary, see Alice Jardine 'Woman in Limbo: Deleuze and His Br(others)', *SubStance*, Vol. 13, No. ¾, Issue 44-45.

45. Rosi Braidotti, *Nomadic Subjects: Embodiment and Sexual Difference in Contemporary Feminist Theory*, New York, Columbia University Press, 1994.

46. Elizabeth Grosz, *Volatile Bodies: Towards a Corporeal Feminism*, Bloomington, Indiana University Press.

47. Ibid., p162.

48. *A Thousand Plateaus*, op. cit., p277.

Guattari as a source in the elaboration of her 'corporeal feminism'.[46] The attractions of Deleuze and Guattari for an anti-essentialist feminism are quite obvious, given their commitment to a position which affirms the multiple capacities of bodies to act in an unlimited number of possible relationships with other bodies, and their refusal of all established norms. In fact, despite the reluctance to take them up which Grosz identified amongst a range of feminist theorists,[47] Deleuze and Guattari's feminism is arguably one of the most clearly stated and unproblematic political positions which they adopt. Their claim that 'all becomings pass through a becoming-woman'[48] has been much fretted-over, but it is easy enough to understand this statement when placed in the context of the wider discussion in *A Thousand Plateaus*. At this point in their argument, the idea of 'becoming' has been clearly associated with the line of flight or deterritorialisation which destabilises fixed norms and identities, and in particular those 'major' identities which express a relation of power between one group, term or entity and various others ('minorities': which are so defined not in numerical terms but in terms of the power differentials between them and the 'majorities', and in terms of the presumed creative superiority of the 'minor'). In this particular section of the book, their privileged figures of 'becoming' are 'becoming-child', 'becoming-animal' and 'becoming-woman'. What each of these figures have in common is that they mark precisely the three things against which the identity of the normative 'Man' of Western imagination has been traditionally defined. To be a man in this context is precisely to be neither child, animal nor woman. Now, particularly to pick out 'becoming-woman' from among these three tropes is merely to repeat the commonplace feminist observation that the feminine is particularly abjected within the terms of patriarchal culture, to the point where normality and masculinity are themselves closely interwoven concepts.[49] As such, any destabilisation of normality involves a swerve in the opposite direction from masculinity, understood as the standard of normality as such. Moving on from this observation, Deleuze and Guattari anticipate much of the debate over 'essentialism' within 1980s feminist theory when they endorse the need for the women's movement to create a 'molar' identity for 'Women',[50] but argue that this should only be a staging post on the way to the general dispersal of sexuality and desire into a proliferation of creative possibilities.[51]

49. An excellent clarification of this position can be found in Félix Guattari, *Soft Subversions*, Chet Wiener and Emily Whitman (trans.), Los Angeles, Semiotext(e), 2009, p143.

50. Ibid., p276.

51. Ibid., p277.

The relevance of Deleuze and Guattari to the concerns of queer theory and anti-essentialist feminism should be very clear here, but it is striking that the key figure who has set the terms of debate in these fields in recent years - Judith Butler - has not made any substantial engagement with them. Indeed, the emergence of a post-Deleuzian 'corporeal feminism' might be seen as an alternative current to that which has been informed by Butler's work, pursuing a line of inquiry which Butler herself hinted at in arguably her most conceptually ambitious work, *Bodies that Matter*,[52] but has really not followed through at all. Butler's suggestion that materiality as such, might be understood as the product of iterative social practices (which would be 'discursive', but not immaterial,

52. Op. cit.

in nature), as the effect of sedimented and continuously-reproduced power relations, is intriguing and persuasive, and has helped many of us to think through some critical questions around the politicality of corporeal experience; but it clearly raises more questions than it answers. What are the mechanisms by which materiality is so produced? How do they relate to biological, geophysical, thermodynamic or biochemical processes? What concept of 'power' makes it possible to understand the relationships between these different orders of process? It is not a criticism of Butler to observe that she has not pursued these particular questions (she has been, without question, busy and productive in the ensuing period). But while Butler has never addressed herself to them, it should be clear already from the foregoing discussion why Deleuze and Guattari should have become key resources for those who have attempted to do so. What is particularly interesting to note from the point of view of our specific concerns in this essay, is that Laclau and Mouffe also arguably made similarly tantalising forays into the theorisation of materiality in the early 1990s, with their subtle and complex discussion of the relationship between materiality and ideality,[53] before going on to pursue quite different lines of inquiry in subsequent work.

In this context, Deleuzian feminist and queer theory have developed very fruitful lines of research, alongside the continued popularity of post-structuralist approaches.[54] Luciana Parisi's *Abstract Sex*,[55] for example, develops the schizoanalytic critique of familialism and of the sexualisation of desire in the light of the work of the radical biologist Lynn Margulis, arguing for a position which recognises the constitutive role of endosymbiositic processes (whereby new modes of interdependence emerge between previously distinct organisms) in the emergence of cellular life. Parisi thus problematises both ordinary biological assumptions about the primacy of sexual reproduction to the formation of life, and the ordinary assumption that 'sex' as such is merely functional to such reproductive processes. Closer to the traditional concerns of Anglophone cultural theory, there clearly remains a great deal of potential for feminist cultural analysis in the deployment of a Deleuzian perspective. For example, the debate over the status of young women as creative agents of the consumer economy or as victims of an hyper-sexualised culture of competition and insecurity[56] could surely derive a great deal from the schizoanalytic perspective, capable as it is of appreciating both the radical force of that positive desire which might find expression in activities as mundane as shopping or dancing, and the insidiousness of those mechanisms of 'capture' and 'territorialisation' which would limit such desire to only such limited forms of expression. More than anything, however, the potential fecundity of post-Deleuzian feminism is indicated by the rich and varied work which it has already begun to produce: arguably the most successful and well-developed branch of Anglophone post-Deleuzian theory, we are delighted to include in this volume several contributions from both leading and emerging figures in this field: Rosi Braidotti, Claire Colebrook, Chrysanthi Nigianni and Patricia MacCormack.

53. Laclau, *New Reflections on the Revolution of Our Time*, op. cit., pp 97-130.

54. See, for example, Camilla Griggers, *Becoming Woman*, Minneapolis, University of Minnesota Press, 1997; Janell Watson and Claire Colebrook (eds), *Women: A Cultural Review*, special issue on Guattari and Gender, 16.3 (Winter 2005-2006); Chrysanthi Nigianni and Merl Storr (eds) *Deleuze and Queer Theory*, Edinburgh, Edinburgh University Press, 2009.

55. Luciana Parisi, *Abstract Sex: Philosophy, Biotechnology and the Mutations of Desire*, London, Continuum, 2004.

56. See, for example, Angela McRobbie, *The Aftermath of Feminism*, London, Sage, 2008.

57. http://www.
darkmatter101.org/
site/category/journal/
issues/race-matter/.

58. Minneapolis,
University of
Minnesota Press,
2007.

59. Ibid., p60.

60. Many similar
insights appear in
Sara Thornton's
Bourdieuian study,
*Club Cultures: Music,
Media and Subcultural
Capital*, Cambridge,
Polity, 1995.

61. The 'Black
Atlantic' is Paul
Gilroy's phrase: see
Gilroy *The Black
Atlantic*, London,
Verso, 1993. For
discussions of
some of the music
mentioned here
from a related 'Afro-
Futurist' perspective,
see Kodwo Eshun,
*More Brilliant than
the Sun*, London,
Serpent's Tail, 1998.

A less well-developed, but clearly emergent, area of research is in Deleuzian studies of race, most notably represented by a special issue of the online journal *darkmatter*[57] and by Arun Saldhana's book *Psychedelic White: Goa Trance and the Viscosities of Race*.[58] Although this book frames its arguments in terms of a typically reductive account of what 'representational' theorists of race have actually said (as if Hall, Gilroy et al have been unaware of the importance of issues of materiality, spatiality, and what is increasingly called, after Foucault, 'biopower'), it also shows the fruitfulness of applying a schizoanalytic perspective to an actual scene of highly complex power relations. Saldhana's emphasis is on race, in particular whiteness, as a lived reality and as a source of pleasures and potentialities as well as as an object of discourse. His study of the finely-grained processes of exclusion and inclusion at work on the Goa trance scene, which saw Japanese ravers included as 'white' while Indian tourists were not, persuasively posits race as a 'viscous' process, following logics of coagulation, dispersal and relative consolidation in very particular contexts; and it deploys a range of Deleuzian terminologies in a largely illuminating way, although at times his excavation of the white privilege of 'being stoned and trippy',[59] and his reduction of sonic and psychedelic experiences to expressions thereof, does feel rather like a Bourdieuan study of habitus and social distinction that has been forced into a 'Deleuzian' box.[60] Saldhana's ambivalence - which is never merely condemnatory - about the insularity and exclusivity of the Goa trance scene is more than understandable, but we perhaps here encounter something of the limit of a method which applies Deleuzian terminologies while remaining resolutely ambivalent about Deleuzian ethical, aesthetic and affective priorities. From the point of view of the latter, it is surely not enough simply to posit Goa trance as the logical conclusion of the experiments with psychedelic culture which peppered the late twentieth century. Some of the most productive and lastingly influential formal innovations in late-twentieth century music arose from the encounter between this tradition and key agents of the 'Black Atlantic': Miles Davis, Sun Ra, George Clinton, Jimi Hendrix, Lee Perry, Larry Levan, etc.[61] So-called 'psy-trance' is notorious amongst followers of other musical styles (and other strands of psychedelic culture) for the intense 'whiteness' of both its sonic forms - which eschew all allusion to the histories of funk, disco, and jazz - and its audiences, and could thus be read as an apparatus of capture of the psychedelic 'war machine', rather than as its final destination. It is surely just this kind of judgement which a schizoanalytic would both enable and demand of a phenomenon like this one.

POLITICS, CAPITAL AND THE STATE

While all of these works are excellent examples of new research informed directly by Deleuzian philosophy pursuing clearly political agendas, most recently-published work in both French and English addresses the question of 'Deleuzian politics' in a somewhat more speculative fashion and at a somewhat higher level of generality. It is worth noting at this stage that there is a well-established current of research in France which treats Deleuze and Guattari's 'schizoanalysis' as a more-or-less clearly defined research programme, and which works to extend its insights into a range of contemporary political, philosophical and cultural questions. This is probably best represented by the ongoing publication of the journal founded by Deleuze and Guattari in the late 1980s, *Chimères* (*Chimaeras*), which rather resembles a Deleuzo-Guattarian version of such left-leaning generalist journals as *Soundings* in the UK and Public Culture in the US. The schizoanalytic intellectual scene has been markedly invigorated by the arrival of another journal in recent years - *Multitudes*, launched in the wake of the success of Hardt and Negri's *Empire*, although the theoretical orientation of its contributors is very often closer to Deleuze, Guattari or Foucault than to Negri. The positions and key personnel of this journal mark it out, like Hardt and Negri's own shared project, as in part a product of and a contribution to the long historical dialogue between Italian autonomism and schizoanalysis, a dialogue which has come to define the orientation of some of the most thoughtful examinations of the relationship between Deleuze's thought and Marxism in recent years.[62] Indeed, the position taken by Thoburn, a contributor to this issue, in his *Deleuze, Marx and Politics*, is that a fundamental compatibility can be identified between the Marxism of the autonomist tradition - with its emphasis on the creative agency of workers in struggle - and the positive emphasis on dynamic creativity and mobility to be found in the work of Deleuze and Guattari. Never collapsing schizoanalysis into autonomism altogether, Thoburn elaborates on a number of the most obviously political or quasi-political themes in the work of Deleuze and Guattari.

A similar task has been undertaken by a range of commentators in recent times,[63] but it is also notable that two edited collections - the first in French, the second in English - have appeared very recently, addressing themselves to the explicit question of the political dimensions of Deleuze and Guattari's thought.[64] These are both fascinating collections, which like the already-existing works by single authors, mostly present a consistent and convincing picture of what is at stake in a 'Deleuzian politics', in particular paying a good deal of attention to the conceptual distinctions between minority and majority, and molarity and molecularity, which organise some of the key arguments of *A Thousand Plateaus*. Although all of the contributions to these volumes are enlightening and well-informed, perhaps the most striking thing about the collections is their relative uniformity of tone and approach, as key concepts - 'geophilosophy', 'control society', 'the refrain', 'creation', 'becoming' - are expounded and their political implications reflected-upon. It must be stressed that I in no way wish to diminish the importance of this kind of conceptual work, and would certainly have no hesitation in recommending either of these important books to all readers. In fact, we have gone so far as to translate and include one of the most interesting contributions to *Gilles Deleuze, Félix Guattari Et Le Politique* [*Gilles Deleuze, Félix Guattari and the Political*] in this

62. Nicholas Thoburn, *Deleuze, Marx and Politics*, London, Routledge, 2003; Jason Read, *The Micropolitics of Capital: Marx and the Prehistory of the Present*, New York, SUNY Press, 2003.

63. E.g. Brian Massumi, *A Users' Guide to Capitalism and Schizophrenia: Deviations from Deleuze and Guattari*, Cambridge, MIT Press, 1992; Ian Buchanan, *Deleuzism: A Metacommentary*, Edinburgh, Edinburgh University Press, 2000; Phillip Goodchild, *Deleuze and Guattari: An Introduction to the Politics of Desire*, London, Sage, 1996; Eugene Holland, *Deleuze and Guattari's Anti-Oedipus*, New York, Routledge, 1999; Paul Patton, *Deleuze and the Political*, London, Routledge, 2000; also various titles in the Deleuze Connections series published by Edinburgh University Press.

64. Ian Buchanan and Nicholas Thoburn (eds), *Deleuze and Politics*, Edinburgh, Edinburgh University Press, 2008; Manola Antonioli et al (eds), *Gilles Deleuze, Félix Guattari, et Le Politique*, Paris, Éditions de Sandre, 2007.

issue: an essay by the Belgian philosopher and poet Véronique Bergen.

What remains relatively absent from these collections, however, as from the small explosion of new 'Deleuze Studies' to have appeared in English in recent years, is any very sustained attempt to bring schizoanalytic concepts to bear upon the analysis of contemporary social formations and the political projects which work to secure, transform or even destroy them. As such, it is important to mention here the work of Maurizio Lazaratto, a Paris-based Italian thinker writing primarily in French, whose work is only known to Anglophone audiences through a handful of translations of short pieces[65] and an informative introductory article by Alberto Toscano,[66] and who remains most famous in this context for his thesis as to the growing importance of 'immaterial labour' (forms of creative, affective, cognitive and communicative work which do not directly produce material commodities) to the post-Fordist capitalist economy. In his more recent work, Lazzarato brings together Deleuze and Guattari with related or relatable thinkers such as Foucault, Tarde and Bakhtin in order to make a detailed analysis of the forms of exploitation and valorisation typical of contemporary capitalism and of the relative efficacy of emergent forms of labour and counter-capitalist organisation.[67] Interestingly, Lazzarato shares with DeLanda and Laclau and Mouffe a rejection of any 'Marxist' emphasis on the totality of social relations or on class identities as the basis for anti-capitalist struggle, and a contrasting emphasis on the contingency and heterogeneity of social formations.

Lazzarato goes much further than these writers, however, in risking some positive judgements upon actual recent 'political experiments'.[68] Most notably, Lazzarato's latest book, examines the dynamics of the *coordinations* - the experiments in self-organisation of casual workers (most notably in the entertainment industry), outside of traditional trade union frameworks, which have taken place in France in recent years; Lazaratto sees these as distinctively 'intervening at the same time on the molar and the molecular side of relations of power',[69] problematising any clear distinction between 'creative' and other kinds of labour, and pushing for the recognition of commonalities typical of post-Fordist economies but not comprehensible in terms of traditional concepts of class (in particular the commonality of 'precarious' workers), and of forms of exploitation not reducible to the inherent logic of the wage/labour relation. Lazzarato's is therefore not just an important analytical intervention, but is directly concerned with the fundamental question of how to develop new forms of labour organisation under the complex and often unstable conditions of advanced post-Fordist capitalism. In Lazzarato's hands, the key conceptual tools identified by most of the writers discussed in this section are deployed specifically in order to make a case for the potential of radically democratic and decentralised forms of such organisation to achieve actual concrete goals.

Lazzarato's is perhaps the most distinctive body of work to draw heavily on Deleuze and Guattari's key political distinctions between micropolitics and macropolitics/molar and molecular/major and minor. Each of these

65. See Maurizio Lazzarato, 'Neoliberalism in Action: Inequality, Insecurity and the Reconstitution of the Social', *Theory Culture and Society*, Vol. 26, No. 6, pp109-33, 2009 and http://affinityproject.org/theories/lazzarato.html. See also Max Henninger's translations in *SubStance* 112 (Volume 36, Number 1), Madison, University of Wisconsin Press, 2007.

66. 'Maurizio Lazzarato and the Metaphysics of Contemporary Capitalism', *Theory, Culture and Society*, Vol. 24, No. 6, pp71-91, 2007.

67. See Maurizio Lazzarato, *Les Révolutions du Capitalisme* [The Revolutions of Capitalism], Paris, Les Empêcheurs de penser en rond/Le Seuil, 2004; *Expérimentations Politiques* [Political Experiments], Paris, Éditions Amsterdam, 2009.

68. Ibid.

69. Ibid., p126.

distinctions points in a slightly different way towards a mode of analysis that recognises different dimensions of political and social organisation which cannot be simply understood in terms of numerical scales: if these distinctions do map onto differences of scale, then, importantly, they are only differences of relative scale in particular contexts. In each case, a tendency towards aggregation, convergence, normalisation and stabilisation in the relations obtaining between different elements is contrasted with a tendency towards disaggregation, divergence, difference and multiplication.

It is worth pausing to consider further some examples of political issues which might be usefully clarified by these distinctions. The shop-level innovation and interaction upon which effective labour organisation depends would be here contrasted with the tendency of large-scale labour organisations towards bureaucratic inertia, but at the same time the tendency towards schism and inefficacy typical of the former would be contrasted with the capacity of the latter to effect significant social reforms through sheer weight of numbers. Deleuze and Guattari's perspective would certainly see any truly effective challenge to capitalist exploitation as depending fundamentally upon the capacity of an organisation to intensify militant participation and creative forms of struggle amongst its rank and file; but it would not be oblivious to the schismatic dangers inherent in any purely fissile, disorganised process of radicalisation, recognising as it does that 'every politics is simultaneously a macropolitics and a micropolitics'.[70] Similarly, the types of experimentation with lifestyle, drugs, sexualities, living arrangements, etc, typical of 'alternative' cultures throughout the history of modernity might be seen as typical of radicalism on a molecular scale, concerned as they generally are with the disentangling of traditional complexes of selfhood, corporeality and personal interrelation; but their vulnerability to persecution, exploitation or simple elimination by 'majorities' - except where they are capable of intersecting with broader popular movements, or with intense currents of social change (consider, for example, the success of those elements of the counterculture which managed to capitalise upon the expansion of commodity-oriented lifestyles typical of emergent neoliberalism in the 1970s) - would also be registered here.

Broadly speaking, it is these distinctions that have emerged as crucial to the formulation of modes of political analysis, or even speculative understandings of forms of political organisation, informed by a Deleuzian perspective. Important examples include Jason Read's *The Micropolitics of Capital*,[71] which (like Thoburn's *Deleuze, Marx and Politics*) identifies Deleuze and Guattari's emphasis on the constitutive function of 'lines of flight' and transformatory processes of 'deterritorialization' for all social formations with the autonomist understanding of class struggle as the key driver of capital's organisational and technical innovations; and the group of authors responsible for the digital book *Micropolitique des Groupes: pour une écologie des pratiques collectives* [*The Micropolitics of Groups: for an ecology of collective practices*],[72] who aim to provide a kind of manual/reference-book for collective self-organisation informed by

70. *A Thousand Plateaus*, op. cit., p213.

71. Op. cit.

72. http://micropolitiques.collectifs.net/

Deleuze and Guattari. Interestingly, this is not the only Deleuzian manual to have been published in recent years. Psychologist Stéphane Nadaud's *Manuel à la usage de ceux qui veulent réussir leur [anti]oedipe* [*Manual for use by those who wish to make a success of their [anti-] Oedipus*][73] purports to offer a critique of contemporary pop psychology from a schizoanalytic perspective, although, notwithstanding some very interesting insights into such issues as the nature of intersubjectivity and contemporary capitalism's culture of memory, it isn't clear that this book draws anything specific from Deleuze and Guattari beyond a general hostility towards capitalism, individualism and psychoanalysis.

73. Paris, Fayard, 2006.

Nadaud's book seems to have been inspired by Foucault's famous preface to the English translation of *Anti-Oedipus*, in which he compares the book not to the great theoretical and analytical treatises of the modern era, but to a work of religious devotion from the seventeenth century: Francis de Sale's *Introduction to the Devout Life*. Having identified the three great enemies which *Anti-Oedipus* attacks as 'political ascetics', 'poor technicians of desire - psychoanalysts and semiologists' and 'fascism', he goes on to describe the work in general as 'An Introduction to the Non-Fascist Life'. Clearly there is a great deal of insight in Foucault's remarks, but they also raise a number of problems, which become much more acute if we try to apply them to the whole of Capitalism and Schizophrenia. For while it may be true, as Foucault asserts in this preface, that there is no fully coherent philosophy to be drawn from its pages - as there might be from the major works of Hegel, Heidegger, even Spinoza - it is nonetheless also true that Foucault's account thoroughly downplays both the evident systematicity of Deleuze and Guattari's approach and the singular object of systematic analysis which emerges from its pages. For as wide-ranging as the investigations are which make up its chapters, and as central to its project as is the critique of all forms of authoritarianism, it is ultimately not fascism but capitalism and the state which emerge as its primary objects,[74] and it is the attempt to invent concepts for the adequate description and analysis of their history, their present forms and their immanent dynamics - at the level of the psyche as well as the economy and the institution - which animates the study from beginning to end. This is why the focus on these issues to be found in work such as Read's, Thoburn's and in *Micropolitique des Groupes* seems so appropriate.

74. See, in particular, *A Thousand Plateaus*, op. cit., pp 424-73.

It is worth drawing out in a bit more detail what the relevance of Deleuze and Guattari's attitude to the state might be for their analysis of contemporary politics, and how much further it can go than a mere denunciation of fascism. Consider, for example, their analysis of the state form as 'apparatus of capture' characterised by a differential set of possible deployments of 'axioms' (basic organisational rules) in relation to the constitutive axiomatics of capitalism and its tendency towards general deterritorialisation. This account explicitly relegates fascism to one relatively specialised variant within a typology of capitalist state formations which identifies 'social democracy' and 'totalitarianism' as its two key 'poles'. Strikingly, Deleuze and Guattari associate 'social democracy' with a multiplication of axioms, bringing different sets of social procedures - rights, obligations, entitlements, demands - to bear upon different social groups (the retired, the young, women, etc) while associating 'totalitarianism' with that reduction of axioms of which they identify neoliberal, 'anarcho-capitalist' Chile as the typical case. The relevance of this formulation to the understanding of recent tendencies in capitalist governance is quite clear, even while they present new types of formation not yet fully imaginable by Deleuze and Guattari. Neoliberal governments such as Tony Blair's have been characterised by highly intrusive interventions in the operation of social institutions and the labour market,[75] although the consistency and homogeneity of their objectives (to ensure the persistence of individualised, competitive market relations in every possible social scene) resemble more the reduction of axioms typical of capitalist totalitarianism than the multiplication thereof typical of classical social democracy.

Deleuze and Guattari's highly complex (and not always necessarily consistent) treatment of these topics derives from a clear appreciation of the increasing complexity of late twentieth-century capitalism and its relationships with state institutions, which was already rendering useless any mechanical understanding of those relationships by the end of the 1970s. What clearly colours all of their writing on these topics, however, is the global context wherein the existence of authoritarian socialism situated within a world capitalist market organises the geopolitical framework within which that world market develops.[76] The end of the cold war and of 'actually existing socialism' in Eastern Europe marked the emergence of a new international order which of necessity demands some revisions of their schemas. Arguably the most high-profile attempt to develop such a revision has been the collaborative work of Michael Hardt (whose first published work was a monograph on Deleuze's thought) and Antonio Negri (himself a friend and collaborator of Deleuze and Guattari, although not always uncritical of them), which owes much to Deleuze and Guattari while also remaining more firmly within a problematic defined by the autonomist Marxism of which Negri was himself a pioneer.[77] Put simply, Hardt and Negri develop a model which understands the mobile and creative power of all of those forces upon which capital accumulation depends - workers, artists, migrants, inventions, science, etc - as ultimately prior and irreducible to processes of capital accumulation as such. For Hardt and Negri this idea ultimately informs a classically Marxian hypothesis as to the tendency of capitalism to generate the forces of its own overthrow, as the 'biopolitical' powers of communication and polycentric organisation which contemporary capitalism builds up tend necessarily towards an expansion of 'the common' (all of those shared terrains of experience, knowledge and resource which make up the stock of the world's culture and ecologies) at the expense of the domain of property.

This highly optimistic reading of the current geopolitical situation is an important corrective to the pessimism typical of most Marxian accounts of neoliberalism[78] - and some of its key assumptions are put rigorously to the

75. For example, manipulating both the national schools curriculum and the benefit system in order to maximise the availability of cheap labour to the service, retail and communications industries.

76. This aspect of their work was further developed by Guattari in important collaborations with both Éric Alliez and Antonio Negri. See Guattari and Negri, *Communists Like Us*, Michael Ryan (trans.), New York, Semiotext(e), 1990; Alliez and Guattari, 'Capitalistic Systems, Structures, and Processes', in Gary Genosko (ed.), *The Guattari Reader*, Oxford, Blackwell, 1996.

77. Michael Hardt and Antonio Negri, *Empire*, Cambridge, Harvard University Press, 2000; *Multitude*, Cambridge, Harvard University Press, 2004; *Commonwealth*, Cambridge, Harvard University Press, 2009.

78. E.g. David Harvey, *A Brief History of Neoliberalism*, Oxford, Oxford University Press, 2007.

test by Jorge Camacho's contribution to this volume - but it is also only made possible by Hardt and Negri's tendency more-or-less to ignore neoliberalism as a specific assemblage, simply overlooking or treating as relatively superficial the panoply of mechanisms by which an axiomatics of property is intensively re-inscribed at multiple sites, from the 'reality' TV shows which promote a wholly competitive set of aspirations as the key means by which desire itself becomes expressed and expressible in public contexts, to the imposition of standardised testing in public education systems, which deploy a competitive set of axioms in order to organise relationships between both students and different institutions, and a consumerist set of axioms to organise relationships between users and workers in education services. The continued importance of Deleuze and Guattari's approach lies partly in its analytical capacity to accommodate Hardt and Negri's emphasis on the creative agency of 'the multitude' with an appreciation of the importance of these other mechanisms of 'reterritorialisation', 'striation' and 'capture'. At the same time, it is just this analytical complexity which at times seems to make it difficult to imagine any clear political strategy being informed by it (although Lazzaratto would seem to point towards such a clear strategy as being presaged by the *coordinations*). So, for example, where Hardt and Negri see a newly radicalised practice of democracy as the means by which 'the multitude' will assert its will against the dominion of 'Empire' (the disaggregated and polycentric network of corporate and state institutions which governs contemporary capitalism), more faithfully Deleuzian commentators such as Thoburn remain sceptical about the value of any embrace of 'democracy' from a schizoanalytic perspective.[79]

79. Thoburn, op. cit.

DEMOCRACY, ECOLOGY AND AFFECT

The key question which emerges here is one of the most vexed and contentious in the field of studies of Deleuzian politics: namely, Deleuze and Guattari's attitude to democracy. While it is quite possible to read in their work an advocacy of that 'plural radical democracy' which Laclau and Mouffe have also famously advocated,[80] it is equally possible to read in Deleuze an aristocratic distaste for democracy which he shares with Nietzsche and much of the philosophical tradition. This is the reading offered by Phillipe Mengue, and it is not difficult to understand his argument. Democracy necessarily implies government by majorities, and as we have seen, 'majority' is, for Deleuze and Guattari, a wholly negative term. Deleuze's express distaste for 'opinion', for 'discussion', his consistent emphasis on the value of the new, the creative and the different, all seem to bespeak an avant-gardism which is ultimately inimical to any politics of popular sovereignty. On the other hand, as Paul Patton has argued in response to Mengue,[81] most of Deleuze's anti-democratic statements can easily be read as expressions of distaste with the inadequacy of actually-existing liberal democracy, informed by the desire for a 'becoming-democratic' which would exceed the self-evident limitations of current arrangements.

80. *Hegemony and Socialist Strategy*, op. cit., pp149-93.

81. Paul Patton, 'Deleuze and Democracy', *Contemporary Political Theory*, 4 (4), 2005.

Taking this further, I would argue that if any mode of self-government emerges as implicitly desirable from the perspective developed by Deleuze and Guattari, then it would clearly be one which was both democratic and pluralistic without being subject to the existing limitations of representative liberal democracy. Deleuze's earlier work may occasionally be characterised by a Nietzschean aristocratic tone. However, where he expresses 'anti-democratic' sentiments in his work with Guattari, these only ever seem to spring from a commitment to that Marxian tradition which understands liberal democratic forms to be deeply imbricated with processes of capitalist exploitation.[82] When weighing up the legacy of this tradition today, it is worth reflecting that the degradation of actually existing 'democracy' under neoliberal conditions in recent decades, especially in the years since the fall of the Berlin wall, has lent much weight to the hypothesis that a 'democratic' politics which has no anti-capitalist dimension can only ultimately fail, as the individualisation of the social sphere and the corporate control of politics progressively undermine the effectiveness of public institutions.[83]

From such a perspective, the problems with existing forms of representative democracy are several. Firstly, in ceding legislative sovereignty to elected bodies for several years at a time, they rely on the artificial stabilisation of 'majorities' of opinion along party lines which do not actually express the complexity of popular desires in any meaningful way. While it is clearly true that democracy as such necessarily demands the temporary organisation of 'molarities' for the purpose of taking collective decisions, the existing set of relationships between individuals and parties does not enable these molarities to emerge with sufficient intensity to effect major change: for example, despite the vehemence of anti-war opinion in the UK in 2003, the government was effectively at liberty to pursue the invasion of Iraq, safe in the knowledge that this intensity would disperse before the next general election. At the same time, these relationships do not enable the emergence of sites of engagement and deliberation which would enable new ideas and practices to emerge, simply delegating political engagement to a class of professional politicians, journalists, and policy-specialists whose job is not to innovate, invent and transform existing relations of power, but to maintain them, and the arrangements which express them. Most crucially, they do not enable the new forms of collective becoming which a more participatory, decentralised, 'molecular' democracy would facilitate, preventing any meaningful institutional expression of those new forms of dynamic, mobile, cosmopolitan collectivity which 'globalisation' makes possible. Instead they seek to actualise that potential only in the politically ineffectual forms of a universalised liberalism or banal forms of multiculturalism, two complementary 'grids' which are imposed upon global flows within the parameters of either the nation state or legalistic supra-national institutions.[84] The drive to find new forms of participative democracy which characterises the leading-edge of contemporary socialist practice,[85] and which has informed not only the politics of the social forum movement[86] but more broadly the entire history of

82. See, for example, *What is Philosophy*, op. cit., p106.

83. See Colin Crouch, *Post-Democracy*, Cambridge, Polity, 2004.

84. For an interesting discussion of related issues, see Dimitris Papadopoulos, Niamh Stephenson and Vassilis Tsianos, *Escape Routes: Control and Subversion in the 21ˢᵗ Century*, London, Pluto, 2008.

85. See Hilary Wainwright, *Reclaim the State: Adventures in popular democracy*, London, Verso, 2003.

86. See Gilbert, op. cit.

radical democratic demands (including, for example, the Chartists' demand for annual parliaments, or the Bolshevik cry for 'all power to the soviets'), surely expresses just this desire for democratic forms not stymied by the apparatuses of majority and individualisation.

This final point draws our attention to the key blind-spot which organises Mengue's argument in particular. Where Mengue sees the only obstacle between Deleuze and a full embrace of liberal democracy as being Deleuze's elitist anti-populism, he apparently sees no obstacle at all in Deleuze's implicit anti-liberalism. This, strangely, is one of the least commented-on aspects of Deleuze's political philosophy. Indeed, the only explicit commentary on this topic that I know of is Daniel W. Smith's 2003 article arguing for an implicit affinity between Deleuze and the liberal tradition. Smith's argument is based on a reading of Patton's *Deleuze and the Political* which is interesting, but which reveals precisely the same blind-spot as Mengue (and, in my view, mistakenly attributes this position to Patton). Rather like Mengue, Smith operates with a definition of liberalism which understands its qualifying characteristics to be a pluralistic rejection of confining systems of social normativity and an emphasis on the value of freedom as a political good.[87] The problem with this argument is that it simply overlooks one of the most important constitutive features of all liberal thought: its assumption that the freedom which it prizes so highly is uniquely and distinctively the property of individuals. There is no question that for the liberal tradition, it is the individual who must be freed from convention and tradition,[88] who is the bearer of rights, liberties and property. There is also no question that for Deleuze and Guattari, the individual is one of the most problematic notions of all. Arguably, this is precisely the point of initial convergence between Deleuze's philosophy of difference and multiplicity[89] (understood as constitutive and irreducible features of all matter) and Guattari's early experiments in post-Lacanian 'institutional analysis'[90] that makes possible their entire collaboration. The freedom which Deleuze and Guattari seek is not the freedom of the liberal subject to buy, sell, and vote, but precisely a freedom from the confines of 'individuality' and property: the freedom of 'singularities' (unique elements of experience which do not necessarily coincide with individual human bodies at all); the freedom of flows of affect and materiality which might or might not coincide with flows of population; the freedom to experience the full complexity of human and non-human interactions in the material world. Theirs is the difficult understanding of agency which runs through Spinoza, Nietzsche and Marx, and which may well (as Hallward notes in his contributions to the round-table presented in this volume) problematise any heroic understanding of collective or individual will, decision and choice, but which is certainly incompatible with any form of liberalism at all; and Chrysanthi Nigianni's contribution to this collection can be understood in part as a meditation on what an entirely different conception of agency from that which would be compatible with any form of liberalism might be. Of particular note here is the complex of problems in thinking through notions

87. 'Deleuze and the Liberal Tradition: Normativity, Freedom, and Judgment,' in *Economy and Society*, Vol. 32, No. 2, 2003.

88. See, for example, John Stuart Mill, *On Liberty*, Oxford, Oxford University Press, [1859] 2008.

89. See Gilles Deleuze, *Difference and Repetition*, Paul Patton Trans, London, Continuum, 1994.

90. See *Soft Subversions*, op. cit., pp 33-53.

91. E.g. *What is Philosophy*, op. cit., p60.

92. William Connolly, *Neuropolitics: Thinking, Culture, Speed*, Minneapolis, University of Minnesota Press, 2002.

of agency which Spinozan materialism (to which Deleuze and Guattari declare their allegiance several times[91]) shares with contemporary neuroscience: a topic explored with explicit reference to Deleuze by the American political philosopher, William Connolly.[92]

The reasons why such a radical anti-liberalism might be necessary today are manifold. For one thing, the dependence of contemporary neoliberalism upon the basic axioms of liberalism is well-documented,[93] and its consequent promotion of a culture of paranoia - of alienation, anxiety and fear - has been well-described by Deleuze and Guattari's most important translator and commentator in English, Brian Massumi.[94] Perhaps even more importantly, however, Deleuze and Guattari's anti-individualism provides arguably one of the most satisfying bases for one of the most important philosophical and political tasks of our time: the formation of a properly ecological perspective on human existence which is not limited by humanism, romanticism or any form of essentialism. It is no accident that Deleuze and Guattari have been inspirational for one of the most important trends in recent social theory, the 'actor network theory' of Latour et al, which attempts to eschew just these qualities in its understanding of the relationships between humans and other elements of the material world (animal, technological, or 'natural').[95] From this perspective, two of the most important of the recent collections to consider the politics of Deleuze and Guattari's thought are those edited by Bernd Herzogenrath - *Deleuze, Guattari and Ecology*[96] - and *An [Un]Likely Alliance: Thinking Environment[s] with Deleuze/Guattari*.[97] As Herzogenrath argues in the introduction to the former, Deleuze and Guattari's 'intelligent materialism' moves beyond both a representational logic and any naive or teleological organicism in its understanding of both 'nature' and 'culture' as operating according to 'machinic' processes of assemblage and aggregation. The series of contributions to this volume presents one of the most convincing cases yet for the capacity of Deleuze and Guattari's thought to address urgent political problems with a unique clarity, and it is worthwhile to note at this point that Guattari's own very latest work concerned itself directly with this set of issues. His short essay *The Three Ecologies* (influenced in part by the work of Gregory Bateson) proposes an analytical approach which considers the interaction between social, mental and environmental 'ecologies' as constitutive of most modes of experience.[98] This highly suggestive approach is proving increasingly influential today,[99] just as Guattari's own entry into active green politics towards the end of his life was to prove prophetic of emerging political priorities for the new century.

Perhaps what emerges most clearly from the preceding discussion of Deleuze and Guattari's politics is the importance of bringing together an ecological perspective with a radically democratic one. While ecological thought can at times descend into a mere celebration of the apparent existence of self-regulating and spontaneously emergent complex systems in the 'natural' world,[100] John Protevi stresses the importance of distinguishing between capitalist and democratic forms of 'self-ordering'. Protevi's warning against the

93. See, for example, Michel Foucault, *The Birth of Biopolitics: Lectures at the Collège de France 1978-1979*, London, Palgrave Macmillan, 2008.

94. See Massumi, 'Potential Politics and the Primacy of Preemption', *Theory and Event* 10:2, 2007; Massumi (ed), *The Politics of Everyday Fear*, Minneapolis, University of Minnesota Press, 1993.

95. Bruno Latour, *Reassembling the Social: An Introduction to Actor-Network Theory*, Oxford, Oxford University Press, 2007.

96. London, Palgrave Macmillan, 2009.

97. Cambridge, Cambridge Scholars Publishing, 2008.

98. Félix Guattari, *The Three Ecologies*, Ian Pindar and Paul Sutton (trans.), London, Continuum, 2000.

99. See, for example, Jo Littler, *Radical Consumption: Shopping for change in contemporary culture*, Milton Keynes, Open University Press, 2008.

100. See Sarah Kember, 'Metamorphoses: The myth of evolutionary possibility' in *Theory, Culture and Society*, Vol. 22, No. 1, pp 153-171, 2005.

101. John Protevi, *Political Physics: Deleuze, Derrida and the Body Politic*, New York, Athlone, p196.

102. Mengue, op. cit.; DeLanda, 'Deleuze, Materialism and Politics', op. cit., pp174-7.

103. Manuel DeLanda, 'Markets and Antimarkets in the World Economy', http://www.t0.or. at/delanda/a-market. htm.

104. See Julian Le Grand and Saul Estrin (eds), *Market Socialism*, Oxford, Clarendon Press, 1989.

105. Colin Leys, *Market Driven Politics*, London, Verso, 2001; Allyson M. Pollock, *NHS plc: The Privatisation of our Health Care*, London, Verso, 2005.

similarity between neoliberal celebrations of markets as self-regulating systems and ecological descriptions of similar systems in 'nature'[101] is highly relevant to the consideration of one of the most contentious political interpretations of Deleuzian thought to have been offered in recent times. Manuel DeLanda, very like Phillipe Mengue, consistently argues that Deleuze and Guttari's commitment to 'Marxism' was a residual and 'Oedipal' commitment typical of their intellectual generation in France, inconsistent with their broader theoretical position and hampering its proper development.[102] DeLanda derives a position from the work of the great French historian of capitalism, Fernand Braudel, which refuses any identity between capitalism and market relations, instead arguing for a radical distinction between capitalism proper (i.e. capital accumulation by extremely powerful institutions or individuals) and ordinary innovative commodity-production. The former both DeLanda and Braudel understand to be dependent upon monopoly practices which they characterise as 'antimarkets', the latter they understand to be dependent upon the existence of relatively egalitarian relations of free exchange typical of ideal 'markets'.[103]

This is reasonable as far as it goes, but from this point the argument becomes more contentious. Braudel suggested that in fact market mechanisms should be used in many spheres of life to encourage innovation and the free circulation of best practice. Now, this was a radical idea when Braudel proposed it in the 1970s, and it was to become typical of the 'market socialism' of social democratic theory in the 1980s.[104] However, the subsequent history of the artificial creation and enforcement of market relations in a range of public services - a core element of the neoliberal programme in many parts of the world - has surely made very clear the naivety of this theoretical perspective. In the UK, for example, there is no evidence that the promised increases in accountability, quality and effectiveness of service-delivery have actually materialised in fields like education and health care, even while marketisation has driven down professional morale, subjected services to a target-driven culture which gives service users no sense of democratic participation, and while partial privatisations have enabled profit-seeking by private corporations. The most informed commentary on this process has persistently pointed to the incompatibility between the commercial marketisation of such services and the promotion of participative and democratic systems of decision-making therein.[105] Despite all this, DeLanda continues to promote Braudel's position as if it had not been subject to three decades of rigorous testing and found distinctly wanting.

What emerges here is the critical elision which Braudel and DeLanda make between egalitarian relations of free exchange in general, and commodified market relations in particular. This is of particular concern to us here precisely because it is Deleuze and Guattari, more than any other thinkers who can enable us to grasp what is at stake in this elision. Deleuze and Guattari's description of the 'rhizome' is arguably the best known description of a polycentric, relatively horizontal set of relations, expressive of the creative potential inherent in sociality as such. As already hinted however, we can easily imagine radically democratic modes of interaction which are rhizomatic in character but which do not take the form of market relations and are not limited by the modes of commodity-exchange (just think of the problems posed for capital accumulation in the music industry by peer-to-peer file sharing). The elision of the rhizome with the market is surely one of the traps which Deleuze and Guattari tried to avoid with their more nuanced understanding of the status of the rhizome in the later chapters of *A Thousand Plateaus*; and yet the persistent rhetorical force of their initial valorisation surely derives from this powerful insight: the rhizome expresses a certain virtual power of the social, of which the market is only one possible form of actualisation. The recognition of this fact is one of the reasons why the collapse of Deleuzian politics into a form of liberalism should be avoided at all costs;[106] though this is clearly the danger which besets Deleuzian philosophy in an era when liberalism remains the default position of academic and journalistic political thought in the West. The capacity to offer a robust alternative to liberalism in the pursuit of a philosophical programme which is nonetheless libertarian in character, and the ability to express such an alternative in terms which are amenable to a radically collectivist and ecological approach which makes no concession to romanticism or organicism, are among the great potential strengths of a 'Deleuzian politics'.

This orientation towards the irreducibly social and collective dimensions of experience is in part the motivation for one of the major impacts which Deleuzian theory has had upon cultural and media studies - and even the more radical branches of political philosophy and critical psychology - in recent years. The 'affective turn'[107] has seen a marked shift in these fields towards a concern with forms of sensory experience which cannot be understood in terms of semantic, linguistic or even rhetorical categories, and Deleuze's work has been by far the most frequently-cited source for this work. While much of it is understandably concerned with emphasising the specific sensory qualities of given communications media - qualities which structuralist and post-structuralist approaches are held to have erased under a general rubric of signification or *différance* - some of the most prominent advocates of this perspective have also deployed this perspective to make far-reaching analyses of the affective dimension of political and cultural formations. Lawrence Grossberg, one of the earliest champions of Deleuze and Guattari within cultural studies,[108] has developed a methodology which draws on Deleuze and Guattari to develop an understanding of the affective elements at stake in relations of hegemony, as evinced most famously in his study of the role played by rock music in the articulation of a conservative consensus in 1980s America.[109] More recently Brian Massumi has, as mentioned above, elucidated the importance played by the cultivation of fear, in particular by the institutional and cultural technologies of the 'war on terror', in the operation of that particularly strange combination of neoliberalism and neoconservatism which defined global geopolitics during the era of the second Bush presidency.

106. Patton's intriguing discussion of the work of John Rawls - which might be seen to mark the point at which the liberal tradition deterritorialises itself in the direction of a becoming-communist - in *Deleuze and the Political*, op. cit., would problematise any absolute dismissal of the liberal tradition as a potential resource for radical thought, but I don't think it would touch upon my fundamental point here as to the incompatibility of classical liberal individualism with a schizoanalytic perspective.

107. Patricia Clough (ed.), *The Affective Turn: Theorizing the Social*, Durham, Duke University Press, 2007.

108. Lawrence Grossberg, 'Experience, Signification and Reality: The Boundaries of Cultural Semiotics' (first published 1982), in *Bringing it All Back Home: Essays on Cultural Studies*, Durham, Duke University Press, 1997.

109. Grossberg, *We Gotta Get Out of this Place: popular conservatism and popular culture*, New York, Routledge, 1992.

110. Protevi, *Political Affect*, op. cit., p 186.

111. Laclau, *On Populist Reason*, London, Verso p131.

112. Hallward, *Out of This World*, op cit..

113. See, for example, Laclau, *Emancipations*, op. cit., pp73-9.

114. The notion of 'actionless action' common to both the Vedic and Taoist traditions would be close to the position which Hallward attributes to Deleuze here.

115. See Gilles Deleuze, *The Logic of Sense*, Mark Lester with Charles Stivale (trans), London, Continuum, 2004.

John Protevi remarks explicitly that almost all recent philosophical work on affect and emotion is characterised by 'an individualist orientation', which his recent own study, informed by complexity theory, cognitive neuroscience and physiology as well as Deleuze and Guattari, works to overcome.[110] The ongoing value of this analytical perspective is not hard to see: just consider the importance of an undifferentiated and programmatically unarticulated 'hope' for 'change' as the driving force of Obama's election victory in 2008. Even while, at the semantic level, 'hope' and 'change' acquired the status for Obama's campaign of what Laclau calls 'tendentially empty signifiers'[111] - standing for nothing but the very possibility of some new political community - they only acquired that status on the basis of the profoundly rhizomatic redistribution of affects which Obama's internet-driven campaigning machine (a true 'war machine' in Deleuze and Guattari's terms) was able to mobilise. This is not to make any judgement on the long-term political efficacy of that campaign or Obama's project.

The analytical value of these observations is clear enough. Whether they can generate strategic solutions to the problems that they identify is another question, but it is ultimately one which can only be answered in practice. Even if we were to accept Peter Hallward's argument - that Deleuze's oeuvre, judged solely on its own merits, cannot generate any such strategies - we would nonetheless have to ask why this should be regarded as a particular failing for Deleuze's thought.[112] In recent times, thinkers such as Derrida and Laclau have emphasised the irreducibility of the decision for any political process, and the inherent risks which beset any decision as such (because we cannot know the results of a decision in advance, or else it is not really a decision at all).[113] However, both Derrida and Laclau would stress - according to precisely the same logic which makes the decision irreducible for politics - that no philosophical system can offer either a fully-comprehensive world-view or a perfectly transcendent viewpoint from which such decisions can be made. Any such political/philosophical decision (which is to say: any political actualisation of philosophical potential) will always involve a certain opening to other spheres of thought, knowledge and experience, and to the complex contingency of events. Hallward argues that Deleuze's is a purely metaphysical, mystical system, whose reverence for the virtual can never endorse the risk inherent in any such actualisation as is involved in a determinate decision: better to remain forever the uncarved block - amongst the angels, in the clear white light of mystical ecstasy, or at least in the pure land of the virtual, where all events are incorporeal and 'creatings' never incarnate themselves as anything so vulgar as actual 'creatures' - than to risk taking concrete form as an actual political action, intervention, institution or subject.[114] There may well be a danger of such an interpretation inherent in any system which is so fascinated with the complex interplay between materiality and virtuality, between sense and incorporeality.[115] But it is surely clear that Deleuze himself always knew this, that his collaboration with Guattari was motivated as much as anything by an awareness that it is only when brought into a relationship of 'transversality'[116] with other bodies of work that his was capable of catalysing or crystallising a political analysis as such. What more radical and self-politicising move could Deleuze have made, in 1968, just at the point of completion of his major ontological works,[117] than to have formed an alliance with the young and relatively unknown pioneer of materialist psychosocial theory, Félix Guattari (who was also, not by chance, a key activist in the events leading up to 'May 1968')? By the same token, all of the writers mentioned in this survey operate by bringing Deleuze's thought into contact with some other such body of thought or practice, however unlikely (autonomism for Thoburn and Read, ecology for Herzogenrath's contributors, Margulis for Parisi, ethnography for Saldanha, neurology for Connolly, Gramsci for Grossberg, Foucault for Lazzaratto, Rawls for Patton, etc, etc), and it is precisely in its evident openness to such productive encounters that the great attraction of his thought lies. From this perspective, there may well be no 'Deleuzian politics' lying in wait in the corpus of Deleuze's own texts; rather, the analytical and organisational elaboration of the political potential inhering in his work may be a task for us, right now, and for those who come after.

Thanks to Nick Thoburn, Angela McRobbie and Chrysanthi Nigianni for feedback and advice.

116. Guattari, *Soft Subversions*, op. cit., pp23-4.

117. *Logic of Sense and Difference and Repetition*, op. cit..

Politics as the Orientation of Every Assemblage

Véronique Bergen

Translated by Jeremy Gilbert

Translators note: In the title, and at several points in the text, I have translated the French 'posture', in a rather unorthodox manner as 'orientation'. Much more usual translations of this word into English would include 'posture' (in either the political or ergonomic sense), 'position', 'positioning', 'stance' (again, in the political or anatomical sense) or 'bearing'. None of these usages in English quite captures the French usage in this text, which would perhaps be most accurately rendered as 'positioning' (although with some of the suggestively anatomical undertones of 'posture' or 'stance'). 'Orientation' has been chosen partly because it carries a similar set of nuances, partly because it sits nicely with the cartographic vocation which Bergen / Deleuze attributes to politics, and partly because it reads less awkwardly in context than any of the more orthodox alternatives, without doing violence to the ideas being communicated.

We will begin with a topological question: where is Deleuzian politics located? Where do its lines run? Through which points do they pass? We can take it as read that politics is not, for Deleuze, a separate field - a space limited by questions of representation, of state, of legitimacy - but an orientation operating at the heart of every assemblage; its lines meeting everywhere where an assemblage - individual or collective, of thought or of desire - operates. Politics characterises *a priori* every assemblage, to the extent that the latter is in itself just a fold in life. If every ideal or desiring assemblage reveals itself to be political in its action as in its effects, if an intrinsic interlinking connects these two terms in a co-definition, then it is to the extent that it bears witness to a mode of existence which consorts with or divorces itself from life. Vitalism, which understands life in terms of flux, in terms of forces and not of forms, carries within itself a politics which it dictates at the same time as fecundating: a politics affiliated to the ethical and ethological question of affirming that which augments the powers of life.

Deleuze's work evolves from an analysis of politics in terms of desires - animated by the question 'how does desire come to desire its own repression?' and by the horizon of revolution - to an understanding of politics in terms of lines, which asks after the *cartography* of an assemblage, understood not only as desiring but also as ideal, perceptual, sensible. In brief, it bifurcates from schizoanalysis into micropolitics. Backed by an ontology configured in terms

    doi:10.3898/newf.68.02.2009

of a Spinozist pantheism,[1] the Deleuzian system grasps the entirety of the real in terms of forces, of fluxes and not of forms or substances / subjects; in terms of relations and not of invariant forces. On the plane of immanence of life, every body, every assemblage, is defined only by a diagram constituted along two axes: the longitudinal axis of movements of speed and slowness which traverse the body, and the latitudinal axis of the body's powers of affecting and of being affected. Prey to those becomings which arise from the line of the Outside, subjected to those connections and interactions which compose or decompose its relationships, augmenting or diminishing its power to act, every assemblage is to be understood in terms of a map drawn from a condition of permanent dynamism. And it is precisely this cartography of individual and collective assemblages, this tracking of a geography and of a physiology cut off from any hermeneutics, which fulfils the Deleuzian definition of the political.

We will begin by explaining the operators which Deleuze deploys in his apprehension of the political. In *Dialogues* and *A Thousand Plateaus*, politics is grasped by way of a double conceptual armoury: on the one hand, the typology of lines (drawn from the literary field, essentially from Fitzgerald in *The Crack-Up*), on the other hand the schema of the molar and the molecular (deriving primarily from Tarde, but grafted onto Ruyer and Leibniz). But, firstly, these two operators reinforce each other such that break lines define themselves as molar, crack lines as molecular; secondly, they converge upon a distinction in nature between the transcendent plane of organisation and the immanent plane of composition. And behind this circumscription of the lines passing through every assemblage, lies the Bergsonian theory of multiplicities (in brief, of the actual and the virtual), the Spinozist ethology of forces and the Nietzschean question of becoming, cut off from history.

To examine a vital assemblage is to pose the political question 'what can an assemblage do, what experimental states can it reach, what are its speeds, the affects of which it is capable, how does it construct its plane, how does it grade its stratified folds, its tangency to chaos, its layout of life-intensifying lines?' This is why the dangers which threaten the desiring machines and the creations of thought will be the same, seeing as the latter present themselves as specific folds in life. That an assemblage presents itself, at such moments, as a stylisation of life from the point of view of a construction of concepts, of functions, or of percepts and affects, means that, in whatever way it positions itself in relation to life, the assemblage is political: in the sense that it disables, negates, impoverishes or exacerbates, affirms, enriches life, of which it is itself only a mode.

Before examining the operator constituted by the three types of lines, mutually-imbricated in every assemblage, we will recall briefly that of the molar / molecular schema. Defined by a difference in nature which equates neither to a difference in scale nor to an opposition between the collective and the individual, the contrast between molar and molecular is to be understood at the level of the distinction between the actual and the virtual,

1. I maintain the existence of an ontology in Deleuze against François Zourabichvili or Monique David-Ménard. Cf. F. Zourabichvili, 'Deleuze. Une Philosophie de l'événement', in *La Philosophie de Deleuze*, Paris, 2004, pp5-12 and Monique David-Ménard, *Deleuze et la psychanalyse. L'Altercation*, Paris, PUF, 2005, pp115-127.

2. C.f. Gilles Deleuze and Félix Guttari, A *Thousand Plateaus*, Brian Massumi (trans), London, Athlone, 1988, pp215-22; Deleuze, *Le Pli*, Paris, Éditions de Minuit, 1988, pp137-140.

between the macroscopic and the infinitesimal: in other words, at the level of organisms and masses, of conscious macroperceptions and unconscious microperceptions, of ensembles of statistics and of singularities, of becoming and history, of the empirical and the transcendental.[2] Here we see that this scheme connects, as was mentioned above, as much to Tarde as to Ruyer or Liebniz. This direct bipolarity in fact translates into an entanglement, an imbrication of these two levels in every assemblage: far from fixing themselves in a dualism, the two poles work on each other in a co-functionality which is subject to an incessant dynamism. Mixing the types of lines - the molar being equivalent to hard segmentary lines, the molecular to quantum lines - the 'molar' and the 'molecular' compose a double mode of being, in immanence, which, in every assemblage, signals the existence of a virtual which insists as pure reserve and an actual without resemblance to the transcendental forge from which it emanates.

The principle operator of Deleuzian and Guattarian politics is composed of the three types of line which are legible in each and every life. Firstly, the molar lines, called break lines, leading to hard segmentation, implicated in binary divisions (from the point of view of social classes, ethnicities, sexes ...), actualised at the level of history; secondly the molecular lines drawn in the milieu of the first, at the thresholds where becomings emerge, occurring in a non-chronological time; thirdly, the lines of flight, abstract, at the steepest gradients, called lines of rupture, meaning a change of threshold, a 'nothing has happened, but everything has changed', a becoming-minor, a becoming-imperceptible, which dissipates the subject to the benefit of a haecceity and which relies on a war machine. The cartographic task to which Deleuze and Guattari commit themselves aims at mapping the composition of lines inherent to every assemblage and evaluating the manner in which the assemblages negotiate the dangers attendant upon each of these lines.

> The study of the dangers of each line is the object of pragmatics or schizoanalysis, to the extent that it undertakes not to represent, to interpret nor to symbolise, but only to make maps and draw lines, marking their mixtures as well as their distinctions.[3]

3. *A Thousand Plateaus*, op. cit., p227.

Dangers of a hardening, of a rigidity, of a macro-fascism on the molar line; of a fall into black holes, into a micro-fascism on the molecular line; of a falling back onto the other two lines or of a collapse into chaos on the line of flight ... the constructivism required for the self-positioning of an assemblage is allied to the cautionary principle in experimentation, to the need for the careful weighing-up of liberatory valencies. *A priori*, nothing can predict the curvature of a becoming: nothing can predict whether, arresting its own movement, it will block itself, trapping itself in a fixed identity; or if it will abandon itself to too brutal a destratification; or if it will allow its line of sorcery to run on, experimenting with new alliances as it does. This exercise of caution, or vigilance, is motivated by a Spinozan intuition with regards to the value of joyous, fecund connections, understanding the adventure of living entirely in terms of the exploration of compositions of bodies with others; this exploration carrying itself forward by way of intensification or retraction, affirmation of life or its negation. In the wake of Spinoza and Nietzsche, then, ethology is the art of selecting good encounters, in the sense that they raise life to the nth power; and conversely the art of detecting the relationships which - compromising the cohesion of the body - depreciate, condemn and atrophy life. Politics is the risky consistency, endlessly to be re-made, to be traced, never to be given for all eternity, that each body confers upon its assemblage: in brief, it is the weaving of the lines into a plane. Politics is thus the singular manner in which each body constructs its diagram and conjugates the fluxes while weighing up the dangers inherent to the three lines. Politics inscribes itself outside of the juridical question and outside an analysis in terms of contradiction: it is neither affiliation to external norms - to transcendent order-words - nor to the search for a public space of law, of communication, or of a scene of mutual recognition (a victory over self-awareness); it is rather the imminent experimentation with a position, an orientation, which leads life (in the case of every assemblage) either to the summit of itself, or into the figure of its opposite. Politics is politics of life - in the double meaning of the genitive, subjective and objective - in the sense that life advances not as a categorical imperative or as a regulatory ideal but as a criterion *index sui*.

The line of flight is characterised by a primacy which is ontological and not chronological: it 'does not come after, but is there from the beginning, even if it awaits its hour, and waits for the others to explode'.[4]

In excess of what is, the lines of flight reconfigure the state of things which they propel in unpredictable directions, which are not given *a priori*. Micropolitics is the truth of macropolitics to the extent that it is the transcendental, the genetic potential of historic, molar facts: history is made by those becomings which except themselves from it, being only the result of evental effulgences, of singularities which have effectuated themselves in the state of things. As the ontological distributions orient the evaluative pragmatic, an axiological privilege is accorded to that which holds itself at height from the transcendental field; in brief, to lines of flight which catalyse the chain of becomings. If being and thought are apprehended in terms of intensive forces and flux, not of forms, if the former are the truth of the latter, which compose only the phenomenal level, then the evaluation of ways of existing, of feeling, of perceiving, of thinking will have for their immanent criterion the augmentation of powers of life. If, via transcendental empiricism, schizoid thought is to be able to capture the processual movement of life, the presentation of being and of thought, short of their representation, then the assemblages of desire and of thought will be evaluated at the level of the intensive effects which they produce. The ontological assertion therefore sees itself validated by a functionalist, ethological criterion: the genealogist evaluates a system of thought in terms of the living forces which it carries

4. Ibid., p205. See also Deleuze and Parnet, *Dialogues II*, Hugh Tomlinson and Barbara Habberjam (trans), Eliot Ross Albert, London, Continuum, p102.

along. Schizoid thought bears witness to an affinity with the differential
foundations of being in that it brings with it an intensification of power to act.
It is life and nothing but life which founds in reason the validity of schizoid
thought: vital intensity is the standard of the consistency of a thought. Even
while being the bearers of the gravest danger - turning into lines of abolition,
lines of death - lines of flight are the liberatory resource of every assemblage, in
that, as Badiou affirmed with regard to Gilles Châtelet, in a vitalist conception,
'the ambiguous closure is worth more than the univocal closure'.[5] It comes
back then to the pragmatics of understanding which fears, which blockages
condemn certain assemblages to contenting themselves with the inheritance
of molar lines imposed from the exterior and to forbidding themselves
from inventing lines of flight, such self-preserving reflexes preventing them
from ever exceeding the limit (reproducing their homogeneity) or passing a
threshold (making the leap into heterogeneity).

5. Alain Badion,
'Les gestes de a
pensée', in *Les Temps
Modernes*, n°586,
janvier-février 1996,
p204.

Having explained the operators with which Deleuze opens up the political,
let us now consider the effects of the cut which he made in it, the impacts of
the assault which he made on it. The political gesture of Deleuzo-Guattarian
thought concedes virtually no ground on this one point: cartography does
not concern itself with questions of interpretation, but takes the radiographic
measure of forces; pragmatics avoids questions of meaning in order to
investigate the singular operation of assemblages. In this seismography of
intensities - where the description exonerates itself of every hermeneutic
inflection - in this panpolitics, the intensive criterion makes a body with itself,
without the possibility of there being anything beyond the criterion of life.
Privileging the bifurcations of trajectories and the mutations of lines, Deleuze
subordinates his reading of existential maps to the exclusive evaluation of the
vital powers to which they bear witness. Such is the first effect of the cut made
in the political by Deleuze. Pulsating in the place where bodies make their
lines run, one can say that that politics is an index of the bearing of bodies.
'Diagnosing the becomings in each present which passes' - becomings which
fall back into history but which escape it in persisting as pure becomings
-: such is the Nietzschean task incumbent upon philosophy, this 'medicine
for civilisation'. Micropolitics is the other name for a politics of the Great
Health, for an ethics traversed by the affirmation of life. The pragmatics
which Deleuze sets to work is a pure description of intensive variations, of exit
vectors and reterritorialisations which shake every assemblage; a mapping
which refrains from teaching any lessons - still less from offering a method
- charged as it is with enlarging and raising up the vital forces. It remains
then to be seen if politics can bring itself back to the specific co-ordinates of
each assemblage, to the measurement of the oscillation between 'more' and
'less' vital intensity, and base itself effectively on this exclusively energetic
criterion.

In this ethology are mixed together two dimensions which at first sight
seem antagonistic: on the one hand, passivity, *amor fati*, the opening to the
powers of the Outside; on the other hand, constructivism. The political

paradox is that of passive volition, of a passivity inscribed in a constructivist choice, an echo of Deleuze's 'only he who is chosen chooses well or effectively'; it is in this paradox that we will locate the second consequence of the Deleuzian understanding of the political. Ad hoc, with no *a priori* formula, with no royal road, this is indeed a matter of entering into a 'pure patient passivity', in such a way as to welcome the event which shatters us from the inside, which ruptures the concordance of our faculties; but also so as to trace its lines, to construct its vital plane, to reach the high point of the crisis which has destabilised the inertia of our codes. The political practice of living thus holds itself between two exigencies: on the one hand, being alert to danger; on the other hand, allowing oneself to be stunned by the incursion of a problem, responding to it even while remaining faithful to it.

With stoicism as its horizon - a stoicism hybridised with *amor fati* - and with the ethic of the mime which it draws in its wake, the politics of Deleuzian thought appeals to the transformatory power of a leap into a place beyond volontarism or resignation: neither an active engagement in planning the future nor a mere acceptance of what is. In this 'neither ... nor ...' we can see the third implication of the Deleuzian vision of politics.

With the ethico-politics of Deleuze, a distinction shatters: that between the beautiful soul - wallowing in the cult of its own, oh-so-pure interiority, cut off from all action on the world - and the artisan, engaged in bodily combat with the course of history. The line no longer passes between the mists of restraint and a militant decisionism (a fanatical, activist engagement with the substance of history) but in the cesura between selective disengagement and inscription in the present. What is ethico-political is the ambition to re-stage the given on another plane: the plane of the virtual, of the evental counter-effectuation. This re-staging goes beyond the impasse between an aestheticism with no impact on the world, and an exclusive concentration on the positivity of what happens which forgets the dimension of becoming. The disengagement of the beautiful soul (who celebrates an incorporeal counter-effectuation which doubles no state of things) and the spontaneous praxis defended by the dialectical donkey (who works only on the actual) are dismissed with one and the same gesture. The protagonists of Henry James' novella *In the Cage* and that of Fitzgerald's *The Crack-Up*, Beckett's late characters, in the grip of exhaustion, Melville's Barteleby, all come to the point where a threshold is crossed, a becoming-imperceptible is entered into: in the sense that nothing has happened at the level of history and its hard segmentations, yet everything has changed at the level of the event.[6] But on the one hand, in no case should one be tempted to map this hiatus - this disengagement between history and event - onto that between exterior and interior, between taking hold of the world and withdrawing into the haze of the imaginary sphere. On the other hand, it is important to underline the fact that transmutation at the level of becoming cannot help but shake up and bend the state of things, seeing as the two dimensions only exist in relation to each other, forming an unstable mixture (whose differences in nature are discerned by the genealogist's eye).

6. See Gilles Deleuze, 'Bartleby, or the Formula' in *Essays Critical and Clinical*, Daniel W. Smith and Michael A. Greco (trans.), University of Minnesota Press, 1997. The essay discusses Melville's *Bartleby the Scrivener*.

As such, the evental 'everything has changed', far from leaving the historical ground unaffected, shakes it and splatters it from all directions: from whence comes the trouble that afflicts contemporaries when Bartleby blinks like the Medicine-Man, whose christ-like figure installed itself at the heart of being *qua* being; from whence comes the perplexity which grips us in knowing that his infirmity, his exterior and interior desertion, his apparent political withdrawal, his absence of will, his vital anorexia, are only the epiphenomena of a great solar health ... A problem which originates with the difficulty of evaluating the real in terms of the virtual and of becoming, and not in terms of history and the actual. In brief, it originates with the difficulty of measuring the nuance between 'nothing happened' and 'everything changed'. The scrivener who has ceased to write exemplifies this co-existence of a slide into apathy, an exhaustion of possibilities, at the molar level, and a settling into being-as-such at the molecular level. If, at the level of history, he seems to settle nowhere, in the hollow of a parenthesis; at the level of becoming he has conquered the elsewhere of an ascent to being. Recall that, in *Difference and Repetition*, Deleuze suggested that only a larval subject, plural, de-centred, expropriated, would be able, without perishing, to endure the trial of the forced violence - coming from the Outside - of a discordance of the faculties. Having formed an alliance with the Outside, having been interpellated by a power which overflows him, Bartleby has released the contours of a people, which is not the fulfilment of the desire for revolution but its renewal and its unalterable persistence, even right where it is swallowed by the course of history. As such, the compromise, the failure, of the revolution at the level of the future leaves untarnished its effulgence at the level of becoming. Bartleby is he who, on the basis of the fundamental impotence which has struck him, exceeds the harmonious relationships on the ontic plane in order to achieve an ontological ascent. Reaching a point of stupefaction, he tears himself from the familiarity of intentional relations oriented towards a subjective or objective pole, and invents a new relation to the world, to others, and to himself; almost a new mode of being without being. From the heart of a limit-experience wherein forms become delirious, wherein motor-sensory schemas and anticipations of perception shatter, he ventures beyond the ontic concordance (between subject and object, subject and subject), and, forced to invent a new mode of existence, a superior regime of thought, accedes to a plane of being *qua* being. The distancing from the empirico-wordly plane is coupled with a breakout from the transcendental plane, and an accession to the plane of being. Somewhat as if the shattered chain of the three lines corresponded to Spinoza's three types of knowledge ... Somewhat as if, drifting on his lines of flight, he had tuned into the third type of knowledge ...

If we can say, with Badiou, that there is no affirmative political doctrine in Deleuze,[7] then it is because - taken in between the unlimited One-All of the plane of life, and the dice-throw (new each time) of its stylisation - it does not carve out an autonomous field ruled by problems, procedures and specific constraints, but rather traverses *ipso facto* every assemblage. If thought, desire

7. Alain Badiou, 'Foucault : continuité et discontinuité', in *La Célibataire*, automne 2004, p66.

and perception are political through and through, then it is because every assemblage is only a declension of life, which expresses itself there in its own contrary or in its highest affirmation.

This essay first appeared as 'La Politique comme posture de tout agencement' in Manola Antonioli, Pierre-Antoine Chardel and Hervé Reginauld (eds), Gilles Deleuze, Félix Guattari et Le Politique, *Paris, Éditions du Sandre, 2007. We gratefully acknowledge permission to reproduce it here. Thanks to Simon Torney for drawing our attention to this essay.*

ON PUTTING THE ACTIVE BACK INTO ACTIVISM

Rosi Braidotti

INTRODUCTION

This paper addresses a paradox: how to engage in affirmative politics, which entails the production of social horizons of hope, while at the same time doing critical theory, which means resisting the present. This is one of the issues Deleuze and Guattari discuss at length, notably in *What is Philosophy?*:[1] the relationship between creativity and critique. It is however a problem that has confronted all activists and critical theorists, namely how to balance the creative potential of critical thought with the necessary dose of negative criticism and oppositional consciousness.

Central to this debate is the question of how to resist the present, more specifically the nastiness, violence and vulgarity of the times, while being worthy of our times, so as to engage with the present in a productively oppositional and affirmative manner. I shall return to this in the final section of my essay. There is a conceptual and a contextual side to this problem and I want to start by discussing each one, before addressing my central concern.

I. THE CONTEXT

The public debate today shows a decline of interest in politics, whereas discourses about ethics, religious norms and values triumph. Some master-narratives circulate, which reiterate familiar themes: one is the inevitability of capitalist market economies as the historically dominant form of human progress.[2] Another is a contemporary brand of biological essentialism, under the cover of 'the selfish gene'[3] and new evolutionary psychology. Another resonant refrain is that God is not dead. Nietzsche's claim rings hollow across the spectrum of contemporary global politics, dominated by the clash of civilizations and widespread Islam phobia.

The bio-political concerns that fuel our necro-politics and the perennial warfare of our times also introduce a political economy of negative passions in our social context. Thus the affective economy expresses our actual condition: we now live in a militarised social space, under the pressure of increased enforcement of security and escalating states of emergency. The binary oppositions of the Cold War era have been replaced by the all-pervasive paranoia: the constant threat of the imminent disaster. From the environmental catastrophe to the terrorist attack, accidents are imminent and certain to materialise: it is only a question of time.

In this context, mass political activism has been replaced by rituals of public collective mourning. Melancholia has become a dominant mood and

1. Gilles Deleuze and Felix Guattari, *What is Philosophy?*, New York, Columbia University Press, 1992.

2. Francis Fukuyama, *The End of History?* Washington D.C., United States Institute of Peace, 1989; and *Our Posthuman Future. Consequences of the BioTechnological Revolution*, London, Profile Books, 2002.

3. Richard Dawkins, *The Selfish Gene*, Oxford, Oxford University Press, 1976.

DOI:10.3898/NEWF.68.03.2009

a mode of relation. There is, of course, much to be mournful about, given the pathos of our global politics: our social horizon is war-ridden and death-bound. We live in a culture where religious-minded people kill in the name of 'the Right to Life' and wage war for 'Humanitarian' reasons.

Depression and burn-out are major features of our societies. Psych-pharmaceutical management of the population results in widespread use of legal and illegal drugs. The narcotic sub-text of our societies is under-studied and mostly denied. Bodily vulnerability is increased by the great epidemics: some new ones, like HIV, Ebola, SARS or the bird flu; others more traditional, like TB and malaria. Health has become more than a public policy issue: it is a human rights and a national defence concern.

While new age remedies and life-long coaching of all sorts proliferate, our political sensibility has taken a forensic shift: 'bare life', as Agamben argues,[4] marks the liminal grounds of probable destitution - infinite degrees of dying. At the same time European culture is obsessed with youth and longevity, as testified by the popularity of anti-ageing treatments and plastic surgery.

Hal Foster[5] describes our schizoid cultural politics as 'traumatic realism' - an obsession with wounds, pain and suffering. Proliferating medical panopticons produce a global patho-graphy:[6] we go on television talk-shows to scream our pain.

In this context ethics emerges as the guiding principle for political action.

Let me sketch a brief cartography of poststructuralist ethics:

Besides the classical Kantians (see Habermas' recent work on human nature[7]), we have a Kantian-Foucauldian coalition that stresses the role of moral accountability as a form of bio-political citizenship. Best represented by Nikolas Rose[8] and Paul Rabinow,[9] this group works with the notion of 'Life' as bios, that is to say as an instance of governmentality that is as empowering as it is confining. This school of thought locates the ethical moment in the rational and self-regulating accountability of a bio-ethical subject and results in the radicalisation of the project of modernity.

A second grouping takes its lead from Heidegger and is best exemplified by Agamben.[10] It defines bios as the result of the intervention of sovereign power, as that which is capable of reducing the subject to 'bare life', that is to say zoe. The latter is, however, contiguous with Thanatos or death. The being-alive-ness of the subject (zoe) is identified with its perishability, its propensity and vulnerability to death and extinction. Bio-power here means Thanatos-politics and results in the indictment of the project of modernity.

Another important cluster in this brief cartography of new ethical discourses includes the Lévinas-Derrida tradition of ethics, which is centred on the relationship between the subject and Otherness in the mode of infinite indebtedness. Best expressed by critical thinkers like Critchley and Butler, this school of thought stresses the vulnerability and passivity of precarious life-forms and the importance of mourning.[11] I have enormous respect for this

4. Giorgio Agamben, *Homo Sacer. Sovereign Power and Bare Life*, Stanford, University Press, 1998.

5. Hal Foster, *The Return of the Real*, Cambridge, MIT Press, 1996.

6. Mark Seltzer, 'Wound Culture: Trauma in the Pathological Public Sphere', *October*, 80 (1999), pp3-26.

7. Jürgen Habermas, *Truth and Justification*, Cambridge, Polity, 2003.

8. Nikolas Rose, 'The Politics of Life Itself', *Theory, culture and society*, 18, 6 (2001), pp1-30.

9. Paul Rabinow, *Anthropos Today: Reflections on Modern Equipment*, Princeton University Press, 2003.

10. Agamben, op. cit..

11. Judith Butler, *Precarious Life*, London, Verso, 2004; Simon Critchley, *Infinitely Demanding. Ethics of Commitment, Politics of Resistance*, London and New York, Verso, 2007.

approach, but the project I want to pursue takes as the point of reference bios-zoe power defined as the non-human, vitalistic, and affirmative dimension of subjectivity. This is an affirmative project that stresses positivity and not mourning.

The last discursive coalition, to which this project belongs, is inspired by the neo-vitalism of Deleuze, with reference to Nietzsche and Spinoza.[12] Bio-power is only the starting point of a reflection about the politics of life itself as a relentlessly generative force. Contrary to the Heideggerians, the emphasis here is on generation, vital forces, and natality. Contrary to the Kantians, the ethical instance is not located within the confines of a self-regulating subject of moral agency, but rather in a set of interrelations with both human and inhuman forces. These forces can be rendered in terms of relationality (Spinoza), duration (Bergson), immanence (Deleuze), and, in my own terms, ethical sustainability. The notion of the non-human, in-human, or post-human emerges therefore as the defining trait of this new kind of ethical subjectivity. This project moves altogether beyond the postmodern critique of modernity and is especially opposed to the hegemony gained by linguistic mediation within postmodernist theory.

In conclusion: in a mournful context where political philosophy rediscovers with Derrida[13] the mystical foundations of Law and political authority; or turns towards Schmitt's political theology,[14] melancholia tends to carry the day. It is in such a context that I want to argue the case for affirmation.

II. THE CONCEPTUAL CASE FOR AFFIRMATION

II.1. *Oppositional consciousness*

The conceptual case of my argument rests on the rejection of the traditional equation between political subjectivity and critical oppositional consciousness and the reduction of both to negativity. There is an implicit assumption that political subjectivity or agency is about resistance and that resistance means the negation of the negativity of the present. A positive is supposed to be engendered by this double negative. Being against implies a belligerent act of negation, erasure of present conditions.

This assumption shares in a long constituted history of thought, which in Continental philosophy is best exemplified by Hegel. The legacy of dialectical thinking is such that it positions negativity as a necessary structural element of thought. This means that the rejection of conditions or premises that are considered unsatisfactory, unfair or offensive - on either ethical or political grounds - is the necessary pre-condition for their critique. A paradoxical concomitance is thus posited between that which one rejects and the discursive practice of critical philosophy. This results in establishing negativity as a productive moment in the dialectical scheme which fundamentally aims at overturning the conditions that produced it in the first place and thus engender positive resistance, counter-action or transcendence.[15] The process of consciousness-raising is crucial to the process of overturning or over-coding

12. Keith Ansell Pearson, *Germinal Life. The Difference and Repetition of Deleuze*, London and New York, Routledge, 1999.

13. Jacques Derrida, *Acts of Religion*, London, Routledge, 2001.

14. Carl Schmitt, *The Concept of the Political*, Chicago, Chicago University Press, 1996.

15. Michel Foucault, *Discipline and Punish*, New York, Pantheon Books, 1977.

the negative instance. This process involves a significant epistemological component in that it requires adequate understanding of the conditions one is critical of. My point is that in the course of time this has resulted in a simplistic equation between critique and negativity and in the reduction of the latter to negation. What I would like to suggest is a change of perspective that aims at re-casting critique as affirmation.

This shift of perspective assumes philosophical monism and an ethical and affective component of subjectivity; it is thus an anti-rationalist position. A subject's ethical core is not his/her moral intentionality, as much as the effects of the power (as repressive - *potestas* - and positive - *potentia*) his/her actions are likely to have upon the world. It is a process of engendering empowering modes of becoming.[16] Given that in this neo-vitalist view the ethical good is equated with radical relationality aiming at affirmative empowerment, the ethical ideal is to increase one's ability to enter into modes of relation with multiple others. Oppositional consciousness and the political subjectivity or agency it engenders are processes or assemblages that actualise this ethical urge. This position is affirmative in the sense that it actively works towards the creation of alternatives by working actively through the negative instance by cultivating the relations that are conducive to the transmutation of values.

16. Gilles Deleuze, *Différence et répetition*, Paris, Presses Universitaires de France, 1968. English translation: *Difference and Repetition*, Paul Patton (trans), London, Athlone, 1968.

In other words: the work of critique must not assume that the conditions for the overturning of negativity are necessarily available in the present time or space. Moving beyond the dialectical scheme of thought means abandoning oppositional thinking. This means that oppositions are not tied to the present by negation and hence emerge out of a different set of premises, affects and conditions. Affirmative politics rests on a time-continuum that indexes the present on the possibility of thinking sustainable futures. The sustainability of these futures consists in their being able to mobilise, actualise and deploy cognitive, affective and collective forces which had not so far been activated. How to ethically assess and format these forces becomes a crucial issue for critical theory - in terms of an ethics of affirmation that is also an ethology of forces. These driving forces concretise in actual, material relations and can thus constitute a network, web or rhizome of interconnection with others. We have to learn to think differently about ourselves. To think means to create new concepts.

To disengage the process of subject formation from negativity to attach it to affirmative otherness means that reciprocity is redefined not as mutual recognition but rather as mutual definition or specification. We are in this together in a vital political economy that is both trans-subjective and trans-human in its force.

Such a vision of the subject, moreover, does not restrict the ethical instance within the limits of human otherness, but also opens it up to inter-relations with non-human, post-human and inhuman forces. The emphasis on non-human ethical relations can also be described as a geo-politics or an eco-philosophy, in that it values one's reliance on the environment in the broadest sense of the term. Considering the extent of our technological development, emphasis on

17. Donna Haraway,
*Modest_Witness@
Second_Millenni um.
FemaleMan© Meets
Oncomouse*, London
and New York,
Routledge, 1997;
Félix Guattari,
Chaosophy, Sylvère
Lotringer (ed),
Los Angeles,
Semiotext(e), 1995;
and *The Three
Ecologies*, London,
Athlone, 2000.

18. Adrienne
Rich, *Arts of the
Possible*, New York
and London,
W.W.Norton & Co.,
2001, p159.

19. Deleuze,
Différence et répetition,
op. cit.

the eco-philosophical aspects is not to be mistaken for biological determinism. It rather posits a nature-culture continuum[17] within which subjects cultivate and construct multiple ethical relations. The concepts of immanence, multiple ecologies and of neo-vital politics become relevant here.

I have argued so far that oppositional consciousness is central to political subjectivity but it is not the same as negativity and as a consequence, critical theory is about strategies of affirmation. Political subjectivity or agency therefore consists of multiple micro-political practices of daily activism or interventions in and on the world we inhabit for ourselves and for future generations. As Rich put it in her recent essays the political activist has to think 'in spite of the times' and hence 'out of my time', thus creating the analytics - the conditions of possibility - of the future.[18] Critical theory occurs somewhere between the no longer and the not yet, not looking for easy reassurances but for evidence that others are struggling with the same questions. Consequently, we are in this together.

II.2. *Positioning Otherness*

The starting point of my case for affirmative politics is the assumption that the proper object of ethical enquiry is not the subject's universalist or individualist core, his moral intentionality or rational consciousness (the gender is not coincidental), as much as the effects of truth and power that his/her actions are likely to have upon others in the world. The ethical relation is central, rather than the universal moral essence of the subject. The emphasis on the relation expresses a pragmatic approach that defines ethics as the practice that cultivates affirmative modes of relation, active forces and values. The ethical good is that which acts as empowering modes of becoming, whereas morality is the implementation of established protocols and sets of rules.[19] This positions Otherness as the key issue.

Contrary to the Hegelian tradition - which is also strong in psychoanalysis - alterity is not a structural limit but rather the condition of expression of positive, i.e. non-reactive alternatives. The other is a threshold of transformative encounters. The 'difference' expressed by subjects who are especially positioned as 'other-than', that is to say always already different from - has a potential for transformative or creative becoming. This 'difference' is not an essential given, but a project and a process that is ethically coded.

My position in favour of complexity promotes consequently a triple shift. Firstly: it continues to emphasise the radical ethics of transformation in opposition to the moral protocols of Kantian universalism. Secondly it shifts the focus from unitary rationality-driven consciousness to process ontology, that is to say a vision of subjectivity propelled by affects and relations. Thirdly, it disengages the emergence of the subject from the logic of negation and attaches subjectivity to affirmative otherness - reciprocity as creation, not as the re-cognition of Sameness. In the rest of this section, I will concentrate on this third aspect: affirmation, or the critique of the negative.

Let me give you an example. Otherness in our culture has historically functioned as the site of pejoration or negativity. Difference is postulated on a hierarchical scale that opposes it to the vision of Subjectivity as Sameness. The subject is expected to be the same as a number of assumed values. In our culture these values are framed with reference to humanist ideals that equate the subject with rationality, consciousness, moral and cognitive universalism. This vision of the 'knowing subject' - or the 'Man' of humanism - posits itself as much by what it includes within the circle of his entitlements, as in what it excludes. Otherness is excluded by definition. This makes the others into structural or constitutive elements of the subject: the other functions as a negatively framed fraction of the same. The others play an important - albeit specular - role in the definition of the norm, the norm-al, the norm-ative view of the subject.

These others are: the sexualised other, also known as women, gays and trans-sex; the ethnic, native or racialised others and the natural, animal and environmental others. They constitute the inter-connected facets of structural otherness, which are constructed as excluded. To say that the structural others re-emerge with a vengeance in post modernity amounts to making otherness not into the site of negation, but rather into polyvalent sites of affirmation. It is a historical fact that the great emancipatory movements of post-modernity are driven and fuelled by the emergent 'others': the women's and gay rights movement; the anti-racism and de-colonisation movements; the anti-nuclear and pro-environment movements, animal rights included, are the voices of the structural Others of modernity. They also mark the crisis of the former 'centre' or dominant subject. In the language of philosophical nomadology, they express both the crisis of the majority and the patterns of becoming of the minorities. It is a case of: 'an/and', not of 'either/or'.

An affirmative ethics for a non-unitary subject proposes an enlarged sense of inter-connection between self and others, including the non-human or 'earth' others. This practice of relating to others requires and is enhanced by the rejection of self-centred individualism. It implies a new way of combining self-interests with the well being of an enlarged sense of community, which includes one's territorial or inhuman, i.e. environmental inter-connections. It is an eco-philosophy of multiple belongings for subjects constituted in and by multiplicity that stands in open disagreement with dominant Kantian morality and its feminist components. This has two corollaries.

The first concerns the question of universal values. An ethics of affirmation is capable of a universalistic reach, though it is critical of moral universalism. It expresses a grounded, partial form of accountability, based on a strong sense of collectivity, relationality and hence community building. There is a simple sense in which contemporary bio-genetic capitalism generates a global form of mutual inter-dependence of all living organisms, including, but not only the humans. This sort of unity tends to be of the negative kind, as a shared form of vulnerability. Bio-technological advances like the Human Genome project, for instance, unify all the human species in the urgency to oppose commercially owned and profit-minded technologies. Franklin, Lury and

20. Sarah Franklin, Celia Lury, Jackie Stacey, *Global Nature, Global Culture*, London, Sage, 2000, p26.

21. Paul Gilroy, *Against Race. Imaging Political Culture Beyond the Colour Line*, Cambridge, MA, Harvard University Press, 2000.

22. Avtar Brah, *Cartographies of diaspora - Contesting identities*, New York and London, Routledge, 1996.

23. Edouard Glissant, *Poetique de la Relation*, Paris, Gallimard, 1990, English translation *Poetics of Relation*, Betsy Wing (trans), Ann Arbor, University of Michigan Press, 1997.

24. Ernesto Laclau, 'Subjects of Politics, Politics of the Subject', *Differences*, 7, 1 (1995), pp146-164.

25. Homi K. Bhabha, *The Location of Culture*, London and New York, Routledge, 1994.

26. Vandana Shiva, *Biopiracy. The Plunder of Nature and Knowledge*, Boston, South End Press, 1997.

27. Patricia Hill Collins, *Black Feminist Thought. Knowledge, Consciousness and the politics of Empowerment*, New York and London, Routledge, 1991.

Stacey refer to this situation as 'pan humanity',[20] that is to say a global sense of inter-connection between the human and the non-human environment in the face of common threats: be it xenophobic populist politicians, or volcanoes, earthquakes and tsunamis. Again, notice the force of the negative here. But affirmation, as usual, is just around the corner.

The positive elements are twofold: firstly, the global re-contextualisation induced by the market economy also produces a sense of inter-connection. Secondly, the renewed sense of inter-connection produces the need for an ethics. The fact that 'we' are in *this* together results in a renewed claim to community and belonging by singular subjects who have taken critical distance from individualism. Far from falling into moral relativism, this results in a proliferation of locally situated micro-universalist claims. This is what Genny Lloyd called: 'a collaborative morality'.

One evident and illuminating example of this is the brand of situated cosmopolitan neo-humanism that has emerged as a powerful ethical claim in the work of postcolonial and race theorists, as well as in feminist theories. Examples are: Paul Gilroy's planetary cosmopolitanism;[21] Avtar Brah's diasporic ethics;[22] Edouard Glissant's politics of relations;[23] Ernesto Laclau's micro-universal claims;[24] Homi Bhabha's 'subaltern secularism';[25] Vandana Shiva's anti-global neo-humanism;[26] as well as the rising wave of interest in African humanism or Ubuntu, from Patricia Hill Collins[27] to Drucilla Cornell.[28] American black feminist theory has been post-secular for a long time, as bell hooks[29] and Cornel West[30] demonstrate.

Thus, the anti-humanism of social and cultural critics within a Western poststructuralist perspective can therefore be read alongside the cosmopolitan neo-humanism of contemporary race, post-colonial or non-Western critics. Both these positions, all other differences notwithstanding, produce inclusive alternatives to humanist individualism. Without wishing to flatten out structural differences, nor to draw easy analogies between them, I want to practice the politics of location and hence try to synchronise their efforts and tune their respective political aims and passions. It is an example of an encounter with otherness as a generative or affirmative force: bio-centred egalitarian post humanism on the one hand and non-western neo-humanism on the other transpose hybridity, nomadism, diasporas, creolisation processes into means of re-grounding claims to connections and alliances among different constituencies.

The second corollary supports my main thesis, that we need to stress the vital politics of life itself, which means external non-human relations, life as zoe, or generative force. The 'others' in question here are non-anthropomorphic and include planetary forces. This runs against the humanistic tradition of making the anthropocentric Other into the privileged site and inescapable horizon of otherness.

This is a point of major difference between nomadic philosophy and a number of Continental philosophers, like Jessica Benjamin[31] in her radicalisation of Irigaray's notion of 'horizontal transcendence'; Lyotard in the 'differed'[32] and his notion of the 'unatoned' and Butler[33] in her emphasis on 'precarious life'. You can approach otherness as the expression of a limit - albeit a negotiable one - which calls for an always already compromised set of negotiations. This is the function of the other's face in Levinas (1999) and, by extension, Derrida's ethics. It is also the position defended both by Simon Critchley on the infinite demand of the Other and the non-negotiable nature of 'justice' and 'hospitality'. I prefer to look instead for the ways in which otherness prompts, mobilises and allows for flows of affirmation of values and forces which are not yet sustained by the current conditions. That is affirmative ethics.

I should add for the sake of scholarly accuracy that Levinas' case is complex, as there are significant resonances between his notion of passivity and Deleuze's affirmation. Levinas' brand of immanence, however, differs considerably from Deleuze's life-oriented philosophy of becoming. Levinas - like Irigaray - inscribes the totality of the Self's reliance on the other as a structural necessity that transcends the 'I' but remains internal to it. Deleuze's immanence, on the other hand, firmly locates the affirmation in the exteriority, the cruel, messy outside-ness of Life itself. Creative chaos is not chaotic - it is the virtual formation of *all* possible forms.[34] Life is not an a priori that gets individuated in single instances, but it is immanent to and thus coincides with its multiple material actualisations. It is the site of birth and emergence of the new - life itself. I refer to this generative force as 'zoe', which is the opposite therefore of Agamben's 'bare life'- in that it is a creative force that constructs possible futures.

Traditional moral reasoning locates the constitution of subjectivity in the interrelation to others, which is a form of exposure, availability and vulnerability. This recognition entails the necessity of containing the other, the suffering and the enjoyment of others. I want to argue instead that an embodied and connecting containment as a moral category can also emerge from the radical redefinition of the same-other relation by the vital politics of life itself, as external and non-human forces: cells, as Franklin[35] argues; viruses and bacteria, as Luciana Parisi[36] points out; and earth others, as Haraway has been arguing for a long time. This post-human ethics rests on a multi-layered form of relationality. It assumes as the point of reference not the individual, but the relation. This means openness to others, in the positive sense of affecting and being affected by others, through couples and mutually dependent co-realities. Containment of the other occurs through inter-relational affectivity.

III. STEPS TO AFFIRMATIVE ETHICS

III.1 *What is affirmation?*
In order to understand the kind of transmutation of values I am defending here it is important to de-psychologise this discussion about positivity, negativity and affirmation, and approach it instead in more conceptual terms.

28. Drucilla Cornell, The Ubuntu Project with Stellenbosch University www.fehe.org/index.php?id=281, 2002. Consulted on 2 January 2007.

29. bell hooks, *Yearning: race, gender, and cultural politics*, Boston, MA, South End Press, 1990.

30. Cornel West, *Race Matters*, New York, Vintage, 1994.

31. Jessica Benjamin, *The Bonds of Love: Psychoanalysis, Feminism, and the Problems of Domination*, New York, Pantheon Books, 1988.

32. Jean-François Lyotard, *The Différend*, Collection "Critique", Paris, Editions de Minuit, 1983.

33. Butler, *Precarious Life*, op. cit.

34. Gilles Deleuze, *Logique du sens*, Paris, Minuit, 1969. English translation: *The Logic of Sense*, M. Lester and C. Stivale (trans), New York, Columbia University Press, 1990.

35. Franklin, Lury, Stacey, *Global Nature, Global Culture*, op. cit.

36. Luciana Parisi, *Abstract Sex. Philosophy, Bio-Technology, and the Mutation of Desire*, London, Continuum Press, 2004.

We can then see how common and familiar this transmutation of values actually is. The distinction between good and evil is replaced by that between affirmation and negation, or positive and negative affects.

What is positive in the ethics of affirmation is the belief that negative affects can be transformed. This implies a dynamic view of all affects, even those that freeze us in pain, horror or mourning. The slightly de-personalising effect of the negative or traumatic event involves a loss of ego-indexes perception, which allows for energetic forms of reaction. Clinical psychological research on trauma testifies to this, but I cannot pursue this angle here. Diasporic subjects of all kinds express the same insight. Multi-locality is the affirmative translation of this negative sense of loss. Following Glissant,[37] the becoming-nomadic marks the process of positive transformation of the pain of loss into the active production of multiple forms of belonging and complex allegiances. Every event contains within it the potential for being overcome and overtaken - its negative charge can be transposed. The moment of the actualisation is also the moment of its neutralisation. The ethical subject is the one with the ability to grasp the freedom to depersonalise the event and transform its negative charge. Affirmative ethics puts the motion back into e-motion and the active back into activism, introducing movement, process, becoming. This shift makes all the difference to the patterns of repetition of negative emotions. It also reopens the debate on secularity, in that it actually promotes an act of faith in our collective capacity to endure and to transform.

What is negative about negative affects is not a normative value judgment but rather the effect of arrest, blockage, rigidification, that comes as a result of a blow, a shock, an act of violence, betrayal, a trauma, or just intense boredom. Negative passions do not merely destroy the self, but also harm the self's capacity to relate to others - both human and non human others, and thus to grow in and through others. Negative affects diminish our capacity to express the high levels of inter-dependence, the vital reliance on others, that is the key to both a non-unitary vision of the subject and to affirmative ethics. Again, the vitalist notion of Life as 'zoe' is important here because it stresses that the Life I inhabit is not mine, it does not bear my name - it is a generative force of becoming, of individuation and differentiation: a-personal, indifferent and generative.

What is negated by negative passions is the power of life itself - its *potentia* - as the dynamic force, vital flows of connections and becoming. And this is why they should neither be encouraged nor should we be rewarded for lingering around them too long. Negative passions are black holes.

This is an antithesis of the Kantian moral imperative to avoid pain, or to view pain as the obstacle to moral behaviour. This displaces the grounds on which Kantian negotiations of limits can take place. The imperative not to do to others what you would not want done to you is not rejected as much as enlargened. In affirmative ethics, the harm you do to others is immediately reflected in the harm you do to yourself, in terms of loss of *potentia*, positivity, capacity to relate and hence freedom. Affirmative ethics is not about the

37. Edouard Glissant, *Poétique de la Relation* (1990), *Poetics of Relation*, Betsy Wing (trans), University of Michigan Press, 1997.

avoidance of pain, but rather about transcending the resignation and passivity that ensue from being hurt, lost and dispossessed. One has to become ethical, as opposed to applying moral rules and protocols as a form of self-protection: one has to endure.

Endurance is the Spinozist code word for this process. Endurance has a spatial side to do with the space of the body as an enfleshed field of actualisation of passions or forces. It evolves affectivity and joy, as in the capacity for being affected by these forces, to the point of pain or extreme pleasure. Endurance points to the struggle to sustain the pain without being annihilated by it. Endurance has also a temporal dimension, about duration in time. This is linked to memory: intense pain, a wrong, a betrayal, a wound are hard to forget. The traumatic impact of painful events fixes them in a rigid eternal present tense, out of which it is difficult to emerge. This is the eternal return of that which precisely cannot be endured and, as such, returns precisely in the mode of the unwanted, the untimely, the un-assimilated or in-appropriate/d. They are also, however, paradoxically difficult to remember, in so far as re-membering entails retrieval and repetition of the pain itself.

Psychoanalysis, of course, has been here before.[38] The notion of the return of the repressed is the key to the logic of unconscious remembrance, but it is a secret and somewhat invisible key which condenses space into the spasm of the symptom and time into a short-circuit that mines the very thinkability of the present. Kristeva's notion of the abject[39] expresses clearly the temporality involved in psychoanalysis - by stressing the structural function played by the negative, by the incomprehensible, the un-thinkable, the other - of understandable knowledge. Later Kristeva[40] describes this as a form of structural dissociation within the self that makes us strangers to ourselves.

Deleuze calls this alterity 'Chaos' and defines it positively as the virtual formation of all possible form. Lacan, on the other hand - and Derrida with him, I would argue - defines Chaos epistemologically as that which precedes form, structure, language. This makes for two radically divergent conceptions of time, and - more importantly for me today - of negativity. That which is incomprehensible for Lacan - following Hegel - is the virtual for Deleuze, following Spinoza, Bergson and Leibnitz. This produces a number of significant shifts: from negative to affirmative affects; from entropic to generative desire; from incomprehensible to virtual events to be actualised; from constitutive outsides to a geometry of affects that require mutual actualisation and synchronisation; from a melancholy and split to an open-ended web-like subject; from the epistemological to the ontological turn in poststructuralist philosophy.

Nietzsche has also been here before, of course. The eternal return in Nietzsche is the repetition, not in the compulsive mode of neurosis, nor in the negative erasure that marks the traumatic event. It is the eternal return of and as positivity. In a nomadic, Deleuzian-Nietzschean perspective, ethics is essentially about transformation of negative into positive passions, i.e. moving beyond the pain. This does not mean denying the pain, but rather

38. Jean Laplanche, *Life and death in Psychoanalysis*, Baltimore and London, Johns Hopkins University Press, 1976.

39. Julia Kristeva, *Powers of Horror*, New York, Colombia University Press, 1982.

40. Julia Kristeva, *Strangers to Ourselves*, New York, Colombia University, 1991.

41. Zygmunt
Bauman, *Postmodern
Ethics*, Oxford,
Blackwell's Publisher,
1993.

42. Susan Sontag,
*Regarding the Pain
of Others*, New York,
Picador, 2003.

43. Paul Gilroy, *After
Empire. Melancholia
or Convivial Culture?*,
London and New
York, Routledge,
2004; Butler,
Precarious Life, op.
cit.

activating it, working it through. Again, the positivity here is not supposed to indicate a facile optimism, or a careless dismissal of human suffering. It involves compassionate witnessing of the pain of others, as Zygmunt Bauman[41] and Susan Sontag[42] point out - in the mode of empathic co-presence.

III. 2. *About pain and vulnerability*

But what about pain? Affirmative politics, with its emphasis on Life as a generative force, may seem counter-intuitive at first. And yet, the urge that prompts this approach is anything but abstract. It is born of the awareness that in-depth transformations are at best demanding and at worst painful. This is not a complaint, nor is it meant as a deterrent against change. I consider melancholic states and the rhetoric of the lament as integral to the logic of advanced capitalism and hence as a dominant ideology. Many leading intellectuals specialise in and profit from this genre.

I do not want to suggest that the politics of mourning and the political economy of melancholia are intrinsically reactive or necessarily negative. A number of critical theorists argue forcefully the case for the productive nature of melancholia and its potential for creating solidarity.[43] I am also convinced that melancholia expresses a form of loyalty through identification with the wound of others and hence that it promotes an ecology of belonging by upholding the collective memory of trauma or pain. My argument is rather that the politics of melancholia has become so dominant in our culture that it ends up functioning like a self-fulfilling prophecy, which leaves very small margins for alternative approaches. I want to argue therefore for the need to experiment with other ethical relations as a way of producing an ethics of affirmation.

Our conservative political context, moreover, has placed undue emphasis on the risks involved in changes, playing *ad nauseam* the refrain about the death of transformative politics. Nothing could be further removed from my project. I simply want to issue a cautionary note: processes of change and transformation are so important and so vital and necessary, that they have to be handled with care. We have to take the pain of change into account, not as an obstacle to, but as a major incentive for, an ethics of transformations.

Let's talk about pain for a moment. Pain in our culture is associated with suffering by force of habit and tradition and is given negative connotations accordingly. Supposing we look a bit more critically into this associative link, however: what does pain, or suffering, tell us? That our subjectivity consists of affectivity, inter-relationality and forces. The core of the subject is affect and the capacity for interrelations to affect and to be affected. Let us agree to de-psychologise this discussion from this moment on, not in order to deny the pain, but rather to find ways of working through it.

If we assume the affective core of subjectivity, for instance with Spinoza's theory of *conatus* or active desire for empowerment, then the aim of ethics becomes the expression of the active or productive nature of desire. It then follows that affirmative politics is not about an oppositional strategy; it is not another discourse about storming the Bastille of phallocentrism, or undoing the winter palace of gender (Lenin meets Butler there in a metaphorical delirium). Politics becomes multiple micro-political practices of daily activism or interventions in and on the world we inhabit. If this is the aim, then what happens to that traditional association between pain and suffering? More specifically, how do we assess the pain linked to political processes of change and transformation? My point is that we need to de-link pain from suffering and re-think its role in constituting ethical relations.

Taking pain into account is the starting point; the aim of the ethical process, however, is the quest for ways of overcoming the effects of passivity, the paralysis brought about by pain. The internal disarray, fracture and pain are also the conditions of possibility for ethical transformation. The qualitative leap through and across pain is the gesture that actualises affirmative ways of becoming. This is a gesture that constructs hope as a collective social project.

It is those who have already cracked up a bit, those who have suffered pain and injury, that are better placed to take the lead in the process of ethical transformation. Their 'better quality' consists not in the fact of having been wounded, but of having gone through the pain. Because they are already on the other side of some existential divide, they are anomalous in some way - but in a positive way: they have already endured. They are a site of transposition of values. Marxist epistemology, post-colonial and feminist standpoint theories have always acknowledged the privileged knowing position of those in the 'margins'. The figure of Nelson Mandela - a contemporary secular saint - comes to mind. As does the world-historical phenomenon that is the Truth and Reconciliation Commission in post-apartheid South Africa. This is a case of repetition that engenders difference and does not install the eternal return of revenge and negative affects. A massive exercise in transformation of negativity, into something more sustainable, more life enhancing.

III.3 *Being worthy of what happens to us*
One of the reasons why the negative associations linked to pain, especially in relation to political processes of change, are ideologically laden has to do with the force of habit. Starting from the assumption that a subject is a molar aggregate, that is to say a sedimentation of established habits, these can be seen as patterns of repetitions that consolidate modes of relation and forces of interaction. Habits are the frame within which non-unitary or complex subjects get re-territorialised, albeit temporarily. One of the established habits in our culture is to frame 'pain' within a discourse and social practice of suffering which requires rightful compensation.

Equally strong is the urge to understand and empathise with pain. People go to great lengths in order to ease all pain. Great distress follows from not knowing or not being able to articulate the source of one's suffering, or from knowing it all too well, all the time. The yearning for solace, closure and justice is understandable and worthy of respect.

44. Lyotard, op. cit.

This ethical dilemma was already posed by J.F. Lyotard[44] and, much earlier, by Primo Levi about the survivors of Nazi concentration camps. Namely that the kind of vulnerability we humans experience in face of events on the scale of small or high horror is something for which no adequate compensation is even thinkable. It is just incommensurable: a hurt, or wound, beyond repair. This means that the notion of justice in the sense of a logic of rights and reparation is not applicable. For the post-structuralist Lyotard, ethics consists in accepting the impossibility of adequate compensation - and living with the open wound.

This is the road to an ethics of affirmation, which respects the pain but suspends the quest for both claims and compensation and resists the logic of retribution of rights. This is achieved through a sort of de-personalisation of the event, which is the ultimate ethical challenge. The dis-placement of the 'zoe'-indexed reaction reveals the fundamental meaningless-ness of the hurt, the injustice or injury one has suffered. 'Why me?' is the refrain most commonly heard in situations of extreme distress. This expresses rage as well as anguish at one's ill fate. The answer is plain: actually, for no reason at all. Examples of this are the banality of evil in large-scale genocides like the Holocaust,[45] the randomness of surviving them. There is something intrinsically senseless about the pain, hurt or injustice: lives are lost or saved for all and no reason at all. Why did some go to work in the WTC on 9/11 while others missed the train? Why did Frida Kahlo take that tram which crashed so that she was impaled by a metal rod, and not the next one? For no reason at all. Reason has nothing to do with it. That's precisely the point. We need to de-link pain from the epistemological obsession that results in the quest for meaning and move beyond, to the next stage. That is the path to transformation of negative into positive passions.

45. Hannah Arendt, *Eichmann in Jerusalem: A Report on the Banality of Evil*, New York, Viking Press, 1963.

This is not fatalism, and even less resignation, but rather Nietzschean ethics of overturning the negative. Let us call it: *amor fati*: we have to be worthy of what happens to us and rework it within an ethics of relation. Of course repugnant and unbearable events do happen. Ethics consists, however, in reworking these events in the direction of positive relations. This is not carelessness or lack of compassion, but rather a form of lucidity that acknowledges the meaningless-ness of pain and the futility of compensation. It also re-asserts that the ethical instance is not that of retaliation or compensation, but it rather rests on active transformation of the negative.

This requires a double shift. Firstly the affect itself moves from the frozen or reactive effect of pain to proactive affirmation of its generative potential. Secondly, the line of questioning also shifts from the quest for the origin or source to a process of elaboration of the questions that express and enhance a subject's capacity to achieve freedom through the understanding of its limits.

What is an adequate ethical question? One which is capable of sustaining the subject in his/her quest for more inter-relations with others, i.e: more 'Life', motion, change, and transformation. The adequate ethical question provides the subject with a frame for interaction and change, growth and movement. It affirms life as difference-at-work and as endurance. An ethical question has to be adequate in relation to how much a body can take. How much can an embodied entity take in the mode of inter-relations and connections, i.e., how much freedom of action can we endure? Affirmative ethics assumes, following Nietzsche, that humanity does not stem out of freedom but rather that freedom is extracted out of the awareness of limitations. Affirmation is about freedom from the burden of negativity, freedom through the understanding of our bondage.

IV. ON THE ADVANTAGES OF DIS-IDENTIFICATION

Transformative ethics involves a radical repositioning on the part of the knowing subject, which is neither simple, self-evident, nor free of pain. No process of consciousness-raising ever is. In feminist theory over the last 30 years we have explored this issue from the initial slogan 'the personal is the political', through the politics of location,[46] into the multiple situated perspectives of today. Feminist theory is double-edged and it involves both critique and creativity. In post-structuralist feminism, this has also been discussed in terms of dis-identifying ourselves from familiar and hence comforting values and identities.[47]

46. Adrienne Rich, *Your Native Land, Your Life*, New York, W. W. Norton, 1986.

Dis-identification involves the loss of cherished habits of thought and representation, which can produce fear, a sense of insecurity and nostalgia. Change is certainly a painful process. If it were not, more people may actually be tempted to try it out. This does not, however, equate it with suffering and hence acquire necessarily negative connotations. To believe this would be a politically conservative position. The point in stressing the difficulties and pain involved in the quest for transformative ethics and politics is to raise an awareness of both the complexities involved and the paradoxes that lie in store.

47. Teresa de Lauretis, *Feminist Studies/Critical Studies*, Bloomington, Indiana University Press, 1986; Rosi Braidotti, *Nomadic Subjects*, Columbia University Press, 1994.

Changes that affect one's sense of identity are especially delicate. Given that identifications constitute an inner scaffolding that supports one's sense of identity, shifting our imaginary identifications is not as simple as casting away a used garment. Psychoanalysis taught us that imaginary re-locations are as complex and as time-consuming as shedding an old skin. Moreover, changes of this qualitative kind happen more easily at the molecular or subjective level and their translation into a public discourse and shared social experiences is a complex and risk-ridden affair. Spinozist feminist political thinkers like Genevieve Lloyd and Moira Gatens[48] argue that such socially embedded and historically grounded changes are the result of 'collective imaginings' - a shared desire for certain transformations to be actualised as a collaborative effort.

48. Moira Gatens and Genevieve Lloyd, *Collective Imaginings: Spinoza, past and present*, London and New York, Routledge, 1999.

Let me give you a series of concrete examples of how dis-identifications from dominant models of subject-formation can be productive and creative events. First of all, feminist theory is based on a radical dis-engagement from the dominant institutions and representations of femininity and masculinity,

49. Paul Gilroy,
Against Race,
Harvard University
Press, 2000; Hill
Collins, *Black
Feminist Thought*,
op. cit.

50. Vron Ware,
*Beyond the Pale. White
Women, Racism and
History*, London and
New York, Verso,
1992; Gabrielle
Griffin and Rosi
Braidotti (eds),
*Thinking Differently:
a Reader in European
Women's Studies*,
London, Zed Books,
2002.

51. Edgar Morin,
Penser l'Europe, Paris,
Gallimard, 1987.

52. Etienne Balibar,
*Politics and the Other
Scene*, London,
Verso, 2002.

to enter the process of becoming-minoritarian or of transforming gender. In doing so feminism combines critique with creation of alternative ways of embodying and experiencing our sexualised selves. In spite of massive media battering and the marketing of political conservatism, there is no credible evidence among European women of a nostalgic desire to return to traditional gender and sex roles.

Secondly, in race discourse, the awareness of the persistence of racial discrimination and of white privilege has led to serious disruptions of our accepted views of what constitutes a subject. This has resulted on the one hand in the critical re-appraisal of blackness[49] and on the other to radical relocations of whiteness.[50] Finally, I would like to refer to Edgar Morin's account of how he relinquished Marxist cosmopolitanism to embrace a more 'humble' perspective as a European.[51] This process includes both positive and negative affects: disappointment with the unfulfilled promises of Marxism is matched by compassion for the uneasy, struggling and marginal position of post-war Europe, squashed between the USA and the USSR. This produces a renewed sense of care and accountability that leads Morin to embrace a post-nationalistic redefinition of Europe as the site of mediation and transformation of it own history.[52]

Beneficial or positive aspects balance the negative aspects of the process. The benefits are epistemological but extend beyond; they include a more adequate cartography of our real-life conditions and hence less pathos-ridden accounts. Becoming free of the topos that equates pain with suffering and links in-depth change to the latter results in a more adequate level of self-knowledge. It enhances the lucidity of our assessments and therefore clears the grounds for more adequate and sustainable relations. This means that the emphasis commonly placed on the force of the negative is out of balance and needs to be reconsidered.

***

The ethical process of transforming negative into positive passions engenders a politics of affirmation, in the sense of creating the conditions for endurance and hence for a sustainable future. Virtual futures grow out of sustainable presents and vice versa. Transformative politics takes on the future as the shared collective imagining that endures in processes of becoming.

53. G.E.R.
Lloyd, *Adversaries
and Authorities*,
Cambridge
University Press,
1996, p74.

This results not in egoism but in mutually embedded nests of shared interests. Lloyd calls this 'a collaborative morality'.[53] Because the starting point with Spinoza is not the isolated individual, but complex and mutually depended co-realities, the self other interaction also follows a different model. To be an individual means to be open to being affected by and through others, thus undergoing transformations in such a way as to be able to sustain them and make them work towards growth. An ethical life pursues that which enhances and strengthens the subject without reference to transcendental values, but rather in the awareness of one's interconnection with others and in multiple modes of interaction with heterogeneous others. The ethical good is the affirmative production of the conditions which will augment our capacity to act in the world in a productive manner - *potentia* as the active engagement with the present, by being worthy of it but also by combining it with the ability and the force to resist the negativity. The ethical-political concept here is the necessity to think with the times and in spite of the times, not in a belligerent mode of oppositional consciousness, but as a humble and empowering gesture of co-construction of social horizons of hope.

A Tragic Note: on Negri and Deleuze in the Light of the 'Argentinazo'

Jorge Camacho

In 1798, when Kant engaged in that prophetic or divinatory exercise of historical reflection entitled 'An Old Question Raised Again: Is the Human Race Constantly Progressing?', he looked for 'an event', 'an historical sign' within the current affairs of the world that would allow him to justify his unrepentant optimism about the prospects of a universal and republican constitution for the human race.[1] He found it in the revolutionary events then taking place in France or, more precisely - and somehow prefiguring the recent theme of fidelity to events - in the 'enthusiasm' that such political process was awakening in people across Europe.[2]

Arguably, a contemporary version of such divinatory optimism is to be found in Michael Hardt and Antonio Negri's recent work, specifically in their political philosophy of the *multitude*. They have postulated a 'materialist teleology' for the recent mutations of capitalist forms of production and communication. From their perspective, the end (seemingly in the double sense of goal and conclusion) of these recent re-configurations is the production of a new political subject capable of precipitating a radical Event. In these conditions, they claim: 'The possibility of democracy on a global scale is emerging today for the very first time'.[3] The comparison with Kant is warranted not simply for the optimism displayed but for the justification adduced: the task of a political manifesto, and for which its prophetic character is deployed, is to participate in the realisation of its own divinations.[4]

If, as Kant did, one had looked a few years ago for an historical sign that Hardt and Negri's optimistic manifesto was indeed justified and participating in the process, the political upheaval then taking place in Argentina could have justifiably emerged as a strong candidate. As one commentator argued, 'the novelty and peculiarity of the social movements that emerged out of the crisis was seen by many as signalling the consolidation and growth of the global struggles against neoliberalism'.[5] The participation of unemployed, women, students and the middle classes in general (which exploded any homogenous conception of proletariat), the vibrant experimentation with novel and immanent forms of political and economic organisation (to a great extent outside of traditional Left institutions), and even a repudiation of the capitalist order in the national and global stage: all of those could have been read as signs that Hardt and Negri's *multitude* was actually waking up in the southern cone of the American continent. A panoply of movements: *piqueteros*, *asambleas barriales*, *fabricas recuperadas* and *clubes de trueque*, gave a concrete illustration of how a multitude (consistent with Hardt and Negri's

1. Immanuel Kant, 'An Old Question Raised Again: Is the Human Race Constantly Progressing?', in Lewis White Beck (ed), *Kant on History*, New York, The Bobbs-Merril Co., p143; see also pp146-47.

2. Ibid., p144; see also xii. The reference for fidelity and events, of course, is Alain Badiou, *Being and Event*, London, Continuum, 2006, Part V, pp201-51.

3. Michael Hardt and Antonio Negri, *Multitude: War and Democracy in the Age of Empire*, London, Hamish Hamilton, 2005, pxi.

4. See Michael Hardt and Antonio Negri, *Empire*, Cambridge, Harvard University Press, 2000, pp63-66; Kant, op. cit., p137.

5. Guido Starosta, 'Debating the Argentine Crisis. Replies to Ana Dinerstein. Editorial Introduction', *Historical Materialism*, 14, 1 (2006), 15ff.

DOI:10.3898/NEWF.68.04.2009

model) could come together as a constituent power. 'The revolt of Argentina', they themselves pointed out, 'was born with the common heritage of the global cycle of struggle at its back, and, in turn, ever since December 2001, activists from elsewhere have looked to Argentina as a source of innovation and inspiration'.[6]

6. Hardt and Negri, *Multitude*, op. cit., pp216-17.

And yet, just as much as the French revolution didn't herald the accomplishment of Kant's vision of cosmopolitan unity, nothing close to the spectacular event that realises 'democracy on a global scale' seems to have followed from the *Argentinazo* or, indeed, from any of the multiple and important struggles against contemporary capitalism that marked the turn of the century and subtended much of Hardt and Negri's analyses. Today, the radical climate in Argentina has largely receded, and the political and economic order of capitalist 'democracy' has managed, for the most part, to reinstate itself there once more. Arguably, despite the strength of its irruption and its exemplary character, which make it a singularity in contemporary history, the revolt can hardly be seen as a process of constitution in itself or, at any rate, as a step or contribution in a progressive and teleological sequence towards national or global post-capitalist democracy.

An important philosophical reference within Hardt and Negri's two-volume manifesto, *Empire* and *Multitude*, is the work of Gilles Deleuze, specifically the second volume of *Capitalism and Schizophrenia* co-written with Félix Guattari.[7] Indeed, for some commentators there seems to be a smooth continuity between the ideas of the French philosophers and the political philosophy recently developed by Hardt and Negri. Nevertheless, anyone who engages more closely with their work may be able to find sufficient and important points of divergence from which political consequences may follow. The exploration of those points may be a good strategy in an exploration not only of Negri's philosophy but also - and more important in the context of this volume - of the problematic status of politics in Deleuze's thought.

7. See Hardt and Negri, *Empire*, op. cit., p415 n4.

In fact, one of these divergences is precisely related to Negri's optimism or, to put it correctly, his philosophical need for a teleological tendency vis-à-vis Deleuze's decidedly non-teleological ontology, which is accompanied by a suspension of historical finalism and consequently points towards an open-ended or 'undecidable' horizon. In a conversation between Negri and Deleuze translated under the title 'Control and Becoming', the former denounces the problematic status of *A Thousand Plateaus* in the context of political philosophy. From Negri's point of view, the intense theoretical exploration undertaken in that work, however important it may be for philosophy, amounts to nothing more than a 'catalogue of unsolved problems' for politics. And he continues: 'I seem sometimes to hear a tragic note, at points where it's not clear where the "war-machine" is going'.[8]

8. 'Control and Becoming. Gilles Deleuze in conversation with Toni Negri'. Available from: http://www. generation-online. org/p/fpdeleuze3. htm. Originally published in *Futur Anterieur*, 1 (1990).

In the light of the 'tragic' fate of Argentina's revolutionary experience, the present article sets out to highlight this philosophical discrepancy and to raise the question about the consequences that could be seen as following from these points of tension. In broad terms, the issues at stake are: multiplicity, immanence and heterogeneity in the political ontology of the multitude; the problem of teleology for ontology in general, and political ontology in particular, as well as its place within a philosophical assessment of contemporary history; the philosophical problem of vitalism in Deleuze's work and its becoming-political in Negri's conception of 'biopolitics'; the status of Marxism as theoretico-political perspective and its concept of capitalism within Deleuze and Guattari's philosophy. There will be no attempt here to construct either an exhaustive historical account or a novel explanation or analysis of the Argentine revolt. The focus of the piece is rather a comparative analysis of a specific aspect of the work of these philosophers in the light of those events. The challenge, of course, is to see whether or not it is possible, via an encounter between Negri and Deleuze, to look in the direction of possible instances of experimentation that, as is always the case, seem to be already taking place.

EVENTS

On 3 December 2001, in the context of a 'zero deficit' programme instituted by the Argentine government under pressure from the International Monetary Fund (IMF), the Minister of Economy, Domingo Cavallo, announced that drastic financial measure later known as *corralito* (for the analogy of money being trapped inside a 'playpen'). Intended to stop the flight of money in order to save banking institutions from bankruptcy, it entailed restrictions on people's access to savings and salaries deposited there: cash withdrawals of no more than $250 per week, no monthly transfers abroad of more than $1000, fixed term savings to be automatically renewed, payments to be done by cheque or debit and credit cards. While it was obvious that such measures would mainly and directly affect the 'saver' middle class, its consequences were widely spread across Argentine society, including workers who failed to receive their salary (supposedly due to the restrictions imposed) and, most significantly, a whole lower stratum of the formal and informal economy entirely dependent upon cash-based trading.[9]

9. See Daniel Pereyra, *Argentina Rebelde. Crónicas y Enseñanzas de la Revuelta Social*, Madrid, El Viejo Topo, 2003, pp96-97.

The grim face of 'zero deficit' continued to appear during the following weeks as national and local governments withheld public workers' salaries, unemployment benefits and all forms of social assistance; middle-class spending power diminished; and unemployment figures rose alarmingly, with the number of people living below the poverty line increasing accordingly. Meanwhile, looting and demands for food on big supermarkets intensified in Buenos Aires and other provinces like Entre Ríos, Salta, Mendoza and Santa Fé, leading at times to arrests and confrontations with the police. On 12 December, the *Confederación General del Trabajo* (CGT) called for a demonstration in front of the Congress using the slogan '*Huelga general hasta que se vayan*' ('General strike until they leave'). This general strike exploded the following day and spread out to cities like Córdoba, Rosario, Tucumán, and Mendoza. 'The climate of civil disobedience', Lobato and Suriano sum up, 'was evident in the continuous demonstrations, the street and highway blocks [*cortes de ruta*], the black-outs, the *cacerolazos* [pan-banging] and the *bocinazos* [car horn-sounding]'.[10]

On the night of 19 December, following a day of widespread unrest, President De La Rúa appeared on television declaring a state of emergency intended to last for thirty days. Even before his speech was finished, a massive *cacerolazo* resounded as people in Buenos Aires stormed to the Plaza de Mayo, and later on, all through the night, to the Congress, to the house of Minister Cavallo, to De La Rúa's official residence, etc. 'All the city of Buenos Aires was an enormous *corte* [*de ruta*], a multitudinous *piquete* [picket line] with hundreds of barricades of burning tires, traffic lights brought down, groups of people protesting in front of banks, multinationals and public buildings'.[11] At one o'clock that morning, Cavallo presented his resignation. December 20 witnessed a strong repressive comeback from the government as police tried to re-establish order, mainly by taking over the Plaza de Mayo and central Buenos Aires. Police tanks, horses, tear gas, rubber and real bullets made their appearance during those clashes: thirty people are estimated to have died around the country during those two days, and many more were injured and arrested. Yet, as Pereyra points out, 'the popular response was very combative'.[12] The emblematic chant began to take shape: '*¡Que se vayan todos, que no quede ni uno solo!*' ('They all must go! Not even one must remain!') President De La Rúa followed up on Cavallo's resignation and took flight from the Casa Rosada on board a helicopter while protests continued on the ground.

Certainly one must be careful, in the face of a spectacular insurrection like this, of interpreting it as a spontaneous irruption or even of treating it exclusively as a response to the financial crisis that preceded it. Argentina's '19 y 20' (as it has come to be known) illustrate quite well what historian Fernand Braudel said of the historical event: 'Infinitely extensible, it becomes wedded, either freely or not, to a whole chain of events, of underlying realities which are then, it seems, impossible to separate'.[13] In this case, such a chain of events and realities - extending through the last quarter of the century - links the process through which Argentina was constituted as a laboratory of neoliberal economic policies with the sequence of progressive revitalisation of social struggles following the period of brutal repression exercised by the military *junta*. In this sense, the Argentine event may be better interpreted as a full stop, marking something like a structural collapse or the end of a secular trend driven by a specific framework of political intervention.

Nowhere else, except perhaps for neighbouring Chile, were the ideal conditions of neoliberalism - a political project of the capitalist class to restore the rate of profit, according to Duménil and Lévy's verdict - more forcefully set in place. Argentina's case fits perfectly with these authors' thesis on neoliberalism as 'the expression of the desire of a class of capitalist owners and the institutions in which their power is concentrated, which we collectively call "finance", to restore - in the context of a general decline in popular

10. Mirta Lobato and Juan Suriano, *La Protesta Social en la Argentina*, Buenos Aires, Fondo de Cultura Económica, 2003, p149; see also pp148-52; Pereyra, op. cit., pp95-99; Ana Dinerstein, 'The Battle of Buenos Aires: Crisis, Insurrection and the Reinvention of Politics in Argentina', *Historical Materialism*, 10, 4 (2002), pp21-23.

11. Pereyra, op. cit., p100.

12. Ibid., p102.

13. Fernand Braudel, 'History and the Social Sciences: The *Longue Durée*,' in Fernand Braudel, *On History*, Chicago, University of Chicago Press, 1980, p28.

14. Gerard Duménil and Dominique Lévy, *Capital Resurgent: Roots of the Neoliberal Revolution*, London, Harvard University Press, 2004, p2.

15. Alberto R. Bonnet, *'¿Qué se vayan todos!*: Discussing the Argentine Crisis and Insurrection', *Historical Materialism*, 14, 1 (2006), p163.

16. Ibid., p161.

17. Dinerstein, op. cit., p15.

18. Bonnet, op. cit., p168.

19. Dinerstein, op. cit., p16; Bonnet, op. cit., p166.

20. Dumenil and Levy, op. cit., p1.

21. Pereyra, op. cit., pp50-57.

struggles - the class's revenues and power, which had diminished since the great depression and World War II'.[14] Accordingly, in Argentina this political project can be traced all the way back to the period of military dictatorship, following into the first democratic administration of Alfonsín, and later to Menem and De La Rua's governments. Following Alberto R. Bonnet's analysis, we will jump into the process already with the ascension of Menem to power and the reincorporation of Cavallo as Minister of Economy.[15] It was then that the neoliberal framework of intervention found its most important weapon in the law of convertibility that paired Argentine peso and US dollar. As Bonnet argues: 'The policies articulated around convertibility must be interpreted ... as a specific case of monetary policies of social discipline imposed at a global level and aimed at the recomposition of profitability through the increase in the level of labour exploitation'.[16] Moreover, the law of convertibility itself was the pivotal centre of a larger set of economic policies, falling neatly into that framework so-called 'the Washington consensus', required to complete the insertion of Argentina's economy into the world market. Dinerstein recounts the means through which a 'great transformation' was achieved: 'tax exemptions, privatisation of the 93 state-owned enterprises, industrial subsidies, the deregulation of financial and labour markets, the flexibilisation of labour, the decentralisation of collective bargaining and tying wages to productivity, the reduction of employers' contributions to union welfare funds and social security, the marketisation of health, social security and work accidents insurance'.[17]

Despite an initial period of successful performance, the stability and competitiveness of Argentine capitalism in the world economy was undermined by a trend towards longer and deeper recessions punctuated by the effects of international financial crises.[18] Under those conditions, economic performance was only sustained on the basis of further and further exactions on society: the reduction of nominal wages, the deregulation of labour markets and flexibilisation of contracts, as well as, most significantly, the dramatic growth of sub-employment and unemployment (the latter reaching 20 per cent in 2000), brought about by bankruptcies or technological and organisational restructuring.[19] In the face of this, Duménil and Lévy seem quite correct when they argue that the neoliberal framework of intervention brings with it the restoration of 'the most violent features of capitalism, making for a resurgent, unprettified capitalism'.[20] Only a growth of social resistance marked the limit to these interventions.

Pereyra traces this process of growth back to the violent episodes of rebellion and repression of state-workers in Santiago del Estero, December 1993, and Jujuy, March 1994, when local governments - in their quest to reduce public deficit, according to the adjustment programs - failed to deliver salaries.[21] Later that year, in July, the *Central de Trabajadores Argentinos* (CTA) and the *Movimiento de Trabajadores Argentinos* (MTA) - two dissident split-offs from the CGT - along with a diverse group of organisations including students, small-scale agricultural and industrial producers, and left-wing parties, called for a federal march to protest against the economic policies of Menem's administration. Most significantly, in June 1996 the Patagonian cities of Cutral-Có and Plaza Huincul witnessed the birth of the *piquetero* movement. The population there was deeply affected by unemployment following the privatisation of *Yacimientos Petrolíferos Fiscales* (YPF) in favour of the Spanish *Repsol*. When the national government cancelled a project for the installation of a plant of fertilisers, they decided to block the *ruta nacional* 22 and maintained it thanks to the involvement of over 20,000 people, despite the government's attempts at repression. The following years leading to the events of 2001 (which there is no space to recount here) saw the extension and intensification of protest against the consequences of the neoliberal intervention mainly pivoting, on one hand, around local or nation-wide, union-led (CGT, MTA, CTA, etc.) demonstrations and general strikes, and, on the other, around the *piquetero* movement. The latter extended its *cortes de ruta* to many provinces including greater Buenos Aires; it also got progressively organised in groups like the *Movimento de Trabajadores Desocupados* (MTD) and the *Federación Tierra y Vivienda* (FTV), reaching its climax in two national congresses in July and September 2001.

The failure of the framework of convertibility was finally expressed in two dimensions: externally, in the default on the ridiculously expanding foreign debt and the consequent pressure exerted by the IMF upon the nation; internally, by the approaching crisis of the banking sector precipitated by the accelerating flight of deposits.[22] This latter, and the politico-economic measures employed to remediate it, as we saw at the beginning of this section, brought with it the final ingredient for a widespread insurrection that was already virtually present. With the addition of the middle sectors to the long list of discontented groups, the legitimacy of the political framework of intervention and of the groups in charge of implementing it could no longer be maintained. The multiplicity of sectors actively opposed now included a diversity ranging from unemployed workers facing conditions of extreme poverty to small-scale producers and traders as well as self-employed professionals affected by the economic crisis and the *corralito*, going through public-sector, industrial, and service-industry workers suffering the consequences of flexibilisation and reduction of wages. It is precisely at this point that we can most easily find a resonance with Hardt and Negri's theory about a new potential political subject. The Argentine insurrection seemingly provided concrete evidence to support the sociology and political ontology of the *multitude*.

POLITICAL ORGANISMS

At its most abstract or formal level, in its ontological wire frame, so to speak, the figure of the multitude is really simple and the construction of its concept has now become almost a commonplace.[23] First of all, the multitude is conceived as a *multiplicity*, following in the wake of Deleuze's proposal of

22. Bonnet, op. cit., p171.

23. See Hardt and Negri, *Multitude*, pp99-100; also Paolo Virno, *A Grammar of the Multitude*, New York, Semiotext(e), 2004, pp21-26.

this concept as a solution to the ancient philosophical opposition between the One and the Many. For Deleuze, 'multiplicity must not designate a combination of the many and the one, but rather an *organisation* belonging to the many as such, which has no need whatsoever of unity in order to form a system'.[24] In political ontology, the multitude *qua* multiplicity is thus consequently distinguished both from the *people* (as the figure of the One or unity) and other concepts that manage only to capture the unarticulated or unorganised Many: crowds, masses. Moreover, the multitude is a figure that articulates heterogeneity (diversity, plurality) as such and thrives on it, unlike the people, which homogenises, and the masses or crowds which, homogeneous or heterogeneous as they may be, remain unarticulated anyway. Most significantly, in political terms, whereas the people is ruled by transcendent and vertical or hierarchical forms of sovereignty like the State, and the crowd remains simply unruly and unorganised, the multitude is the embodiment of immanent and horizontal or non-hierarchical forms of organisation (its topology is that of distributed networks). The multitude is active; the other figures are more on the passive side. Finally, and most importantly, the masses or crowds are only stupid; the people, in turn, is dumb - for they relinquish their capacities to speak and think to a transcendent head like the State and other institutions of representation; however, the multitude, as conceived by Hardt and Negri, is endowed with emergent properties: a *collective intelligence*.

Still, as they explain, this is only the multitude under its eternal aspect, *sub specie aeternitatis*: a possibility that has haunted all historical situations. An exploration of this possibility in the contemporary world must always fall back on its material or economic conditions. Thus, an indispensable step taken by Hardt and Negri is to account for the process of class re-composition that has recently shaped the proletariat - understood as all those 'directly or indirectly exploited by and subjected to capitalist norms of production and reproduction' - as a potential multitude.[25] They propose a new model for the sociology of this *postmodern* proletariat that decentres the figure of the industrial worker, raises the figure of the 'immaterial' worker to an *economically* hegemonic position and accounts in equal measure for the role of women, the unemployed, the emigrant, the poor. Arguably, it was this latter, outward expansion of the proletariat that was more significant for the Argentine situation.

The formation of the *piquetero* movement coincides with the growth of the unemployed sector - which went from 16 per cent in 1988-1989 to 40 per cent in 2002.[26] With unemployed workers cut from the site of production and from its gremial affiliations, a movement of a new kind was born with new locales, methods and forms of organisation, different and relatively disconnected from the precedent organisations of the left. The route or highway and the neighbourhood effectively replaced the factory as pivotal locales. This constituted the material condition for the heterogeneous composition of the movement: it included not only workers who had lost their jobs but also young people that never even managed to get their

24. Gilles Deleuze, *Difference and Repetition*, London, Continuum, 2004, p230, emphasis added.

25. Hardt and Negri, *Empire*, p52; see also p51, 4-5 n12 and pp284-94.

26. Dinerstein, op. cit., p16.

first one; to a great extent it included also precarious, self-employed and employed workers; most importantly, it granted a key role to women who, in those critical conditions of survival, acquired a central role in the family and the community, and constituted the initial thrust and driving force behind the movement. Furthermore, a central feature of this movement, as Pereyra explains, was 'an exemplary democratic system of decision-making by means of assemblies where all the participants in the *piquetes* took part, irrespective of sex, age or labour activity, be they active workers or unemployed'.[27]

27. Pereyra, op. cit., p55.

The question of direct democracy was also a central problem for the movement of *asambleas barriales* ('neighbourhood assemblies'). This was a unique movement for it was the only one that properly emerged in the wake of the crisis, having its origin in the *cacerolazo* that exploded in Buenos Aires on 19 and 20 December. To the extent that its locale was also not the workplace but the city, the neighbourhood itself, its composition was equally heterogeneous along different lines: gender, age, economic activity, employment status, etc. (although it was the preferred form of mobilisation for the middle classes). The development of this movement displays a curve marking a stage of growth and intensification in the early days, then a process of articulation among different assemblies - punctuated by inter-neighbourhood assemblies in Buenos Aires and a National Popular Assembly - and finally a long tendency towards relative decline. The outward dimension of this movement was the expression of a diversity of demands of which perhaps the most significant was a call for the articulation of local assemblies into a proper Constituent Assembly. The inward dimension, centred on the *asambleas de base*, was directed to a great extent to fill the void left by a withering State regarding the provision of public spaces and services. State- or privately-owned buildings and sites were occupied to improvise a diversity of communal resources. An important feature of the movement of *asambleas barriales* was its problematic relationship with left-wing parties. Having found a space for political involvement that was disconnected from political parties, the activists that had never belonged to any party (or had even explicitly left them for various reasons) progressively found their assemblies infiltrated by individuals and interests of those same organisations. Indeed, the level of participation declined precisely in relation to the degree of involvement of traditional parties. The issue at stake was perhaps the experience of direct democratic participation, which was directly concomitant with the heterogeneous composition of the assemblies and the specific challenges and needs to which it constituted a response. As a text from the *Colectivo Situaciones* formulates it: 'The neighbourly strategy of horizontal and democratic forms of elaboration, far from operating on the basis of a moral exigency or from being an arbitrary invention, constitutes a practical necessity'.[28]

28. Egardo Fontana, Natalia Fontana, Verónica Gago, Mario Santucho, Sebastián Scolnik, and Diego Sztulwark (Colectivo Situaciones), *19 Y 20 : Apuntes Para El Nuevo Protagonismo Social*, Buenos Aires, Ediciones de Mano en Mano, 2002, p170.

To the extent that the organisations that conformed these two political movements constituted a departure from 'old left' institutions like industrial-worker unions (homogeneous) and political parties (vertical representation) and were, at least at times, explicitly cut-off from them, also to the extent that

29. See Raúl Zibechi, *Genealogía De La Revuelta: Argentina: La Sociedad En Movimiento*, Buenos Aires, Letra Libre Nordan Comunidad, 2003, pp205-209.

30. Hardt and Negri, *Multitude*, pp104-105.

31. Ibid., p104.

32. See Juan Grigera, 'Argentina: On Crisis and a Measure for Class Struggle', *Historical Materialism*, 14, 1 (2006), p245.

33. Hardt and Negri, op. cit., *Empire*, p49.

34. Ibid., p28; also Virno, op. cit., pp106-111.

35. See Paolo Virno and Michael Hardt, *Radical Thought in Italy: A Potential Politics*, London, University of Minnesota Press, 1996.

36. Hardt and Negri, *Empire*, op. cit., p336.

37. Ibid., p404, emphasis added.

38. See Hardt and Negri, *Multitude*, op. cit., pp91-95, 338-340.

they articulated heterogeneity, and articulated it in a horizontal, immanent fashion, they can be seen - indeed, they have been seen - as providing a concrete manifestation of the multitude imagined by Hardt and Negri.[29] However, as they themselves explain, multitude is first of all a concept of class, and the contours and composition of a class are dependent upon instances of political struggle: actual or potential.[30] 'Class is and can only be a collectivity that struggles *in common*'.[31] From this perspective, it may be possible to think that in Argentina the neoliberal offensive described above called a class into being. Perhaps this is what a popular phrase captured - one that reminded those involved that unemployed *piqueteros* and the middle-sectors were fighting the same struggle: '*Piquete y cacerola: la lucha es una sola*'. This commonality, however, remained for the most part theoretical: no concrete, enduring articulation across movements was achieved.[32]

It is precisely at this point that Hardt and Negri's theory becomes, in their own words, an 'ontological drama'.[33] How can the multitude come into being as a subject that struggles and decides in common? To respond to this question Hardt and Negri continue and develop the work of other Italian authors, like Paolo Virno, who find in the process of postmodernisation or informatisation of production the emergence of what Marx called 'general intellect'.[34] For all of them, more than just fixed capital, 'general intellect' must be seen as the sum of all the cognitive capacities through which value is produced. In the same movement, this concept is deployed to postulate a 'collective intelligence' proper to the postmodern proletariat: its capacity to produce in common, in cooperative and communicative self-organised networks.[35] In the wake of these transformations, the proletariat is seen as progressively composed and articulated *for* communism. This is the real material condition on which the possibility of the multitude to act in common rests. Economic self-organisation, Hardt and Negri believe, is already the material condition of possibility for political subjectivation.[36] The main aspect of the ontological drama is to be found here: how can this multiplicity, this network of singularities that produce in common as a collective and distributed intelligence, become a *subject* proper, capable of acting purposively? As they write, 'The question is really how the body of the multitude can configure itself a *telos*'.[37] Most importantly, having set themselves so many ontological requirements, a further question arises: how can it become a political subject without collapsing into homogeneity and unity, without transforming collective intelligence or general intellect into a concentrated and unified *volonté générale*?

The examples provided by Hardt and Negri, in accordance with the schema of a political vitalism, all come from biology: they refer specifically to those models of distributed intelligence represented by insect colonies and swarms as well as neural networks in the brain.[38] Nonetheless, as fast as they are posed, these examples prove incapable of providing a model given that, quite clearly, neither insect nor neuronal societies can be seen as proper illustrations of the heterogeneity or articulation of singularities that Hardt and Negri celebrate. Malcolm Bull has highlighted this problem in the theory of the multitude. The fact is not only that insect colonies are homogeneous but also that, in accordance with such homogeneity, in those 'societies' there is no discrepancy between individual and collective interests. Following this path, Bull points towards a theoretical impasse in the philosophy of the multitude (indeed, in political thought in general) between the perspective of private interest that highlights the collective intelligence supervening networks of production and exchange - and thus, according to Bull, links Spinoza with free market ideologies - and the one of collective will, concerned with proper political subjectivation or agency, which must forcefully be conceived on the basis of ontological unification - leading thus, to the ideology of people and State. 'From Cicero onwards,' he writes, 'it was axiomatic that only when unified into a people could a multitude become a political agent'.[39]

In conceiving the multitude as a body that configures for itself a *telos* and constitutes itself as a subject, Hardt and Negri necessarily fall back into what can be seen essentially as a Kantian complex of problems. The properly subjective moment is conceived as the self-production of the multitude (*qua* subject) in a manner that is essentially *autopoietic* in the sense of Humberto Maturana and Francisco Varela's organism-centred definition of life. Indeed, it seems quite clear that the problem of the becoming-subject of the multitude, whereby it *constitutes for itself a telos*, could only be solved by the introduction of a model, also extracted from biology, but radically different from those preferred by Hardt and Negri: the organism. For Kant, as is well known, it was the challenge of reflecting upon organic, living beings that forces us to introduce teleological judgments.[40] In turn, it is Hardt and Negri's introduction of teleological judgments that forces a conception of the multitude into the model of an organism. Varela himself, arguing for a realist construction of Kant's thoughts on teleology, argues that it is precisely the autopoietic nature of the organism - involving self-organisation and self-production but also autonomy and unification vis-à-vis an external milieu - that allows it to be a 'creator of "*real* teleology"'.[41] This is the only model that yields the possibility of subjectivation that Hardt and Negri would like to see in the multitude. As Varela writes: 'Organisms are subjects having purposes according to values encountered in the making of their living'.[42] As far as it seems conceptually possible, internal teleology can be revived only in the context of a framework that highlights - far more than Hardt and Negri's ontology does - not only organisation but also autonomy and individuation. Furthermore, the reflection upon organisms as 'final ends' (*Endzwecke*) leads Kant towards the question of nature itself being endowed with an 'ultimate end' (*letzte Zweck*), that is, man.[43] The possibility of an external, historical teleology towards a 'universal civic society' is thus rescued and postulated, now grounded exclusively on the human capacities for rational and free thought.[44] In a rather similar way, Hardt and Negri link the internal teleology appropriate to the becoming-subject of the multitude with an external historical teleology: 'democracy on a global scale'. And the ground is the same: 'Human faculties and historical teleologies exist only because they are the result of human passions, reason, and struggle'.[45]

39. Malcolm Bull, 'The Limits of Multitude', *New Left Review*, 35 (2005), p38-39.

40. Immanuel Kant, *The Critique of Judgement*, Oxford, Oxford University Press, 1952, pp19-26.

41. Andreas Weber and Francisco Varela, 'Life after Kant: Natural Purposes and the Autopoietic Foundations of Biological Individuality', *Phenomenology and the Cognitive Sciences*, 1 (2002), p102, emphasis added.

42. Ibid.

43. Kant, op. cit., p86-100.

44. See Immanuel Kant, 'Idea for a Universal History from a Cosmopolitan Point of View', in Lewis White Beck (ed.), op. cit.

45. Hardt and Negri, *Multitude*, op. cit., p221.

Discussing the problem of the material constitution of Empire, Hardt and Negri mention Foucault's work along with Deleuze and Guattari's as two cases in a line of 'partially successful attempts' on which they build in order to articulate the problem of 'biopolitical' production. Foucault, they explain, opened up the path towards an investigation into the nature of 'biopower' and 'biopolitics'. Yet his limitation resides in his failure to recognise who or what is the productive 'bios' driving these social mutations. Deleuze and Guattari, in turn, are praised for having made that 'bios' immanent to the machines of the social field, but are criticised precisely for failing to recognise a *telos* for social production, conceiving it exclusively in terms of an horizon of 'continuous movement': insubstantial, impotent, indeterminate and chaotic.[46]

46. Hardt and Negri, *Empire*, op. cit., p28.

In a recent survey of contemporary thought, Alex Callinicos has pointed towards a fundamental continuity linking Negri's theory with Deleuze and Guattari's philosophical framework, specifically with the reconstruction of Foucault's thought developed by the former. Indeed, we have seen already the extent to which Deleuze's ontology of immanence and multiplicity casts a long shadow over Hardt and Negri's political ontology of the multitude. Another important issue at stake in this philosophical relation, according to Callinicos, is a conception of resistance as 'an expression of Life'.[47] For this reason, Negri's work - and specially *Empire* vis-à-vis *A Thousand Plateaus* - entails for him something like a becoming-political-theory of Deleuze's 'vitalist ontology'.[48] Nonetheless, a proper account of the specific traits for which Deleuze's ontology deserves such qualification is lacking in Callinicos' discussion, as it is, indeed, in many recent commentaries that make the same accusation. In what way is Deleuze's ontology a vitalist one? We will attempt one possible response here, recognising that - as many introductions and critical discussions of his work illustrate - any attempt to disclose a kernel of Deleuze's philosophy is bound to be limited by a necessarily selective and perhaps idiosyncratic reading.

47. Alex Callinicos, *The Resources of Critique*, Cambridge, Polity, 2006, p142.

48. Ibid., p143.

In a proper search for Deleuze's vitalism, much needs to be said about the old debate between vitalists and mechanicists in the philosophy of biology; about Deleuze's relationship with Bergson and his (and Guattari's) notion of *Nonorganic* or *Anorganic* Life; about his life-long philosophical search for the plane of immanence and ontological univocity, which concluded with an enigmatic invocation of 'a Life' that precedes all individuations; about Badiou's contention that in Deleuze's philosophical universe, Life is the proper name of Being.[49] More feasible here is to focus on a more restricted sense, closer to Negri's work and to our concerns here, in which Deleuze's philosophy may be said to articulate a vitalist disposition. To put it bluntly, it entails the conviction that the first ontological fact is this: *life thrives*. Or, at least: *life strives*. In this formula, life - defined along the lines of Deleuze's Bergsonism, as a movement of self-differentiation or internal difference[50] - is primary and substantial; formed matter (or, the organism, stratification, the

49. Alain Badiou, 'Deleuze's Vitalist Ontology', in Alain Badiou, *Briefings on Existence*, Albany, State University of New York Press, 2006, p68.

50. Gilles Deleuze, *Bergsonism*, New York, Zone Books, 1988, pp94-95.

State, Power: in sum, the actual structure of the world) is only secondary, an after-effect, an arrest. The political aspect of this ontological disposition is clearly articulated. The key formula is this: *lines of flight are primary*.[51] Almost a pseudonym for difference or life, these lines, the operators or 'cutting edges of deterritorialization and creation,' are primary to the apparatuses of capture: the State, capitalism, etc. In 'Control and Becoming', Deleuze explains: 'we think any society is defined not so much by its contradictions as by its lines of flight, it flees all over the place'.[52] A vitalism so defined provides an ontological diagram that resonates with a major concern found in Negri and the other Italian thinkers emerging from *operaismo*: power (as *'potenza'* or *'puissance'*), the whole problem of constituent power, specifically as it takes the form of *exodus*.[53] At least partially, it may be seen as the basis for a theoretical nugget of Negri's framework: the conviction that struggle 'anticipates and prefigures' the forms or structures in which Capital or capitalist power will be embodied in the future.[54] From the perspective of this political vitalism, we could say, it is life that always speaks the *first word*.

Nonetheless, Deleuze and Guattari write: 'there simultaneously occurs upon the earth a very important, inevitable phenomenon that is beneficial in many respects and unfortunate in many others: stratification … Strata are acts of capture … but the earth, or the body without organs, constantly … flees and becomes destratified, decoded, deterritorialised …'.[55] So, capture and stratification are real and inevitable, perhaps just as much as Life is. Yet, inasmuch as they are inevitable, capture or stratification must be seen always as temporary effects. Thus, it is possible, in addition to what has been stated above, to find in Deleuze a conviction that Power (as *'pouvoir'*) or capture will never have the *last word*? Or, more precisely, that there will never be a *last* word? Perhaps this is what Badiou refers to when he speaks of Deleuze's 'ontological optimism': 'no closure is ever complete'.[56] And he seems right to track this 'optimism' back to Deleuze's polemical reading of Nietzsche. Indeed, a third and not unquestioned formula can be found here: *the eternal return of difference*. At this point, vitalism as the theory of the primacy of lines of flight takes the place of a philosophy of history with the category of *becoming* as its kernel. As explained in *Difference and Repetition*, Deleuze finds in Nietzsche a 'philosophy of the future'; specifically in the theory of eternal return or recurrence he finds 'an untimely belief or belief of the future'.[57] In his hands, the theory of the eternal return is pitched against two philosophies of history or, more precisely, against a Modern philosophy of history that opposes its own linear and progressive, perhaps teleological, model to an Ancient, cyclical conception of history (partially misunderstood as the return of the Same).[58] In relation to this latter interpretation, Deleuze most famously argues that eternal return 'is the expression of a principle which serves as an explanation of diversity and its reproduction, of difference and its repetition'.[59] This is why: 'The eternal return is the being of becoming'.[60] On the other hand, in relation to the Modern conception of history, Deleuze points out that Nietzsche's eternal recurrence 'presupposes' a critique of the idea that becoming reaches

51. Gilles Deleuze and Félix Guattari, *A Thousand Plateaus: Capitalism and Schizophrenia*, London, Athlone, 1988, p531 n39.

52. Deleuze and Negri, 'Control and Becoming', op. cit..

53. See Virno and Hardt, *Radical Thought in Italy*, op. cit..

54. Hardt and Negri, *Empire*, op. cit., p51, 427 n12.

55. Deleuze and Guattari, *A Thousand Plateaus*, op. cit., p40.

56. Badiou, op. cit., p69.

57. Deleuze, *Difference and Repetition*, op. cit., p6, p303.

58. Ibid., p302.

59. Gilles Deleuze, *Nietzsche and Philosophy*, London, The Athlone Press, 1983, p49.

60. Ibid., p71.

61. Ibid., p47.

'a terminal or equilibrium state', 'an end or final state'.[61] It is in this way that Deleuze's own construction of the eternal return (of difference) or becoming testifies to his more general belief in an inexhaustible future: a philosophy of an open-ended and unforeseeable history, a history that remains forever open in the relay between lines of flight and acts of capture.

This is precisely the point at which Negri, with all his teleological concerns, would prefer to part company with Deleuze's vitalism. We have already seen how *Empire* decries Deleuze and Guattari for conceiving social reproduction only as 'continuous movement ... as a chaotic, indeterminate horizon marked by the *ungraspable event*'.[62] We have also seen how, in 'Control and Becoming', Negri articulates the same critique - possibly referring to the closing pages of the plateau 'Apparatus of Capture', where capitalism appears marked by an 'undecidable' horizon without resolution or closure in sight, for it releases lines of flight as much as it conjugates them, and conjugates them as much as it needs them to be released; he complains: 'I seem sometimes to hear a tragic note, at points where it's not clear where the "war-machine" is going.' Deleuze's answer sure sounds tragic and, arguably, pre-emptively devastating for what was to be Hardt and Negri's philosophy of the multitude with all its optimism and prophetic vocation: 'What's so shameful is that we've no sure way of maintaining becomings, or still more of arousing them, even within ourselves. How any group will turn out, how it will fall back into history, presents a constant "concern." There's no longer any image of proletarians around of which it's just a matter of becoming conscious.'

62. Hardt and Negri, *Empire*, op. cit., p28, emphasis added.

This is a tailor-made comment, utterly appropriate to reconnect with our Argentine example. In a text compiled by the *Colectivo Situaciones*, the activist and political theorist Sandro Mezzadra is quoted describing his return to Argentina in 2005: 'Coming back to Buenos Aires in October, after more than a year, the impression has been disconcerting ... It is really difficult, going about the streets of the city, to find the traces - evident until last year - of the great explosion of collective creativity determined by the development of the movements after the insurrection of 19 and 20 December 2001'.[63] In the same text, the collective of authors describes regretfully a process of 'normalisation' whereby, we could say, history kicked in again. The reconstruction of governability reinstated once more a distinction between those governing and those governed. With the ascension of Néstor Kirchner to power, they explain, the fundamental role of social movements was recognised for the first time while, in the same movement, they were repositioned in a traditional relationship with the State. The constitutive power was cancelled and reduced to the elaboration of demands 'to which then only the political system can give an answer'.[64] Other commentators have similar diagnoses of the 'tragic' outcome of the Argentine revolt. Bonnet, for example, explains how the struggle and demands of the two main movements, *piqueteros* and *asambleas*, were 'routinised', channelled 'into the boundaries of capitalist democracy'.[65]

63. Colectivo Situaciones, 'Diagrama Argentino de la Normalización: Trama y Reverso', Available from: http://194.109.209.222/colectivosituaciones/articulos_18.htm

64. Ibid.

65. Bonnet, op. cit., p180-81.

Following up on these conclusions, it is possible to argue that, in many important respects, the events of the Argentinazo, as they unfolded, may be taken as a better illustration of Deleuze's 'tragic' metaphysics - although not necessarily of the ethics that so many have found immediately following from them - than of Negri's teleology of the multitude. Perhaps the model of a *haecceity*, a loose and momentary figure of individuation dear to Deleuze, grasps the Argentine revolt better than an image of the becoming-subject of a postmodern proletarian class. Deleuze, as is well known, would be quite content with doing away with or, at least, displacing the organism and the subject as the only (or preferred) categories to asses proper ontological and political status. As *haecceities*, multitude or movements 'cease to be subjects to become events'.[66] And just as internal teleology or subjectification would be abandoned as the only measure for the true relevance of movements, so would the external teleology and progressivism that subtends much of Negri's philosophy of history. From this perspective, the Argentinazo would not be seen only as an unaccomplished or defused, 'tragic' event in what should have been a progressive and teleological tendency, but as a *revolutionary becoming* worthy of being thought in itself without any reference to external, historical teleologies: 'a line of becoming has neither beginning nor end, departure nor arrival, origin nor destination'.[67] Giorgio Agamben addresses a critique to Negri on the basis of similar ontological convictions: 'What I always disagree with Toni about is this emphasis placed on productivity. Here we must reclaim the absence of *opera* as central. This expresses the impossibility of a *telos* and *ergon* for politics. Movement is the indefiniteness and imperfection of every politics ... movement is atelic, an imperfect act, without an end'.[68]

Negri might be right to hear a 'tragic note' when such an open-ended and undecidable horizon is evoked, but perhaps for reasons other than those seemingly subtending his complaint. In Nietzsche's philosophy or, at least, in Deleuze's reconstruction of it, the proper 'tragic' outlook is distinguished from the Christian one - which, arguably, still provides the basic structure to Negri's thought. This latter revolves around a justification of Life on the basis of a redemption or resolution to be found on a higher plane. The former, that is, the true tragic disposition, entails 'the affirmation of life instead of its higher solution or justification'.[69] Hardt and Negri explicitly attempt to avoid the former; they write: 'We are not proposing the umpteenth version of the inevitable passage through purgatory (here in the guise of the new imperial machine) in order to offer a glimmer of hope for radiant futures'.[70] Yet, to the extent that their theory does not constitute something like a scientific prediction, they inevitably produce a *justification* of contemporary life under capitalism on the basis of a 'to come' that remains, despite all philosophical efforts, simply chimerical.[71] On the other hand, it may be argued that Deleuze and Guattari's philosophical engagement with capitalism, at least in the aspects already mentioned, provides neither a justification nor a celebration - as some too readily assume - but, in the properly 'tragic' way, an *affirmation* of it, in the way that one affirms life along with 'even the harshest

66. Deleuze and Guattari, *A Thousand Plateaus*, op. cit., pp260-262.

67. Ibid., p293.

68. Giorgio Agamben, 'Movement', (2005) Available from: http://www. generation-online. org/p/fpagamben3. htm

69. Deleuze, *Nietzsche and Philosophy*, op. cit., p13.

70. Hardt and Negri, *Empire*, op. cit., p47.

71. Antonio Negri, 'Kairòs Alma Venus Multitudo', in Antonio Negri, *Time for Revolution*, London, Continuum, 2004, pp248-261.

72. Nietzsche quoted by Deleuze, *Nietzsche and Philosophy*, op. cit., p16.

73. 'Control and Becoming', op. cit., emphasis added.

74. See Manuel DeLanda, 'Markets and Anti-markets in the World Economy' in Stanley Aronowitz, Barbara Martinsons and Michael Mensen, *Technoscience and Cyberculture*, London, Routledge, 1996, available from: http://www.t0.or. at/delanda/a-market. htm; also, 'Deleuzian Interrogations: A Conversation with Manuel DeLanda, John Protevi and Torkild Thanem', available from: http://www.dif- ferance.org/Delanda- Protevi.pdf

75. Fernand Braudel, *The Wheels of Commerce, Civilization and Capitalism: 15th-18th Century, Vol. 2* London, Collins, 1982, p581.

76. Ibid., p233.

suffering'.[72] Affirmation, of course, is not acceptance but the first step in a path of experimentation, and thus, a precondition for politics.

NON-CAPITALISM

In the encounter that we have been building upon, Deleuze's response to Negri's complaint begins with an interesting remark: 'I think Félix Guattari and I have remained Marxists ... You see, we think any political philosophy must turn on the analysis of capitalism and the ways it has developed.' At least three things can be highlighted in this response. First, Deleuze seems to conceive the political moment of philosophy as primarily an analytical endeavour, and thus, not necessarily a normative, programmatic or strategic one. Indeed, he then proposes that one of the tasks of such an analytical or, perhaps we could say, cartographic approach is 'to try and *follow* the lines of flight taking shape at some particular moment or other'.[73] The second important element in the response is the idea that politico-philosophical analysis must bear on capitalism and its historical development. Third, and most importantly, the idea that the framework provided by Marx and his followers is considered to be the appropriate one for developing a political philosophy. Accordingly, it is safe to say, some of the most fruitful efforts to produce a more explicitly political development out of Deleuze and Guattari's conceptual framework have focused on the relationship they maintained with Marx and various Marxists traditions including, of course, the Italian one to which Negri belongs.

There is, however, another figure that constantly reappears when Deleuze and Guattari turn to the development of capitalism but, perhaps simply due to the contemporaneousness of their work, never acquired a central status or exerted a proper influence on their conception of capitalism. We are referring to Fernand Braudel and his research on the history of early modern capitalism; specifically, to the aspects of his work that constitute an explicit alternative to important aspects of Marxist history and theory.[74] The relationship was not unilateral for, in the second volume of his monumental study, Braudel quotes them approvingly on a very important issue: 'I am tempted to agree with Deleuze and Guattari that "after a fashion, capitalism has been a spectre haunting every form of society" - capitalism, that is, as I have defined it'.[75] Interestingly, Braudel's approval is not unconditional and his qualification is important. A long work in itself would be required to do justice to the complex historical and theoretical issues at stake in this short commentary. However, a few words should be said here about it. Through this brief discussion we will be able to turn towards one dimension of the Argentine movements that hasn't been addressed so far.

One of Braudel's main manoeuvres is to have broken with what he calls a 'post-Marxian orthodoxy' that wouldn't allow historians 'to talk about capitalism before the end of the eighteenth century, in other words before the industrial mode of production'.[76] In *Anti-Oedipus*, Deleuze and Guattari follow such an orthodox definition of capitalism as an industrial mode of production: capitalism, they say, is defined by 'industrial capital ... [it] doesn't begin ... until capital directly appropriates production'.[77] Most importantly, for them, it is only at this point, and from this point onwards, that capitalism appropriates for itself the totality of social forces: 'it is solely under these conditions that capital becomes the full body, the new socius or the quasi cause that appropriates all the productive forces'.[78] Later on, in *A Thousand Plateaus*, they continue to conceive capitalism as 'commensurate with society in its entirety'.[79] For Braudel, on the other hand, something that truly deserves the name of capitalism already had a long history before the industrial passage highlighted by Deleuze and Guattari had taken place: he explains, 'I am therefore in agreement with the Marx who wrote (though he later went back on this) that European capitalism - indeed he even says capitalist *production* - began in thirteenth-century Italy'.[80] If he is willing to distribute capitalism more widely, historically speaking, it is because his conception differs from Deleuze and Guattari's in two important aspects. First, capitalism in the past and always in principle, is not essentially an industrial mode of production: before industry, it 'elected residence' in other areas, namely commerce and specifically long-distance trade, because 'these were the only areas which favoured the reproduction of capital'.[81] Second, capitalism in the past, but always in principle, was not a '"system" extending over the whole of society'; it occupied only the commanding heights of the economy, 'the realm of investment and of a high rate of capital formation'.[82] This leads to his famous three-tiered division: below, 'material life' (roughly, self-subsistence and production for direct consumption); in the middle, the 'market economy', a properly competitive field of transparent exchange and small profits; finally, on the top, the capitalist 'countermarket' or 'antimarket': 'an accumulation of power (one that bases exchange on the balance of strength, as much as, or more than on the reciprocity of needs) a form of social parasitism which, like so many other forms, may or may not be inevitable'.[83]

All this could be seen just as a matter of terminology. But the fact is that Braudel wanted to effectuate something like an *incorporeal transformation*, to 'impose a new set of divisions on things and actions', as Deleuze would say.[84] Moreover, this was a new division that he was willing to maintain for the present; he wrote: 'we should not be too quick to assume that capitalism embraces the whole of western society, that it accounts for every stitch in the social fabric'.[85] Most importantly, it was a division that he considered important as a guide for the future. Well aware that neither is capitalism 'likely to collapse of its own accord' nor does the proper market economy pose a threat in itself (in fact, possibly the contrary), Braudel recognised capitalism as a problem that was economic and political at once. In doing so, he suggested two equally necessary, parallel and interrelated approaches to the problem. On the one hand, we could say, a specifically *political* field of anti- or counter-capitalist intervention that would require organisation and articulation between organisations, indeed even the seizure of State power (beyond

77. Gilles Deleuze and Félix Guattari, *Anti-Oedipus : Capitalism and Schizophrenia*, London, Continuum, 2004, p246.

78. Ibid., p247.

79. Deleuze and Guattari, *A Thousand Plateaus*, op. cit., p452.

80. Fernand Braudel, *The Perspective of the World, Civilization and Capitalism: 15th-18th Century, Vol. 3*, London, Collins, 1984, p57.

81. Braudel, *The Wheels of Commerce*, op. cit., p239.

82. Ibid., p232.

83. Ibid., p22. For an overview of this division see Fernand Braudel, *Afterthoughts on Material Civilization and Capitalism*, London, The John Hopkins University Press, 1979, pp39-75.

84. Gilles Deleuze, *Expressionism in Philosophy: Spinoza*, New York, Zone Books, 1990, p321; see also Deleuze and Guattari, *A Thousand Plateaus*, pp80-85.

85. Braudel, *The Perspective of the World*, op. cit., p630.

86. Braudel,
Afterthoughts, op. cit.,
p64.

87. Braudel, *The
Perspective of the
World*, op. cit., p632.

88. Ibid.;
also Braudel,
Afterthoughts, op. cit.,
p115.

any metaphysical or ontological prejudices). Braudel explicitly reminds us: 'Capitalism only triumphs when it becomes identified with the state, when it is the state'.[86] On the other hand, he highlighted as well the importance of a specifically *economic* field for non-capitalist experimentation (beyond any ideological prejudices, we could add). 'If people set about looking for them,' he argued, 'seriously and honestly, economic solutions could be found which would extend the area of the market'.[87] Indeed, doesn't Bull's aforementioned conflation between the theory of the multitude and the ideology of the free market take on a new light when looked at from this perspective? At the end, it is clear, Braudel's 'ideal' was not highly original (socialism on top, market at base) nor was he too optimistic about its prospects.[88] Still, an interesting question remains: what happens if we take seriously the division he proposed for our politico-philosophical, analytical or cartographic task? What lines of flight seem worth trying to follow?

One central aspect of the Argentine revolt is that, as it developed, the specifically political struggle of various movements became progressively enriched by properly economic instances of experimentation. These appeared most clearly articulated in the movements of *fábricas recuperadas* ('seized factories') and the *clubes de trueque* ('barter clubs') - of which, unfortunately, we were unable to say anything here - but also in what came to be known as *emprendimientos productivos* (roughly, 'productive undertakings') within the *piquetero* movement and similar experiments initiated by *asambleas barriales*. This dimension of the Argentine post-crisis development is highly complex and contested, packed with hopes but also with problems; to name a few: the relationship of these practices with the State, the formal and established market economy and the capitalist anti-market; the problem of the articulation between different instances of non-capitalist production and exchange distributed across movements; the clash between more anarchist and properly socialist ideologies, and so on.[89] Some commentators emphasise the fleeting nature of these experiments while others perceive them as the longer-lasting and most effective contributions to have arisen out of the revolt. Raúl Zibechi, for example, describes some current efforts to maintain and expand on these practices in the city of Buenos Aires while, quite accordingly, finding in them a renewed and enhanced expression of that non-capitalist economic life that Braudel insisted upon. 'In a sense, these experimental endeavours are recuperating the original nature of the market, described by Fernand Braudel and Immanuel Wallerstein as characterised by transparency, modest profits, controlled competition, freedom, and, above all, the domain of "common people"'.[90]

89. The best critical
overview is Grigera,
op. cit.; see also
Pereyra, op. cit.,
pp173-192.

90. Raúl Zibechi,
'Worker-Run
Factories: From
Survival to Economic
Solidarity', Americas
Program Citizen
Action in the
Americas, 12 (2004),
p6, Available from:
http://americas.irc-
online.org/am/1543

***

EXPERIENCE

As was stated, this article set out to explore specific and divergent elements of Negri and Deleuze's political ontologies, namely, the question regarding teleology in the two senses employed by Kant: internal teleology or purpose-driven action, and the external teleology of historical development as such. Prior to this problem, we explored also certain convergences between these two authors' vitalist metaphysics. Convergences and divergences were illuminated by our chosen example. We saw how the social movements that exploded in Argentina around 2001 served as a good illustration of the sociological and ontological requirements of Hardt and Negri's theory of the multitude. For these authors themselves, as well as for other commentators, there is a fundamental continuity between this theory and the metaphysical framework developed by Deleuze alone and in his work with Guattari. Multiciplicity, immanence, heterogeneity and vitalism were selected as important points of connection. Yet, we saw also that when Hardt and Negri invoke the problem of the subject or subjectivation - a category that Deleuze and Guattari seem content to dispense with - the two metaphysical frameworks diverge.

When it comes to the point where a theory of subjectivation is necessary, Hardt and Negri's political philosophy reaches an impasse, what they call an 'ontological drama'. The collective intelligence they postulate for postmodern forms of capitalism, despite all their claims, still seems far from the collective will that a genuine process of subjectivation would necessitate. For the postmodern proletariat *at large* (as imagined by Hardt and Negri), to *act in common* or in concert may be enough for economic production and exchange but certainly not for producing a proper, teleologically oriented subject. Arguably, the impasse or drama of this passage can only be remedied or bridged with a theory and strategy of properly *political organisation* that is lacking from Hardt and Negri's work. Taking our cue from Varela's equation of the subject with the organism, we could argue that subjectivation is proportional to the degree of organisation and individuation that a multiplicity may achieve. From this perspective, it is only political organisms, that is, institutions (although not necessarily those of the State) that are genuinely and effectively *telos*- or purpose-driven. In this regard, there are both positive and negative lessons to be learned from Argentina's movements.

If there was subjectivation, aims and even achievements, those coincided with the degree of organisation within movements and groups inside movements. For many analysts, the great absence was that of articulation across movements and organisations. For the most part, a multitude, a society-wide action in common, remained wanting or, at any rate, was only loose and temporary. It is precisely in this wide and spontaneous dimension, perhaps negative from the point of view of organisation and individuation, that we find an illustration of Deleuze and Guattari's metaphysical categories. The *Argentinazo* as a whole may be seen as a huge revolutionary becoming: pre-individual, a-subjective and a-teleological movement. The figures preferred by the French philosophers, for example, haecceities and war machines, may be seen as ontological categories characterised by minimal degrees of organisation and individuation. Up to this point, it must be stressed, these must be seen primarily as analytical categories and not yet, not necessarily and not immediately, as evaluative, normative or strategic ones. Even if Deleuze and Guattari themselves do seem to favour the open-ended movement of the war machine, the ontological and ethical moments can be kept separated. The limitations or weak efficacy of pre-subjective and non-teleological movement is well illustrated in the Argentine episode. And yet, haecceity and becoming are worthy of being thought of and evaluated in themselves without reference to internal or historical teleologies.

There is much talk among the people involved in the movements about the experience produced, shared and accumulated during the *Argentinazo* and its ongoing sequels. Pereyra writes: 'These fights left an experience, they forged a new generation of popular fighters that gave shape to new organizations, and allow experiments with other forms of struggle that might occasionally achieve partial successes'.[91] 'Experience' here should be raised to the level of a philosophical and practical concept that would be the corollary for a non-teleological conception of history and becomings. Ultimately, the conclusion put forward by Deleuze in his encounter with Negri is this: there where no resolution is in sight, where lines of flight and becomings are primary but always as well fall back into history, a 'constant concern' is necessary.[92] As we have seen, Braudel agrees with Deleuze and Guattari that capitalism has haunted all societies; a corollary is suggested: what holds for the past holds for the future, capitalism will always, *at least virtually*, exist. This is, we have argued, a tragic affirmation. Inasmuch as capital remains actual, Deleuze and Guattari's proposal is simple: to 'relaunch new struggles whenever the earlier one is betrayed'.[93] It is in light of this tragic and open-ended horizon that experience seems an important concept. Experience or experimentation (etymologically: to try, to test, to undergo) entails a movement of probing in the virtual space, the space of potentials. There lies the criterion by which to evaluate a non-teleological becoming: what is it that was found? The experience is not limited to those involved; it is carried forward in the form of learning for the new struggles that will be relaunched. From this perspective, even if history is conceived in a non-teleological way, it surely can be seen as cumulative.

Following Braudel we have asked about the possibility of opening up and sustaining properly economic, non-capitalist experiments as a necessary companion for the equally necessary, properly political instances of counter-capitalist intervention. This is the dimension of the Argentine experience that we have chosen to highlight at the end of our politico-philosophical, cartographic or analytical exercise. But all the experiences accumulated during these becomings amount to significant discoveries in the technologies, economic and otherwise, of non-capitalist life.

91. Pereyra, op. cit., p43.

92. 'Control and Becoming', op. cit.

93. Deleuze and Guattari, *What is Philosophy?*, London, Verso, 1994, p100.

QUEER VITALISM

Claire Colebrook

This essay is about vitalism and the ethical urgency of returning to the problem of life. This urgency, I will argue, far from being a recent, radical and necessarily transgressive gesture, has always underpinned (and presupposed) highly normative gestures in philosophy, literature and cultural understanding. Indeed, the very notion and possibility of the normative, or the idea that one can proceed from what *is* (life) to what ought to be (ways of living) has always taken the form of vitalism. For the purposes of this essay, then, I will define vitalism as the imperative of grounding, defending or deriving principles and systems from life *as it really is*. From this it follows that there will be two forms of vitalism, for there are two ways of understanding this notion of 'life as it really is'. For the most part 'life as it really is' is reduced to *actual* life: here, vitalism begins from living bodies (usually human, usually heterosexual, usually familial) and then asks what it means to live well. We could refer to this, following Deleuze and Guattari, as an active vitalism because it assumes that 'life' refers to acting and well organised bodies. However, there is another way of understanding 'life as it really is,' and this is to align the real with the virtual. For Deleuze and Guattari this leads to a passive vitalism, where 'life' is a pre-individual plane of forces that does not act by a process of decision and self-maintenance but through chance encounters.

By understanding life *as virtual* we no longer begin with the image of a living body, and are therefore able to consider forces of composition that differ from those of man and the productive organism. Those queer theories that account for the self as it is formed in the social unit of the family fail to account for the emergence of the self and the genesis of the family; in so doing they remain at the level of the actual and of active human agents. Passive vitalism is queer, by contrast, in its difference and distance from already constituted images of life as necessarily fruitful, generative, organised and human. A passive vitalism is also queer in its transformation of how we understand the work of art. The notion of the 'aesthetic' has its origins in perception - referring to - and also to the subject. For Kant, the work of art is to be judged only in its capacity to enliven the subject's capacity to give order and synthesis to the world; beauty is the experience of material as perfectly harmonious with the subject's conceptualising powers, while the sublime refers to an experience that allows the subject to feel its own striving for form and order. The work of art returns us to the constituting power from which the lived world unfolds. This emphasis on art as disclosing the active power that originally forms the world *as this meaningful world for 'us'* is maintained in all forms of post-Kantian aesthetics that takes us back to the structure, language or matrix that gives sense to 'our' world.

1. Gilles Deleuze and Felix Guattari, *What is Philosophy?* Hugh Tomlinson and Graham Burchell (trans), New York, Columbia University Press, 1994, p213.

2. In *Difference and Repetition* Deleuze argues that there is a radical potential in Platonism - where Ideas are pure potentialities from which differentiated beings are actualised - that is lost in Aristotle's criticism of Platonism. For Aristotle, rather than Ideas, it is categories which define each being; and these categories are referred back to a (human or at least subject's) good sense and common sense that identifies common and repeatable features. Deleuze, *Difference and Repetition*, Paul Patton (trans.), New York, Columbia University Press, 1994.

3. Deleuze and Guattari's preference for the passive vitalism of Leibniz/Ruyer allows us to make some connection to neo-Platonism, and also allows us to answer Alain Badiou's criticism of Deleuze's ultimate appeal to a Platonic One (Badiou, *Deleuze: The Clamor of Being*, Louise Burchill (trans), Minneapolis, University of Minnesota Press, 2000). Leibniz synthesised Platonism with the mechanical materialism of his time, and did so by insisting that even if the world

(AT LEAST) TWO VITALISMS, TWO HISTORIES, TWO PHILOSOPHIES

In *What is Philosophy?* Deleuze and Guattari argue for a tradition of passive vitalism (beginning with Leibniz and extending to Ruyer) which counters the dominant tradition of vitalism, which runs from Kant to Claude Bernard:

> Vitalism has always had two possible interpretations: that of an idea that acts, but is not - that acts therefore only from the point of view of an external cerebral knowledge ... or that of a force that is but does not act - that is therefore a pure internal awareness ... If the second interpretation seems to us to be imperative it is because the contraction that preserves is always in a state of detachment in relation to action or even to movement and appears as a pure contemplation without knowledge.[1]

Before looking in detail at what the aesthetics of such a passive vitalism might be, and how such an aesthetic might open a way of thinking beyond modernist norms of art, we would do well to define the dominant vitalism that 'acts but is not.' Deleuze and Guattari suggest that this vitalism begins with Kant. This would already make it different from the vitalism that, perhaps, has always been Western philosophy's spontaneous gesture. We can discern a vitalist normativity in the very ethic of philosophy's definition of itself against sophistry, dogma and opinion. Philosophy refuses to accept the ready-made and received judgments of gossip and chatter and instead strives to legitimate truth by tracing its genesis, whether that be from Platonic ideas, categories of universal reason, or the structure of the world. If language circulates without justification, or is repeated without an animating and intuiting intent that would ground what is said in an ongoing and truth-oriented experience, then language falls into an automatic, inhuman and merely technical repetition. The doctrine of Platonic Ideas is, after all, an ethical and political manoeuvre that would aim to ground assertions, identities and claims in an originating and animating force: the Idea which grants each being its proper form allows us to decide what any being *is,* and the ways in which it ought to become, according to its preceding and governing essence.[2] Not surprisingly, neo-Platonism will render the vitalist potential in Platonic ideas more explicit.[3] Neoplatonism regards every being in this world as an emanation of the One, and in so doing neither detaches a world of matter from a divine transcendence, nor denies any being a participation in holiness. In contrast with a strict Platonism, Neoplatonism tends to suggest that the One is not above and beyond its emanations, but is given only through each of its expressions. Thus vitalism in its most general sense would be a commitment to the animation or spirituality of everything that lives, and would be contrasted both with forms of atomist materialism that reduced matter to that which operates only through mechanical and external relations rather than its own immanent force, and with Cartesianism, which separates mind from body, regarding the latter as devoid of any inner life.

Both of these modes of vitalism - an anti-atomism and an anti-Cartesianism - were prevalent in the seventeenth century, and could often take on a quite revolutionary strain.[4] Rather than seeing order as necessarily imposed from above on an otherwise chaotic and unruly world, vitalism granted each aspect of the world its own striving potential directed to order and relations. Against Cartesianism and the disenchantment of the world, modern vitalism drew on Neoplatonism to argue for each being's tendency towards the expression and fulfilment of the divine. It is possibly requisite to correct, then, one notion which dominates the history of ideas: that modernity is governed by a Cartesianism which places mind and matter as distinct worldly substances, seeing matter as operating mechanically and mind as being a power to represent and organise the relations of the rationalised matter. Instead, there is an (at least) equally prevalent continuation of an emphasis on the world's immanent spirit, its striving towards the good, and the contribution of every living being in its difference and specificity towards the efflorescence of the whole.[5] It is this expressivist tradition that Deleuze draws upon throughout his diverse corpus in his references to Leibniz and Spinoza. However, Leibniz and Spinoza stress a univocity - or *one* life - that expresses itself in both mind and body, rejecting any Cartesian substance that would be simply, distinctly or merely mechanical. For that expressivist tradition the world of distinct and separate entities flows from the one expressive life which becomes what it is only in its production of diverse and emanating bodies, all of which have their origin or true being only *as expressions* of a prior animating One. For Deleuze, though, this ultimately expressive ground is not a grounding unity or single substance but a power for differentiation; it is Nietzsche, according to Deleuze, who will radicalise the expressivism and univocity opened by Spinoza and Leibniz. The latter philosophers refused to posit any substantial distinction between emanating life and its dazzling array of expressions, but it was Nietzsche who regarded the emanating life as a plane of forces effecting itself through styles and dramas.

We can make a first note towards the distinct contribution of Leibniz's passive vitalism in contrast with the general doctrine of Platonic and neo-Platonic emanation. Leibniz, like Deleuze after him, will not posit two distinct substances. For Leibniz, the reasoning, perceptive and 'singing' monad is what it is only in the passions, affections, perceptions that it expresses.[6] Reason, mind or spirit are not the same as matter, but the relations of material bodies are like the ground bass upon which each monad unfolds its own melody, each of which contributes to the overall harmonious symphony of the world. Whereas neo-platonic emanation posits each individual being as deriving from and expressing a One, Deleuze (like Leibniz) refuses to posit a unity that would be other than each perceiving and affected point of view; the world is just this multiplicity of viewpoints, each of which is a truth of a whole that is nothing other than this expressive multiplicity. To refer to Deleuze as a Platonist in a de-realising or unworldly sense - as a philosopher who wishes to overcome the gritty actuality of this world in favour of some mystical unity - is to fail to

is composed of nothing more than bodies as movements, we need to account for the incorporeal force that enables movement (Christia Mercer, *Leibniz's Metaphysics: Its Origins and Development*, Cambridge, Cambridge University Press, 2001). Complete reasoning entails that we give a justification for all the affections and actions of *every* body. This can only be achieved - not by accepting ready-made definitions - but by giving each event a place in the infinite world, and regarding the infinite world as nothing other than all the perceptions through which it is expressed. If Deleuze will follow Leibniz and Plato in referring actual events back to their enabling potentiality which is their real cause, he will reverse Platonism by seeing that plane of virtual potentialities not as some *prior* or distinctly theological ground, but as a co-present and always insistent potentiality for variation.

4. In *Political Descartes: Reason, Ideology and the Bourgeois Project* Antonio Negri defines the Cartesian separation of the subject from a world of meaningful powers as a break or crisis that destroys an initially revolutionary tendency to ground human knowledge and power on the material power of the cosmos. Negri,

Political Descartes: Reason, Ideology and the Bourgeois Project, Matteo Mandarini and Alberto Toscano (trans), London, Verso, 2006, pp107-112.

5. On vitalism in the seventeenth century and its opposition to Cartesian materialism and mechanism, see John Rogers, *The Matter of Revolution: Science, Poetry, and Politics in the Age of Milton*, Ithaca, Cornell University Press, 1996. On the Spinozist contribution to the enlightenment, rather than an enlightenment dominated by Cartesian or Kantian rationalism, see Jonathan Israel, *Radical Enlightenment: Philosophy and the Making of Modernity, 1650-1750*, Oxford, Oxford University Press, 2001.

6. Gilles Deleuze, *The Fold: Leibniz and the Baroque*, Tom Conley (trans), Minneapolis, University of Minnesota Press, 1993, p132.

7. Badiou, *Deleuze*, op. cit; Hallward 2006.

8. Deleuze, *Difference and Repetition*, op. cit.

take into account what I will refer to as the *queer* nature of Deleuze's vitalism.[7] Every body in this world is possible as an individual because it gives some form and specificity in time and space to a potential that always threatens to destabilise or de-actualise its being. This is what Deleuze refers to as *real* conditions of existence and allows us to think of his philosophy as offering a positive sense of queer being, or what Deleuze also refers to as ?being.[8] That is, in addition to the actual bodies that populate this world in time and space there is also the virtual plane that is thoroughly real and that is infinitely different; it exists in each body as its potential for variation, a potential that is actualised not by the decisions that body makes but by the encounters it undergoes.

In concrete terms, we might begin by thinking of gender. Active vitalism, at least in the form that Deleuze and Guattari trace back to Kant, regards all concepts and categories as originally imposed by the subject upon an otherwise meaningless life. Active vitalism might regard gender as one of the ways in which life or the social 'constructs' categories that differentiate an otherwise general or undifferentiated humanity: so the criticism of stereotypes (as clichés or rigid forms imposed upon life) would lead to an overthrow of rigid categories in favour of what we really are (as unique individuals) or would expose that there are no such things as individuals, only effects of gender as it is represented. Genders and kinds are known in the vague and general opposition between male and female, distinctions that are imposed upon life and that need to be reactivated by being traced back to their social and familial origins. By contrast, for Deleuze and Guattari's passive vitalism genders, kinds and stereotypes are not categories imposed upon life that might be overcome or criticised in the name of a universal and self aware humanity; instead, it is life as a multiple and differentiating field of powers that expresses itself in various manners. Differentiation is not a false distinction imposed on an otherwise universal humanity. On the contrary, every female is an individuated actualisation of a genetic potential for sexual differentiation, and every aspect of that female body - ranging from chromosomal and hormonal composition to the stylisation of dress and comportment - is one highly individuated way of actualising a potentiality. So every woman is an actualisation of a potentiality to be female, while the difference between straight and gay gives further specification or distinction, and this would continue on and on to the smallest of differences, marking out not only each body, but also all the events, souls and affections within bodies. There is, then, no opposition between sexual difference and queerness. It is not the case that causes, such as feminism, that would aim to affirm the possibility of women's becoming would - as gender differentiated - be opposed to movements of queerness that would strive to liberate bodies from gender *norms*. The key to Deleuze's passive vitalism and the aesthetics that it mobilises lies in thinking difference beyond the kinds and generalisations of a politics of active vitalism. Whereas active vitalism would seek to return political processes to the will, intent and agency of individuals or subjects, passive vitalism is micropolitical: it attends to those differences that we neither intend, nor perceive, nor command.

Again, to return to a seeming tension between queer politics and gender politics, we might consider movements of trans-sexualism, cross-dressing and the politics of sexualities. On an active vitalist model the very identification of oneself as, say, 'woman' or 'queer' would be internally contradictory. In order to achieve political recognition I must at once be recognised *as* this or that being participating in some movement of identifiable collective will, but I must also realise that the demand for recognition from the normative matrix compromises my claim as a subject. The vital, on this model, is the spirit or subjective act that is always belied or compromised by actuality. It follows, then, that there would be a conflict between the vitality of political claims and the intrinsic compromise of political actuality. It also follows that those selves who would embrace certain kinds or distinctions - men who want to be regarded as naturally homosexual, women who want to be recognised as masculine, and bodies who regard their individuation as possible only outside or beyond gay, lesbian or gendered kinds - would have competing and exclusive political agendas. What is presupposed is a distinction between the active enunciating self of politics - the active subject whose claims must be heard in opposition to normativity - and the enunciated or represented individual defined by sex, gender, sexuality or other terms such as race, ethnicity or belief. Such an opposition is captured in what Gayatri Spivak refers to as strategic essentialism: on the one hand we acknowledge that politics requires kinds or essences, but we also see such terms as the effect of strategies, or activist decisions made for the sake of political efficacy. Such a term creates an ongoing problem and contradiction for any political movement that undertakes an overthrow or revolution in terms of transgression, for acting in the name of a subordinated term must begin from the already determined and subordinated field of positions.

The same problems and tensions apply to the tired dialectic between philosophies of rights on the one hand and multicultural and racial political claims of difference on the other. That is: there are those who would defend a 'subject,' universalism or radicalism opposed to all constituted identities (and would therefore reject any multiculturalisms or relativism that merely allowed competing bodies to exist alongside each other). At the same time there are those who oppose any such appeal to the subject, philosophy or critique *as such* insisting that one only knows the subject as this or that specified, individuated and socially determined form. In the first mode of critique in opposition to actualised terms in favour of a constituting decision we could place Alain Badiou and Slavoj Zizek, both of whom insist that there is no intuitable domain of life in itself, for being is just that void that is given only in its disappearance. But for every insistence on the subject as a power that must be inferred as that which gives birth to the decision there are also a range of political debunkers who regard such appeals to an originating act as one more ideological obfuscation or mysticism; for all we have is an actual political field of determined bodies, always already given in terms of race, sex and gender. It is no surprise, perhaps, that today a series of 'philosophers' berate the ways in which multiculturalism (or the claim for difference) precludes an ethics of decision and the subject. For Alain Badiou subject events occur *not* through processes of inclusion and the allowance of any lifestyle whatever, but through acts that decide - with no prior justification in actuality - that a new situation has occurred; subjects are nothing other than such decisions.[9] The entire possibility of ethics is not grounded on life and actuality, but on a subjective decision or break. Badiou's ethics of the subject is ostensibly an anti-vitalism, insistently opposed to the grounding of political claims on some already existing actualisation of being or life. But it is just the vibrancy of the subject's difference from the world as already actualised, the radical distinction of the subject as negation of an already lived order that places Badiou in stark contrast both with the undifferentiated and generalising inclusiveness of a weak multiculturalism that would seemingly appeal to differences among individuals, *and* the passive vitalism of Deleuze and Guattari who would regard the subject of identity politics and activism as not yet fully individuated. Far from seeing the subjective event as occurring in a break with the world of differences, as Badiou would do, or from regarding the profusion of different cultures and bodies as the very force of life, Deleuze and Guattari put forward a vitalism that is neither that of the decision nor of the differentiated body. Their vitalism is passive in its attention to the barely discerned, confused and queer differences that compose bodies.

Deleuze and Guattari's insistence that there is a vitalism that one can discern in Kant alerts us to a long-running privileging of the decision and the re-awakening of the subjective act in the face of a fall into everyday normality and normalisation. An active vitalism strives to overcome the imposed norms that would reduce an individual's autonomy, but also takes into account the vitality of traditions, cultures and practices that constitute bodies as individuals and agents in the first place. A passive vitalism, by contrast, is one of re-singularisation or counter-actualisation: every differentiated political claim, whether that be in the name of the human, a sexualised or gendered individual, or a racial minority may begin with a molar politics, but has the potential to become minoritarian, and it is this potentiality of queering that is properly vital.

INDIVIDUATION

Both vitality and queerness are crucial to Deleuze's philosophy of individuation. First, vitality: a body is identifiable or individuated *not* because it takes the undifferentiated potentiality of life and then subjects itself to a norm. It is not the case, as Judith Butler would have it, that in the beginning is a radically undifferentiated becoming that can become an autonomous being only by being recognised *as* this or that generality in some social matrix.[10] Butler's notion of the performative self is directly opposed to a simple active vitalism: there is no grounding and pre-social 'sex' which is then represented

9. Alain Badiou, *Ethics: An Essay on the Understanding of Evil*, Peter Hallward (trans), London, Verso, 2001.

10. Judith Butler, *Giving an Account of Oneself*, New York, Fordham University Press, 2005.

in language or signification. There is no subject or proper self who then acts and speaks; instead, in the beginning is the act or performance *from which* we conclude or posit that there must have been a pre-linguistic subject. Sex, then, is not some materiality or ground that issues in or is belied by gender; for it is only through gender that we can conclude that *there must have been* some instituting act. Further, and more importantly for Butler, genders or social norms cannot simply be removed or destroyed in order to reveal the true and real subject; a subject exists and has being only insofar as it is effected as a relatively stable and recognised social kind. And if the self is constituted as recognised then it requires some reference to the heterosexual matrix of normativity, even if it marks its own being as a negation or refusal of that matrix. For Butler, then, social differences are at once the means through which subjects are constituted as recognisable performing, speaking and acting selves; at the same time *as performance* the subject is always also a potentiality for destabilisation or unsure repetition of the normativity that is its founding condition. Queerness then lies in the difference between performance and performed; the social differences we recognise would be stabilisations or reifications of a performative power that is nothing other than the capacity to destabilise differentiated kinds. Difference, then, is negative: both the difference between kinds, and the difference *from* social kinds; but there is no difference itself as some posit or intuitable power.

When Deleuze insists on vitalism he insists that life tends towards difference, creating further and further distinctions. This is so much the case that he follows Leibniz in seeing the world as composed of souls that descend infinitely. My body is a soul or monad because it is capable of perceiving and being affected in an absolutely singular manner: no other body has the same unfolding of time and space, the same perceptions and affections as mine. And within this body are a thousand other souls: a heart that will beat according to all the hormonal, nutritional, climactic and nervous perceptions it endures (and so on with every organ, and so on with every organ's cells, and so on with every microbiological event). Far from a body being individuated through subjection to norms, a body is absolutely individuated above and beyond (or before) any of the generalising norms that the laziness of common sense applies. This vitality is therefore *essentially* queer. The task of thinking is not to see bodies in their general recognisable form, *as* this or that ongoing and unified entity, but to approach the world as the unfolding of events. Take an encounter between two bodies: you, a straight man, consider your sexuality to be properly vital, contributing as it does to heterosexual reproduction. I, however, as a lesbian female regard my sexuality as properly vital: not subjected to rigidifying norms of biological reproduction I am capable of creating myself in ways far more imaginative and varied than any social norm might dictate. The dispute *between* two such bodies would concern a proper image of life (as biologically reproductive, or imaginatively productive) and would be disjunctive: either I answer to the norms of social reproduction as they exist, or I create other norms and ideals. And one could go on adding other bodies to this terrain: I might be a gay man, assured that my homosexuality is genetically determined, or a trans-gendered individual considering myself to be capable of living a gender while maintaining a sex. One could see such a dispute as devolving upon just how we determined the relation between life and norms: either we regard life as having a genetic reality that would determine sex regardless of social performance, or would see social performance as the determining and decisive force that makes possible any individual body. Determining sexual political disputes in this way - as rejecting the norm of the heterosexual nuclear family but doing so in favour of some more radical determining force - merely substitutes one normative image of life (familial, productive) for another (genetic, socially constructed, performatively constituted). Either life is and ought to be oriented to reproduction, or life is capable of variation, or there are genetic determinants that preclude a realm of pure decision.

What such a way of thinking depends upon is what Deleuze and Guattari diagnosed as an exclusive use of the disjunctive synthesis: *either* one subjects ones desire to social norms *or* one falls back into the dark night of the undifferentiated.[11] They opposed this transcendent, exclusive and illegitimate use to their own immanent, inclusive and vitalist disjunctive synthesis. Here the relations between terms are neither exclusive (either male *or* female, either social/political *or* genetic, either real *or* constructed) nor transcendent (where such terms organise and differentiate life, and do so on the basis of some grounding value, whether that be genetics, reproduction, liberty or the human). That is to say, we could argue that queer politics in one of its dominant forms remains committed to a transcendent and disjunctive use of the synthesis and is therefore profoundly oedipal: *either* you recognise yourself as a being within the familial order of male-female *or* you risk falling into psychosis. It is the family as the basic unit that also relies on an active vitalism: in order to become individuated 'we' must recognise ourselves as part of a symbolic order, for we have no self or being outside the human and self-governing world of father-mother-child, and political action must proceed from a desire that begins, initially, from a relation between self and other than can *then* open onto a broader political field of historical, racial and social forces. Judith Butler, for example, reads Antigone's rebellion against the State as at once familial, negative and activist: the very possibility of making a claim, of speaking and being heard, requires that Antigone be situated as a sister and daughter, but it is just that positioning that is rendered negative, impossible and activist by Antigone's speaking *for* the claims of her brother. She at once speaks as a familial subject, dutifully promising to bury her brother, while also negating or perverting that subjectivity, by speaking against her father who would refuse her that sibling bond: 'If kinship is the precondition of the human, then Antigone is the occasion for a new field of the human, achieved through political catachresis, the one that happens when the less than human speaks as human, when gender is displaced, and kinship founders on its own founding laws'.[12] One could extrapolate from

11. Gilles Deleuze and Félix Guattari, *Anti-Oedipus: Capitalism and Schizophrenia*, Robert Hurley, Mark Seem and Helen R Lane (trans), Minneapolis, University of Minnesota Press, 1983.

12. Judith Butler, *Antigone's Claim: Kinship Between Life and Death*, New York, Columbia University Press, 2000, p82.

here, as Butler does, to the structure of political speech in general: in order to speak and be recognised I must be situated in a social body, but 'I' have being only in my negation or queering of that recognised normativity. The subject is active only in its taking up, and then negation, of a norm that is at once its condition for being and its condition for *not* being. To be is to be *dis*obedient, acting and speaking only within the frame of a presupposed obedience against which one is defined:

> The claiming becomes an act that reiterates the act it affirms, extending the act of insubordination by performing its avowal in language. This avowal, paradoxically, requires a sacrifice of autonomy at the very moment in which it is performed: she asserts herself through appropriating the voice of the other, the one to whom she is opposed; thus her autonomy is gained through the appropriation of the authoritative voice of the one she resists, an appropriation that has within it traces of a simultaneous refusal and assimilation of that very authority.[13]

13. Butler, *Antigone's Claim*, op. cit., p11.

Like Freud, Butler's conditioning matrix of obedience is familial (even though she uses the ambivalence of one's familial relations to argue for a necessary mourning and melancholia in one's object choice); to take on a gendered body as one's object choice both creates one's own sexuality in relation to an other, and entails a renunciation of other gender and sexual potentials.

For Butler the socio-political world extends from the initial coordinates of the family. Deleuze and Guattari, by contrast, insist on a schizoanalysis that sees the family as a stimulus for historical political coordinates, and sees the 'global persons' of the family as possible only through a process of historical, political and racial contraction. The father, for example, is not the basis from which the political figure of the king, the despot or the dictator is extrapolated; on the contrary, it is only possible for us today to understand ourselves as individuated through our relations to our mothers and fathers because an entire history of domination has increasingly displaced its complex, political and collective desires onto private familial images.

MICROPOLITICS

For Deleuze and Guattari schizoanalysis reverses this process: we need to see the ways in which our seemingly familial and oedipal conditions - the child constituted as a gendered individual in a family dynamic - is a compression of historical and political forces. In practice this would require opening any relation among bodies to the historical, political, 'micro' and vital (or infinitely small) potentials from which they are composed. The attention shifts from persons and norms, to the thousands of souls from which we are effected. So, the heterosexual man who defends his being on the basis of reproductive norms only lives and feels this normativity because his body is composed of passions, affections and orientations which it is the task of Deleuze and

Guattari's 'schizoanalysis' to break into its various components. We would need to analyse the composition of each of 'man's' defining souls: images of the nuclear family, which have a figurative (Christian, bourgeois, popular science) dimension; notions of life which are also inflected by theology ('be fruitful and multiply'); political discourses (the family as economic unit); and racial notions of man as the rational, democratic and white individual towards which all human civilization is 'progressing.' In order to form some notion of 'the human' one needs to take all the capacities for genetic variation and assume some underlying unity. This 'man in general,' according to Deleuze and Guattari is achieved historically and politically by unifying complex differences into some single figure. The same applies to 'woman,' 'lesbian,' 'trans-sexual' or - in some cases - 'queer.' If the latter term denotes a group of bodies who seek recognition on the basis of their relation to, or difference from, other bodies then 'queer' forms a majoritarian mode of politics: a political force that reduces difference for the sake of creating a political subject group. If, however, 'queer' were to operate *vitally* it would aim to signal the positive potentialities from which groups were formed: there could only be lesbian women because certain differences are possible (such as sexual difference, and difference in orientation), but that would then lead to further and further difference, not only to each individual but within each individual.

Minoritarian politics moves in the opposite direction from recognition and aims to maximise the circumstances for the proliferation and pulverisation of differences. In terms of policy and representation this would have concrete consequences: one would not strive to attain a representative polity - include more women and gays in parliament - but would see politics not as representation (of women's issues, gay rights, minority values), but as mobilisation. What processes could operate in the absence of any ideal image, figure or grouping of human normativity?

As a concrete example, we might look at reproductive rights, and the question of whether same sex couples should be allowed access to IVF. One way of approaching this would be through rights, access and - perhaps - broadening notions of what counts as a family. Such an approach could also take into account pragmatic considerations about distribution of resources, the quality of life for children of same-sex couples given the prevailing norms, and might also have to deal with the competing rights of religious and ethnic groups. 'Queer' in this context would count as one variable among others, and questions of life would be considered in terms of relations among persons: how do we compare and negotiate the competing demands for, and quality of, various notions of what counts as a good life? How do we balance the claims of one group - those bodies who affirm their right to be queer - with another, such as those Christian agencies who have requested exemption from equal opportunity law when it comes to dealing with adoption by gay couples? How do spiritual rights compete with sexual rights? Such questions and problems negotiate *interests*, already constituted political positions that mark out and, according to Butler, enable political agency. By contrast, a Deleuzo-Guattarian approach would consider life beyond the concept of the person, and would therefore define its vitalism as queer, as having to do with all those potential differences that exceed and infinitely divide each body. Desire, they insist, is both pre-personal and necessarily revolutionary; so one would take *any* political interest such as the demand by a gay couple for a child, and then look at its multiple constituting desires. These may be in part revolutionary - a destruction of the family unit as the sole site for reproduction, a refusal of the norms of social recognition, and even an affirmation of life beyond one's own body - but also in part reactionary, in the desire for inclusion in the social field as it currently is, in the maintenance of the family, now as a sexually diverse unit of social production, and in the racial commitment to one's own kind. Desire is essentially revolutionary precisely because it is the matter that is formed by social relations; even when desires are reactionary - such as the racial deliriums that underpin the manifest political interest of having a child of one's own - they are nevertheless distinct from the social machine that takes up those desires into its own workings. To say, as Deleuze and Guattari do, that we are composed of a thousand tiny sexes is to place race, politics, history and sexuality *within*, not between or among, individuals. Any body's desire, and therefore its relation to other bodies' desires, is composed of multiple and divergent series. My relation to other sexes may have familial determining points; one might relate to something like 'masculinity' through the image one has of one's father. But every father, in turn, presents a certain racial, economic, political and sexual complex. The father who comes home complaining about all the migrants who have taken away his employment, all the single mothers who are destroying the welfare system, who then treats his successful upwardly mobile son with resentment, while fearing his daughter's relation with her black schoolmate gives the child an entire racial-cultural-economic field through which sexuality is negotiated.

There is no such thing as 'a' life, and a vitalist queer politics is a vitalism that negotiates the multiple affections and attachments that compose any field. We would have to add to any consideration of same-sex couples and reproductive rights a critical approach to family as such: questioning the prima facie value of a child of one's own, of family units, of reproductive medicine as a form of bio-capital. The same would apply to any issue of queer politics, which ought not be considered as a negotiation among competing political groupings, nor as a 'pragmatic' relation between the necessary accession to norms and the desire for autonomy.

Micropolitics is a form of pragmatism insofar as it focuses on life, but this is a life of passive vitalism where we attend to all the minor, less than human, not yet personalised desires that enter any field of social relations. If pragmatism refers questions of truth and right back to the life that is maximised and enabled, the pragmatism of micro-politics considers the lives of which we are composed. We would need to take something as general and majoritarian as the right to reproduction and look at the desires from which it is composed, some of which would be 'sad' or reactive (my desire to be like every other normal family, and which diminish my power by referring my body to what it is not yet and may never be); but other components would be joyful (if I imagined an other life as creating potentialities beyond my own imagination, perhaps also compelling me to feel different affects beyond those of autonomy and self-management). Every body is queer, not because there is no body that actually attains the ideal embodied in any norm (say, where there is no woman who fulfils the figure of 'woman'); rather the queerness is positive. No body fully knows its own powers, and can only become joyful (or live) not by attaining the ideal it has of itself - being who I really am - but by maximising that in ourselves which exceeds the majoritarian, or which is not yet actualised. Counter-actualisation or re-singularisation takes bodies as they are, with their identifying and determining features, and then asks how the potentials that enabled those features might be expanded. If I identify myself as having a certain gender or sexuality then I can either regard this (in active vitalism) as a form of strategic essentialism, where I decide to adopt an identity for the sake of political efficacy while remaining aware that who I am as a subject is radically different from any identifying term; *or* (as in passive vitalism) I would recognise that gender, sex and other defining features emanate from histories, passions and relations that I have not lived but which might be retrieved.

From the position of passive vitalism one would need to look at the composition of bodies as themselves encounters. Deleuze's book on Leibniz cites a seemingly politically and sexually neutral example: a body at a desk is at once composed of inclinations towards a drink in a club (anticipating the hum of the surrounds, the coolness of the drink, the conviviality of the atmosphere) competing with the desire to continue writing (the anticipated sense of a job done, the interest in solving a problem). What is required in such a situation is a 'differential calculus' for it will always be the smallest imperceptible *inclinations* that lead to a decision one way or the other. The same idea can be extended politically. Our sympathies, affects, desires and acceptances as social and political beings are composed of micro-perceptions that barely come to awareness. One of the key ways in which Deleuze and Guattari see such counter-actualisation coming into being is through art.

THE AESTHETICS OF VITALISM

In many ways the link between art, vitalism and political renewal is rather tired and seems to run directly against everything that might be revolutionary in Deleuze and Guattari's political theory. Particularly dominant in the broad understanding of Romanticism and modernism, vitalism appealed to a life force that would be capable of destroying or enlivening the reified categories of the understanding. Vitalism, in its Romantic and modernist modes was also an appeal to various forms of defamiliarisation and impersonality. That is to say, for everyday efficiency and action we cannot afford to live the intensity and complexity of life, and so we create concepts and languages to manage and diminish the forceful chaos of existence. Art, however, by using language or figures in unfamiliar or unworkable combinations can reawaken us to the creative force from which such systems emerged. In its Romantic form vitalism was active and subjective: whereas everyday understanding reduces us to so many socio-political and atomised individuals, the work of art intimates a creative power or genius that is given only after the effect intimating the subject who *must have been* the author of a synthesis. This was how Kant described beauty in nature, where the delight in form prompts us to posit some notion of design, even if that creating power is felt reflectively, rather than known. In modernism, the vital power that was reawakened by art was achieved through impersonality, with the work of art suggesting a creative spirit behind the created form - a spirit given only in its *not* appearing. Such high modernist or Romantic modes of defamiliarisation and renewal that would reawaken the creative force from which our lived world has been synthesised are essentially normalising insofar as they refer back to the subjective or grounding conditions from which works must have emerged and which can be retrieved, recognised and re-lived as our own. The human in general is just that spirit or power that must be felt, but not known, above and beyond any work of genius.

By contrast, Deleuze insists on real and immanent conditions, and also on the virtual or vital, not as an active underlying ground but as a 'swarm' or chaos that, far from grounding or returning life to its animating power, *deterritorialises* life beyond any of the seemingly proper forms that we know. What I hope to demonstrate is that vitalism in its active form has dominated general concepts of the aesthetic at least since Kant. This active form of vitalism, which refers systems and identities back to a constituting power, is also highly normative: life has a proper trajectory towards fruition and the realisation of its proper form; art is the process whereby deviations, failures or corruptions of the vital power may be retrieved and re-lived. Deleuze and Guattari's passive vitalism, by contrast, challenges the idea of a single, unifying, productive and fertile life force whose proper trajectory is fruition, expansion and revelation. In a number of contexts Deleuze describes the deterritorialising vitality of life as 'sterile,' 'divergent,' 'self-enjoying,' and 'surveying'. That is, the vital is not that which springs forth from itself to synthesise, unify and produce its world; it is receptive in its feeling of that which is not itself, often yielding nothing more than the isolated or punctuated affect of encounter.

To summarise so far: there are two ways in which we might think about vitalism and personality, both of which involve dissolution. First, in the tradition of active vitalism personality is that which remains the same through time, allows us to be recognised as this or that individual being and which also (as socially enabling) is existentially or virtually disabling. Personality, or recognising oneself *as human*, is required and enabled by seeing oneself as an instance of humanity in general, but this requires a certain sacrifice or even mourning for one's singularity or specificity. Kant insists that one must have a sense of one's phenomenal personality but must also recognise a free noumenal, supersensible and moral personality that we cannot know or perceive but can only think after the event of decision. In contemporary discourses of the subject, such as Judith Butler's, one must subject oneself to enabling and recognisable norms. To be recognised by, and with, others requires some determined personality. But those necessary norms and figures of personhood are at odds with the act, performance or event which brings them into being. On this account, personhood comes into being through moments or decisions which are perceived only after the event as the outcome of a performance that must be posited as having been. We do not see, live or intuit performativity itself, only its effects. A politics and vitalising imperative follows: do not be seduced by normativity. Recognise that the self who is performed and recognised is at odds with the less stable - one might say 'queer' - vital self who acts (who 'acts but is not').

I would suggest that this form of active vitalism, as critique and negation of norm, image, figure or stereotype is not only the dominant in theory, but also in popular culture and public policy. That is, there is today a widespread suspicion regarding the passive reception or incorporation of images; indeed, we might even say that capitalism is just a continuous production of 'images,' a constant destruction of any definitive, transcendent or external quality in favour of an incessant process of newly consumable images. One is always defined on the one hand as *either* male or female, while also experiencing oneself as that consuming subject who is *neither* male, nor female: a unique subject as point of consumption. Against that negation of the image we could posit Deleuze and Guattari's positive use of the conjunctive synthesis: I am girl *and* woman *and* lesbian *and* masculine *and* effeminate *and* ...; here the self is not some radical alterity before and beyond images but a potentiality to include, transform and vary all the races, sexes and peoples of history.

In its active vitalist form the self is always, ideally, a purely formal principle of decision irreducible to any image. The good citizen is not seduced by rigid norms, does not passively allow himself to be imprinted by pre-given figures and relates to social and representational systems critically. In policy, for example, governments increasingly express concern regarding negative and pernicious images, whether these concern the representation of the acceptability of certain practices - binge drinking, smoking, the sexualisation of children - or the direct war on life-impeding images, or the image as life-impeding per se. In the UK, the Body Image Summit of 2000 sought to police the overly stringent body ideals imposed upon girls and women and led to later campaigns to ban the promulgation of overly thin or 'size zero' models. The assumption that an image or model is a *norm*, or an image of what the viewer ought to be, is unquestioned; such an assumption relies upon a definition of the self as at one and the same time determined by the consumption of images, while properly being other than the generality of the image. Only if the representational and normative sphere is achievable by the bodies it organises will we have a healthy body politic. If the model, ideal or imaged persona is radically at odds with actual bodies then individuals either *diminish* their own being through submission and subjection *or* are not recognised as subjects at all.

What has been lost is the fictive, virtual or incorporeal power of the image: is it not possible to see a body of 'heroin chic,' of androgynous subtlety, or even childlike frailty *not* as an ideal self, but as ideals that float freely from actual bodies, varying the imaginative range of what counts as human. Would the problem then be *not* that body-images are insufficiently normal - not like real women - but are insufficiently queer, too close to actuality? One might imagine a higher degree of inclusion and disjunction, with more bodies that are increasingly less realistic, yielding more of a sense of the model or image *as* image/model, not as some active representation of a life that must know and recognise itself and always remain in command of the production of affects. The war on reified and passively-ingested images leads to, and presupposes, a vitalist ethical imperative that would aim to re-awaken the sense of the produced status of the image: one ought not regard any actuality - be that the heterosexual matrix or humanity in general - as a final or essential form. (Indeed there are no essences, only existence.) The true self is not the subject who is recognised so much as the act, performance, decision or 'lived' which is other than (although only known through and after) the norms which give it being.

If this form of active vitalism demands a becoming-impersonal it does so only in recognising that while we may require personality to live and speak socially and politically, we are always irreducible to (and other than) such ideals. This mode of active vitalism has specific consequences for activist politics, and results in a certain style of problem: where there is always an 'on the one hand / on the other hand' structure. The very notion of 'queer' is always a queering *of* some norm: on the one hand I say 'no' to normativity, while on the other hand I demand recognition from the very matrix of recognition whose system allows me to speak. This structure of compromise (or negation and recognition) also plays out in concrete issues: are demands for civil partnership (for example) ways of enlivening social bonds, or are such appeals for inclusion negations of one's non-heterosexual status? Do movements of sexual or gender re-orientation inject an instability or performativity into the norms of male and female, or are we not seduced too easily into already defined gender roles? Such problems concern the degree of *act* in relation to the image: is our relation to the norm properly productive (introducing or exposing a potential deviation or queerness) or are we not, in remaining activist at the level of sex/gender/sexuality passively obedient to already constituted categories? Such a structure is theorised by Butler as a necessary acceptance of recognition and submission, alongside an instability or excitability internal to those very normalising procedures. But such structures are not unique to queer theory (a fact which should give us pause for thought: for Alain Badiou a subject *is* just this decision or event within an enumerated scene to institute a new mode of numeration. For Slavoj Zizek the subject is this impossible, barred, excluded and negative remainder that occurs in the failure of any image or object to capture desire.) By contrast, as I have already suggested, the Deleuzo-Guattarian approach differs in its very style of problem, which is not to interrogate the relation between body and norm according to the appropriate degree of its vitality (whether it really issues from a proper force of decision or is not further subjection). Instead of seeing the self in relation to perceived norms (a self which is defined as other than any of its perceptions), Deleuze and Deleuze and Guattari make two key interventions.

First, for Deleuze there are not bodies, selves or subjects *who* perceive, for the self is composed of perceptions, each of which just is its imaging of other perceiving souls: the heart has its life by responding to the hormones, rhythms, flows and movements that create it as a point of view, while the body is at once a perception of all those barely perceived durations within, and the affectations that it encounters without. Instead of subject-norm relations, we deal with multiplicities and singular points: networks of perception and imagination which create points of view, and that can - at singular points - produce entirely different relations and configurations. Second, once bodies - all bodies - are no longer bodies with organs (the eye that sees in order to negotiate a world mastered by the hand, relating to other subjects through the voice of reason), we can take the image beyond organic and centred thinking to look at the power of micro-perceptions: not just the domain of body-images and imposed norms, but all those barely discerned perceptions that compose all images, and that exist and insist beyond the human.

BECOMING VULVA: FLESH, FOLD, INFINITY

Patricia MacCormack

Patriarchal and psychoanalytic discourses have oriented the dissemination of privilege and power which facilitates the dominance of male subjects, not through selection of those particular subjects but through the systems which structure society and ideology. These abstract systems default to valuing certain 'masculine' qualities and foreclose the possibility of the recognition of true difference by describing alterity only as different from. Gilles Deleuze and Félix Guattari see the male subject as the most in need of deconstruction in order to facilitate the mobilisation of ethics. Luce Irigaray describes the masculine structuration of society as phallologocentric, where knowledge and power are oriented around such qualities inherent in masculinity, such as singularity, solidity, visual total apprehension and transcendental signification. Deleuze, Guattari and Irigaray have all offered alternatives - Deleuze and Guattari call to the becoming-woman of dominant subjects, Irigaray describes the model of the two lips which exchanges the symbolic phallus for a feminine-genital model. In this article I will offer another model which negotiates the traditional antagonism between these two theoretical suggestions. Using Deleuze's work on 'the fold', I will posit 'becoming-vulva'. The vulva mediates the feminine-genital elements of Irigaray's two lips with Deleuze's structure of the fold to become a relationship between disparate perspectives and elements. Becoming-vulva is available to all subjects while resisting the vaguely essentialising fetishisation of the term 'woman'. As a metamorphic and volatile structure becoming-vulva is necessarily experimental and thus this article will attempt to offer entrance points into other forms of becoming without demanding a prescriptive technique.

Anatomically defined, the vulva is the visible external female genitalia. By external what is meant is all that isn't within the pelvis, so the vaginal aperture is included. Divergent from psychoanalysis and classical sculpture, external female vulva is visible only through exploration. It is two sets of lips, clitoris, vagina, anus, g-spot and apocryphal elements. It is the spreading out and convergence of labia. It is the unity of the clitoris and its concealment of the urethra, a single organ as palimpsest. The vaginal 'aperture' is a volitional hole, both penetrable and ingurgitant. The general perinea, the indiscernibility between what constitutes the vulva (not the thigh, not the belly) and what constitutes the surrounds (not vulva) and the internal aspect of the vulva, which reflects the infinite potential found in the exploration of all internality (seen in such activities as speculum sex, fisting, and douche and enema play among other things) offer an organ far removed materially and conceptually from the hypostasis of the phallus. Being as a body is a formalisation of flesh into smaller forms which have function and signification: head as seat of logic, face as signifying plane of subjectivity, race, age, genitals as signifier of gender and possible sexuality and sexual configurations in relation with other subjects. The vulva is informal both as a non-reified biological form and as a mode of expression. Becoming investigates and exploits the relations between forces of subjugation and seeks tactics to reorient strata of desire - how does a vulva desire differently to a phallus or a vagina or clitoris within phallic paradigms? Vulvas are materially formed of multiple folds of flesh. The body becoming-vulva is involuted and undone, creating what Deleuze in *Difference and Repetition* calls a larval sexuality - immature and transformed at every synthesis, which acts not toward a thing but toward its metamorphosis, toward encountering the self which is sensed but not wholly perceived, toward the imperceptibility within repetition where all elements within syntheses are dissipated, disoriented and reoriented with each turn, each folding and each alteration in the aspects of involution. Pleasure is folding with the planes of flesh. Beyond metaphor becoming-vulva enfleshes as fold every part of the flesh, every nerve every tissue mass, every artery, every organ, the unfolded skin as libidinally provocative. In the event of thinking over knowing vulva is present but not present to itself, sensed but not perceived and known. Skin may be peeled, planes touched, parts intensified or moved around, corporeal minutiae explored and every plane of the body reorganised into a new configuration with new function and meaning. Becoming-vulva makes skin-flesh of the world, not the self upon a becoming.

Becoming-vulva is, put simply, entering into an alliance with the fold, flesh and force of the indeterminacy of this desiring disorganising organ. It is difficult to conceptualise 'a' vulva in the same way as one can conceive of 'a' penis. One can however have vulvic male genitalia. The use of the word 'cunt' as opposed to 'vulva' comes as a response to 'cunt' being the limits of linguistic profanity in Western culture, where the actual signifier of non-specific female genitalia is exchanged for the signifier of a repulsive or offensive or, more resonant with its affinity with women, disorderly or disobedient subject, particularly male (essentially men most often call other men 'cunts', 'pussies' and 'girls' when they fail to fulfil an expectation). The transference from philologically smooth vulva to the hard consonants of cunt converts the speaking of the word itself from the open vowel teeth to tongue to the guttural and teeth to teeth. Can we redeem cunt from its expropriation from female anatomy to majoritarian insult? Cunt doesn't really refer to any body part - while it insinuates genitals it isn't specific. Like the feminine it is vague, threatening, neither demarcated nor determined. The disobedience of the vulva is intimately related to the transgression of paradigms of the singular, the onomastic, the visual and the functional which the vulva performs. This paper uses the term 'vulva' as a navigation of the tensions between Deleuze and Guattari's problematic term 'woman' with Irigaray's model of the two lips. I argue that Deleuze and Guattari's concept of the demonic and Deleuze's work on Leibniz and the fold can create fruitful political relations with feminist issues and Irigaray, acknowledging the imperative becomings of all subjects, their histories and memories, creating a structure which is not a term which describes becomings to come but an abstract experimental terrain which is a configuration of all subjects, here and now.

Negotiating the pitfalls and problems in using the subject position woman I will argue that a vulvic paradigm can bypass these risks as it works directly (and only) with structure rather than any phantasmatic notion of a particular kind of subject which has both been oppressed and denied validation or self-authorisation of her own subjectivity. Just as phallologocentrism coalesces the dominance of the visible, the phantasy of transcendental truth incarnated in the solid, demarcated, objectifying, investigating and penetrating symbol of the phallus, so the vulva privileges fluidity, connectivity, aspectual apprehension, tactility and the other senses.

By way of contextualising becoming-vulva I turn to the fruitful field created by relatively recent work by feminists who have negotiated Deleuze (both with and without Guattari) and Irigaray. Irigaray uses the configuration of the two lips to elucidate connections between language, self as manifold, flesh and inevitable but not object-activated becomings.

> In order to touch himself, man needs an instrument; his hand, a woman's body, language … and this self-caressing requires at least a minimum of activity. As for woman, she touches herself without any need for mediation, and before there is any way to distinguish activity from passivity. Woman 'touches herself' all the time and moreover no-one can forbid her to do so, for her genitals are formed of two lips in continuous contact.[1]

Becoming-vulva, while taking its cue from Irigaray's model of the two lips, concerns itself more with temporality in its focus on mobilisation and in reference to space, to perspectival apprehension. The vulva is made of the fold of two lips and with every move the relation and orientation alter. That is, where Irigaray critiques the compulsion to either-ing: either illuminated or invisible, he or she, you or me and one or two, it is the interstitial aspects of the neither and beyond one or two that becoming-vulva exploits on the way to pure immanent one-ness, and Deleuze's input comes from extensive relation. Deleuze's fold extends and proliferates the potential futures of the lips. In addition to the lips' structure as creating a morphological pleasure in and for the self, the fold 'is inseparable in itself from the power to affect other forces (spontaneity) and to be affected by others (receptivity)'.[2] It is compelling at this stage to refer the reader to Deleuze's pictorial sketch of Foucault's foldings and inside of thought (1999, p120). The similarity between this image and the undifferentiated vulva is astonishing. This diagram is made of four elements which could be oriented to feminist theory. Line of the outside refers to the vulva's affectuation of and by other elements. Citing Blanchot and resonant with Irigaray Deleuze states this zone has become 'intimacy and intrusion' (1999, p120). Strategic zone refers to the powers of

1. Luce Irigaray, *This Sex which is Not One*, Gillian Gill (trans), Ithaca, New York, Cornell UP, 1985, p24. Subsequent references cited in the text.

2. Gilles Deleuze, *Foucault*, Seàn Hand (trans), London, Athlone, 1999, p101. Subsequent references cited in the text.

thought as creation over knowledge as pre-formed constitution masquerading as reflection, (always by the structure that allows it to emerge). Deleuze states these are fictions but no less capable of affectuation shifts in the folds. More satisfying than exchanging the masculine for the feminine or aspiration to equality (which allows only sameness) strategy encourages specific and singular aims for feminine liberation without essentialising woman. Strata in the fold is fold structure without hierarchy or the geo-atrophy constituted by history. The fold is the zone of subjectivation, being as the experiment in thought. It is also the point in the diagram which most resembles the vaginal aperture, and, perhaps sympathetically, Deleuze's naming of the hole as voluminous manifold multiplicity shows that even the most traditional parts of female genitalia can - indeed must - be the very sites of reconfiguration. Beyond, (but not better than) Irigaray's two lips, this aperture attacks the very site of paradigmatic oppression. There is no preferred site of liberation, this diagram is the vulva as all at once and not limited by an enclosing line around it limiting it to one form. Of course Deleuze does not associate his diagram with female genitalia, but I find the incidental collision of the two structures enticing.

While many feminists working with Deleuze and French feminists point to the thousand tiny sexes of Deleuze's thought, becoming-vulva attempts to extend Deleuze's idea of 'invagination as a pleating',[3] verbing the vagina in an (admittedly vaguely phallic in the persistence of the 'vaginal' terminology) attempt toward female morphology as movement. Politically this would take becoming-woman as always and urgently political in relation to relevance and immediate social issues. For Grosz, where 'multiplicities of (more or less) temporary alignments of segments' form (and we might read segments in the becoming-vulva aspects of folds),[4] 'it is … no longer appropriate to ask what a text means, what it says, what is the structure of its interiority, how to interpret or decipher it. One must ask what it does'.[5] This perspective addresses issues of singularity, which we are all already complicit with and resistant to at once: our folds of negotiation and our position in relation to such issues. The 'woman' of becoming-woman is no longer an instrument because t(he)y who enter becoming is/are as lost on many fold-planes as t(he)y is/are volitional (without aim or destination) on others. Deleuze states 'the world was an infinity of converging series, capable of being extended into each other, around unique points…singularity is inflection and curve' (2001, pp60, 90). When Irigaray seeks to have 'another look' at psychoanalysis (pp34-67) she neither limits nor orients looking but invokes a look at a singularity from other points, points of others, which will be perspectival points and where the concept of the unique point is a matter of relevance of a particular singular structure apprehended from multiple others. The gaze converges and negotiations form folds within gazes as with the unique singularity they contemplate. Olkowski states 'each perception is a complex multiplicity that includes not only the object perceived but the expanded circuits , the deeper and more distant regions of memory'.[6] Perhaps put very simply becoming-

3. Gilles Deleuze, *The Fold: Leibniz and the Baroque*, Tom Conley (trans), London, Athlone, 2001, p6. Subsequent references cited in the text.

4. Elizabeth Grosz, 'A Thousand Tiny Sexes', in Constantin Boundas and Dorothea Olkowski (eds), *Gilles Deleuze and the Theatre of Philosophy*, London, Routledge,1994, p198.

5. Ibid., p199.

6. Dorothea Olkowski, *Gilles Deleuze and the Ruin of Representation*, Berkeley, University of California Press, 1999, p114.

vulva is the convergence-action-potential aspect which navigates movement and demand from the two-lips. An issue, for example, which concerns 'real life' women, could be a unique singularity and each subject inflects with that singularity along divergent planes, not visible to each other, nor to themselves as a unified subject. Women, after Deleuze, are not 'things' but continuity. Planes affect and synthesise with each other based on inflective folding and refolding.

Becoming-vulva interrogates phallologocentrism as a structure beyond identity with which all subjects participate. This has a twofold effect - it recognises that participation rather than position in the structure is where reification and revolution is enacted and it shows the imperative availability of feminist structures for male subjects, thus revolt comes from all directions, not simply from those which are directly served by shifts in the structure. Unlike becoming-woman, a vulva is a series of connexions between the various elements of female genitalia. Massumi[7] emphasises the risk Deleuze and Guattari take as disregarding real lived conditions. Braidotti,[8] and Goulimari[9] urge a shift from becoming any 'thing', because of the problems in Deleuze and Guattari's use of 'woman' to becoming-minoritarian which would catalyse all subjects based on context-historical and specific powers and risks of each unique project of becoming. Jardine[10] isolates the focus on women as a result of their being in 'limbo', neither recognised as subjects nor allowed ownership of the fluidity and other transgressive elements inherent within their minoritarianism. The place of woman is in-between, the state is void. The unfolding of this void is from atrophied fetish - even if it is a post-structural fetish - to mobilised unfurling into infinity (creating the possibility of infinity by its movement within a space and through time). Inherent within all these (generally sympathetic) criticisms is the difficult disjuncture where structure and subject collide. Materiality emerges through signifying systems and these systems are themselves material, thus the collision is never between two but creates an involuted encounter that dissipates molecules of each as more or less intensified in regard to moments of thought and actualisation. The tactical selection over the subject-thing 'woman' for the paradigmatic vulva makes a voluminous rather than absent or male-defined space, a feminist space that is imperative for all sexes to participate with and which can allow all subjects to have similar intensive aspects of political unity without themselves being the same. Deleuze and Guattari's reminder that women themselves must become-woman risks formulating a chronological evolution of becoming as a temporal project - which woman, what intensities make up woman? Is asking defeating the very purpose of the ambiguities of the noun, without asking what are we doing? Irigaray critiques the very asking of the question itself as making a woman-ing impossible (pp120-121). She says: 'I don't know whether the [male] person who asked the question wants to try again or not …' (p121).

The many folds of the vulva create connections, multiplying Irigaray's model of the more-than-and-less-than-one two lips. Like the penis and its relation to the phallus, the vulva is an organ that is known but not (in polite

7. Brian Massumi, *A User's Guide to Capitalism and Schizophrenia: Deviations from Deleuze and Guattari*, Cambridge Mass, MIT Press, 1992.

8. Rosi Braidotti, *Patterns of Dissonance*, Elizabeth Guild (trans), Cambridge, Polity, 1991.

9. Pelagia Goulimari, 'A Minoritarian Feminism? Things to Do with Deleuze and Guattari', *Hypatia*, 14: 2 (1999), 97-120.

10. Alice Jardine, 'Woman in Limbo: Deleuze and His Br(others)'. *SubStance*, 13:44-45 (1984), 46-60.

company) seen. It is the ultimate phantasy of nothing to see and the horror of seeing it is too much - unlike the penis the vulva is neither funny nor virile but confounding. This is true both metaphorically and in popular parlance actually. The vulva is not visible when the human body is erect. The concentric resonances of erect phallus-erect human-erected-speech erected-knowledge can be reconfigured through the vulva being there but not necessarily seen, thus the categories of human and knowledge also contort. Because the vulva is made up of folds, shared language is always expressed from one fold and is neither independent of the perspective of the speaker's position nor entirely apparent to that speaker - language, rather than seen as coming from outside as a transcendental structure, frees itself to inherent independent ambiguity at the crease where two folds are juxtaposed, fused only through inflection not assimilation or metonymic juxtaposition. Incommensurability is therefore always part of the vulvic structure, neither a failure nor celebrated rupture. The vulva is female but in aspects thus becoming-vulva allows one minoritarian subject woman to share one aspect or fold with another based on a common political or ideological activist-desire, Deleuze's continuity thus incorporates other elements, a continuity between what is traditionally discontinuous. Continuity is constituted by particle-intensity elements, not forms.

Becoming-vulva emphasises the movement of the two lips as our folding with them and our fold-planes forming connections which we cannot see but which affect the singularity nonetheless, as we perceive relations with elements of other planes that do not perceive themselves but affect, to infinity. In relation to the fold-unfold-foldings of becoming-vulva is the fold itself as a fluid inflection, what Irigaray has called blurring and mucosal. This resists the risk in creating yet another binary from the mechanics of fluids versus solids. Mucosal describes the fluids emergent of and from the vulva which connects the vulva's folds with itself and blurs demarcations of externality, while Irigaray claims sperm has been associated with a form of object, but because it is within spermal fluid threatens to 'crumble' the penis (p113). Crumbling creates a becoming-vulva of the penis because the penis does not disappear, only dissipates as a unity.

Braidotti points out that unique singularity is not universalism but what Deleuze would call singularity as *potential*, singularity as expression,[11] relating expression to Irigaray's concept of the unconscious which means singularity as political anchoring point that is, in becomings 'flows like symbolic glue between the social and the self ... it flows but it is sticky'.[12] Perhaps Irigaray expresses the stickiness of each fold, where we neither select nor apprehend the planes to which we stick, and where angles are sticky and infinitely fluid, so that fold is always folding, just as becoming-vulva is morphology-in-action. This all occurs in the space which is here and now, neither exchanged economy nor deliberate nomadic immigration or defection, but a process which celebrates rather than asks 'where does this element of the vulva begin and end?' just as one asks where as subject do I begin and end? Deleuze and Guattari's lauding of multiplicity in becoming-vulva is always and only the

11. Rosi Braidotti, *Metamorphoses*, Cambridge, Polity, 2002, p66.

12. Ibid., p143.

multiplicity of aspectival-folds and movements within the one. The point of convergence between the two-lips and becoming-woman resolves the phallocentric tendency to bring 'multiplicity back to the economy of sameness, oneness, to the same of the one' (p131). This point for Irigaray is the shift from solid to fluid, and the creation of a territory that is not 'woman' ripe for male colonisation. She uses the term pleasure to critique desiring machines. Becoming-vulva could be described as the ethico-political imperative within pleasure, that is, the desire for that which we cannot know but which needs mobilisation within a particular political territory in reference to particular real life issues - folds - that are aspects of the one which is neither unity nor multiplicity, and where becoming-woman is one trajectory that twists, involutes, emerges and explores the labyrinth of the fold. Some of these turns may be deeply unpleasurable for the majoritarian. Becoming-vulva creates all these turns as a structure, or what Irigaray sees as the urgently needed woman's *terrain* of becoming - the 'unterritorialized spaces where her desire might come into being' (p141) - rather than becoming which demands one term, such as 'woman'. 'The process of imitation may set up analogies between ourselves and what we imitate but cannot engage us in creative becomings. Irigaray says something similar when she insists that our encounters with others - in particular the feminine other to whom we would like to relate - must involve mutual becomings rather than specular identifications'.[13]

13. Tamsin Lorraine, *Irigaray and Deleuze: Experiments in Visceral Philosophy,* Ithaca, Cornell University Press, 1999, p182.

While Deleuze and Guattari are explicit that becoming is adamantly not imitation, Irigaray asks how man can become what woman never had, that is, her own pleasure (p141)? None of us are but we all occupy becoming-vulva. Vulva is a noun, yes, but a mucosal inapprehensible one, and indeed a word not frequently used in common parlance in the same way as woman. As a fold structure we also do not occupy one versus many spaces but one space which stretches, folds, inflects and thus multiples are aspects not sets of singulars which can co-opt other singulars. In this sense Deleuze would emphasise the fold as a consistency-relational space more than the hybrid form posited in *A Thousand Plateaus*. He calls this a dimension, not a physical environmen (1999, p109). The vulva thus could be a dimension-form, and Irigaray's terrain a material dimensional reality, in excess but not ignorant of 'real life' dimensions. Indeed as Deleuze offers the singularity of dimensions there can no longer be a doubling of real versus abstract places. They are always both, like the fleshy vulva configuration.

'Woman' cannot cause becomings, inflection with certain, specific, politico-historical planes invoke becomings, and the becoming-minoritarian of the majoritarian is a question of resistance to or desire for mucosal folding: not a question of terminology but becoming-vulva is the terrain rather than the term. All elements occupy the terrain and so becoming-vulva describes tensions, thresholds, activity-affect-passivity-syntheses, and action-potential, not a project involving a thing. The terrain of the vulva is always there and perhaps a more appropriate element would be to apply Deleuze and Guattari's becoming-imperceptible, as the vulva-terrain is discursively affective but not perceptible as noun, smooth singular space or uni-localised place for occupation, against the 'kingdom' of women (for becomings). However, as Deleuze and Guattari claim concepts come from problems, to remain in the field of politics as problems, I will return to the tactical use of the vulva as noun. How the vulva is desired towards becoming the vulva, momentarily, will 'be' a concept before describing a larger abstract territory.

These ideas are simply a series of sketches of issues. I neither wish to vindicate nor condemn Deleuze and Guattari, but many of the issues are ones which have also plagued feminism. When feminists ask 'what do we want', the 'we' is far more problematic than the want. This has been the nexus of innumerable and continued discussions. The problems within a male discursive navigation of women can itself offer a traversal line of flight where different perspectives of the same issue and different issues from a sympathetic perspective create assemblages rather than antagonisms - a vulvic fold, not one element's demand to penetrate and colonise the other with language, thought and flesh. Becomings are assemblages, and, like the horror of the vulva tamed as vagina/castration site, are always more than and less than one, infective, leaky, scary, literally round-ed up, to resemble inside-out penis apertures. Before they ever mention woman, in *A Thousand Plateaus* Deleuze and Guattari invoke female genitalia: 'Comparing a sock to a vagina is OK, it's done all the time, but you'd have to be insane to compare a pure aggregate of stitches to a field of vaginas'.[14] The connective aspect of the stitches, and their inside-outside folding-emerging is expressive of the vulva, and recalls Lyotard's möebian skin which: 'rather than being smooth, is on the contrary (is this topographically possible?) covered with roughness, corners, creases, cavities which when it passes on the first "turn" will be cavities, but on the "second" lumps' (pp2-3). It is indeed topographically possible - but as Deleuze and Guattari state you have to be insane - so the vulva-field is a schiz-territory. Does the mucosal unconscious require an insane-'man'? Deleuze and Guattari claim nouns domesticate multiplicities and jeopardise the assembling connections of their intensities, just as the vagina domesticates the vulva as its own multiplicity while smoothing it as aperture and ignoring all its other folds to prevent any intensive connections with the penis as phallus (because, most obviously and perhaps most imperatively needing to be challenged) the penis is domesticated by the phallus. The domestic chore ... the woman reduced to only mother or wife darning to repair the smoothness of the sock, utters 'darn this sock!'.

Irigaray demarcates particular qualities of the morphology of the phallus as preventing the opening of a space of difference. The prevalence of the visual, the solid, the demarcated, the relegated, the known, the phantasy of objectivity, even the question itself ablate and atrophy fluidity, connectivity, accountable subjectivity, thought, the multi-sensorial and speech which is not through the language of the same/one. The lips are always and already in a condition of pleasure and they need nothing other than themselves. Any additional connections create extensions and becomings as third, fourth, fifth

14. Gilles Deleuze and Félix Guattari, *A Thousand Plateaus*, Brian Massumi (trans), London, Athlone, 1987, p27. Subsequent references cited in the text.

elemental terms. Man's need for woman as a tool places onus on the tool as a signifier, not of something that is, but something that is to be *used*. Man cannot touch himself and thus his self is always object and objective. He is neither mani-fold nor in reflective relation to himself. Activity and passivity are forces which occur within the same space as resistance-expression. Most importantly woman touches herself as her condition of being, not as autonomous choice. The phallus rents the two vulva lips apart and penetrates the vagina, shifting woman's relation to herself to one as object for male sexuality and her many folds as quickened into a mournfully empty aperture. Male language forces itself between the mouth lips of women, compelling her to listen and speak only in the language and always flawed. The use of a tool performs two functions. The first is to nomenclature the expressive aspect of content within a phallic discourse, the second to prevent it acting beyond or without that discourse and especially, acting for itself (which is the self it does not and cares not to 'know', but to think or touch).

The crux of the difficulty with these many issues can be summed up by Deleuze and Guattari's navigation of content and expression. Content is pragmatic, action and passion, while expression is semiotic - the regime within which content operates and through which action-passion is potentialised. 'Incorporeal transformations' (1987, p504) attribute certain qualities to content-forms. Content and expression form a strata which is cut through by a line of flight which deterritorialises expression and thus materially transforms content by connecting it to another assemblage - a different refrain - or operating within its own territory to reconfigure it. This second deterritorialisation is most pertinent to becoming vulva in that it is the reciprocal territory of expression-content within singular concepts that can orient the accountability of a majoritarian in becoming-woman without leaping straight onto and hijacking the woman's own becoming-refrain or, worse still, teaching her the refrain she has been extricated from in phallologocentric culture. But neither deterritorialisations are entirely extricated. It is thinking Irigaray's two lips as two-two lips, folded into infinity - the genital to mouth lips where semiotic female speech and pleasure are one fold configuration; the mouth to another mouth connection where my top lip is the others other lip and speech cannot be spoken with one mouth but two mouths creating one expression; the vulva to vulva connection where women speak together their own pleasure independent of men and thus within a different system of language, this language being explicitly corporeal, 'she has two mouths and two pairs of lips'.[15] This resonates with Wittig's claim that without alterity there can be no definition, and, while Irigaray sees difference as imperative in feminism (which is why she has been maligned as advocating compulsory heterosexuality) Wittig's nomenclaturing of lesbians as not women fares little better than Deleuze and Guattari's claim that all men should be minoritarian-women. For Irigaray it is alterity in itself, not between two defined entities, that is key. The sharing between the unlike evinces the alterity rather than ablating it. The genital lips speak as the mouth lips, a language which is silent to phallologic audibility. She speaks of breathing

15. Luce Irigaray, *The Irigaray Reader*, David Macey (trans), Oxford, Blackwell, 1992, p170. Subsequent references cited in the text.

together, the sexual pant but also the trembling breath that awaits but does not need to know what it awaits, speaks as imagination, creation.

> The only guide there being the call to the other. Whose breath subtly impregnates the air, like a vibration perceived by those lost in love. Their senses awake, they boldly go forward by ways where others see only shadows and hell. They go forward and sometimes a song comes to their lips. From their mouths come sounds which mean nothing.[16]

16. Ibid., p217.

The vulva breathes beyond speech or silence. The vulva is the wound, too much, not enough, too visceral, not present. Freud's dark continent, castration, Lacan's specular lack and Irigaray's elucidation of the larger philosophical trajectories in dominant culture that make the way we understand genitalia a symptom rather than the cause of the blind spot. Deleuze sees folds as crucially 'free of any intentional gaze' and the phallic compulsion to look and thus know is thus antagonistic to the fold.[17]

17. Deleuze, *Foucault*, op. cit, p109.

Repudiation of inappropriate objects - for Deleuze and Guattari anything that is irredeemably other, woman, girl, animal, and asemiotic elements without signification such as colour, harmonious music without melody - prevents unfolding-refolding from producing a hybrid third term or self as part of a greater in-between and less than its own ideational subjectivity. Folding with another incommensurable element - what Deleuze and Guattari call an inter-kingdom or unnatural participation - makes the subject more than and less than one dividuated, apprehensible and knowable, therefore phallic, self. Deleuze, after Spinoza, claims ethics comes from what is produced between the encounter of two entities, not from two entities addressing each other according to a larger, established and prescriptive structure. The fold relation cannot help but produce because traditional structures do not allow for these unnatural inter-kingdom relations. They are prohibited or named perverse. According to Irigaray women are oppressed because they must accede to larger structures - as wife, as mother but never as for-herself. Only when women can be a for-herself can she enter into productive relations. Parts of women's former folds have been constituted by phallologocentrism so while the past does not guarantee the future it also doesn't forget it. The for-herself as mani-fold allows feminism to avoid the trap of essentialising what woman 'is'. All that woman is a condition independent of phallologocentric structure because within that structure 'woman' is relegated to wife, mother and so forth. Irigaray is adamant: 'woman would be wife and mother without desire' (1992, p117). Thus becoming-vulvic is a shift in patterns of desire.

FORM AND FORCE-FOLD

Form
Forms are shadows only when seeking to apprehend the solid is impossible, knowledge prevented and the self relegated to hell - perhaps a feminine realm,

where Deleuze and Guattari's demons reside. Meaningless sounds are words without syntax, devoid of the nouns that are the little phalluses of speech. Deleuze, after Spinoza, sees belief in the possibility of seeing, knowing and controlling and the ethical difference between love - which is imagination and creation - and hope, which is always for the pre-formed, always simultaneously hope for and through slavery, causality and the elusive.[18] A vulva is already a pack animal, a demonic schema between various connected elements. We may know what to do with a vagina, but what do we do, what can we do (what can't we do) with a vulva? - 'the demon functions as a borderline of an animal pack, into which the human being passes or in which his or her becoming takes place by contagion' (1987, p247). The vulva's borderline sexual organ undifferentiated pleasure fold requires the affected connected to enter into alliance, to be infected by the vulva's molecular possibilities of sexual acts and pleasures and signification and semiosis as acts of pleasure in power. The whole desiring body must be more than one and folded to enter into alliance with the vulva - a sorcerer body. Otherwise the vulva is reduced to the little penis clitoris and the absent-penis sheath.

Becoming implies:

> An initial relation of alliance with a demon ...There is an entire politics of becomings-animal, as well as a politics of sorcery, which is elaborated in assemblages that are neither those of the family nor of religion nor of the State. Instead they express minoritarian groups, or groups that are oppressed, prohibited, in revolt or always on the fringe of recognised institutions, groups all the more secret for being extrinsic, in other words, anomic ... becoming-animal takes the form of a Temptation, and of monsters aroused in the imagination by the demon (Deleuze and Guattari, 1987, p247).

The vulva is a tempting form. Its tempting aspect is traditionally one of the reasons for its danger and the imminent downfall of the (usually majoritarian) tempted. The vulva is also a monster, all the more monstrous for simultaneously being so tempting, evoking the fascination of ambivalence - elaborated in feminist teratology, particularly Braidotti's work. Without using the term however, and beyond the everyday monstrosity of traditionally oppressed subjects, Deleuze and Guattari invoke monster structures - hybrids, demons, abstract entities.

For all the ways the vulva transgresses and traverses dominant phallic paradigms it is both prohibited and perceived as revolt-ing (in both senses of the word). The vulva, as opposed to the obedient vagina, will not be defined by production (family), chastity (Church) or an acceptance of subjugation (state). It cannot be seen with a speculum. It is, nothing more than the everything which is an assemblage of folds, organs, elements, textures, tastes and involutions with its disciples. It is, materially and conceptually, a rupture and rupturing. The vulva is a demon - convoked by the sorcerer fascinated

18. Gilles Deleuze, *Spinoza: Practical Philosophy*, Robert Hurley (trans), San Francisco, City Lights Books, 1988, p26.

with the possible but unknowable futures the vulva offers, tempted by the vulva's seduction against the warnings of family, church, state. But like a demon the vulva must also be evoked. It will not come unless it is desired and it cannot materialise unless through the desires of the sorcerer. The idea of the vulva is the temptation, but its evocation is the demon with which the unholy alliance is formed and the becoming-vulva facilitated. Many demons in a variety of literature and lore are vulva-like. Many demonic forms follow the basic tenets of the vulva as somehow gender ambiguous, as assemblage or fold, as both tempting and dangerous. Against the singularity of the phallus and the majoritarian subject, 'My name is Legion: for we are many' said Satan (Mark 5:9, also referenced in Deleuze and Guattari, 1987, p239); and so is the vulva and the affinities we form with it. Leviathan is one example of a demonic form becoming-vulva. Leviathan, like vulva, translates from Hebrew as 'that which gathers itself together in folds'.[19]

If vulva is infinite and indefinite, how can we refer to it as being of a form? Deleuze and Guattari state of form as a turning point in thought:

> a *form in itself* that does not refer to any external point of view ... so many *inseparable variations* on which it confers an equipotentiality without confusion ... under its first aspect of absolute form, appears as the faculty of concepts, that is to say, as the faculty of their creation.[20]

The vulva here does not appear prior to the act of thinking and its appearance is concept-aspect, which is also the act of creating it as a perception-thought-force. The vulva is infinite determinates and its dimensions become the reformation of the single plane through perception *as* creation. Unlike the phallus, which has already been folded into a particular configuration to the extent that to create it as a concept is subsumed by its immediate presence to its own transcendent form. Shifting from knowing to thinking female form as aspectual foldings necessitates the death of majoritarian subjectivity, which is why theorists refer to the fatal results of the ancients' attempt to locate female pleasure in demonic women; Medusa's gaze,[21] the Sirens' call[22] and the gaze of Orpheus demanding Eurydice come into the world of the male gaze.[23] Because the vulva is internal, external, relatively smooth mons verenis full frontal, occluded and splayed labia, and various other possible configurations depending on positioning, to see it through one perception or orientation is impossible. The body must actually be reformed or refolded to catch a glimpse of all the vulva's various aspects.

Force

Can we say we have a memory of vulva in the same way as we refer to the meaning of the phallus as a historical artefact? 'Man constitutes himself as a gigantic memory, through the position of the central point, its frequency (insofar as it is necessarily reproduced by each dominant point) and resonance (insofar as all of the points tie in with it' (Deleuze and Guattari,

19. Gustav Davidson, *A Dictionary of Angels*, New York, Simon & Schuster, 1967, p173.

20. Gilles Deleuze and Félix Guattari, *What is Philosophy?*, Hugh Tomlinson and Graham Burchell (trans), New York, Columbia UP, 1994, pp210-211.

21. Hélène Cixous, 'The Laugh of the Medusa', in E. Marks and I. DeCourtivron (eds), *New French Feminisms: An Anthology*, New York, Schocken, 1981.

22. Michel Foucault, 'Thought from the Outside', Brian Massumi (trans) in M. Foucault and M. Blanchot, *Foucault/Blanchot*, New York, Zone Books, 1997.

23. Maurice Blanchot, *The Gaze of Orpheus and Other Literary Essays*, Lydia Davis (trans.), Barrytown, NY, Station Hill Press, 1981.

1987, p293). The phallus is a memory which paradigmatically resonates with systems. Memories of a sorcerer are invocations, memories of a phallus are recognitions.

Forms fold and refold, recreating their own forms by their capacity to influence themselves. At the same time they influence external elements and external elements influence them. In the act of creating the vulva toward its various becoming potentials, the vulva's dimensions fold and refold. 'A fold is always folded within a fold, like a cavern in a cavern [but not fractal of same, rather what Lyotard would call a labyrinth] ... correlative to elastic compressive force. Unfolding is thus not the contrary of folding but follows the fold up to the following fold' (Deleuze, 2001, p6). For each form there are those forms which impress upon it to offer its form as the act of creation and reaction through those forms which buttress it; mouth, genital, skin, object, breath, heat, vibration, cold, absence, pressure, vacuum. Lyotard's möebian bands: 'open up the so-called body and spread out all its surfaces ... the labia majora, so also the labia minora ... and this is not all, far from it, connected onto these lips a second mouth is necessary, a third mouth, a great number of other mouths, vulvas'.[24] As with becomings, Lyotard includes the organic, inorganic, the sonorous and the coloured, adjectives disanchored from nouns, inflections and always there are concealed planes and elements, connections which are not apparent. Through becoming-vulva the act of conceptualising a vulva, which has no transcendent form, creates another dimension to the act of becoming; a constellation of conceiving as creating, while becoming. In order to become, form must be reoriented from analogy to transformation through contagion. However because the vulva form is itself unstable, demonic becoming is launched.

Fold

The folding of two matters refers to the involution of two forms and their impact within and upon each others' memory, future and present form and force. The fold is not the result but the act of force of forms. Becoming-vulva is how we are vulva and vulva is us, how we reform vulva and as vulva, and how vulva reforms us and as us. While each form becomes the other, their specificity and for feminism their memory is essential to their becoming. The forms do not homogenise or forget but retain specificity and yet assemble. 'If two distinct things can be really inseparable, two inseparable things can be really distinct' (Deleuze, 2001, p12). Woman already has a vulva (rather than being had by the phallus, both duped and biblically) distinct and indistinct from her form. The fold of vulva, thought and self creates a simultaneity of differential elements and integration. According to Leibniz, unlike inanimate forms which are components of assembled parts, organic elements cannot have their choices inferred in advance, thus an organic element is required in becoming, through relations with organic or inorganic elements, as yet undeveloped, larval. '[There is] no universal reason or law of nature...from which any creature, no matter how perfect and well informed about this mind,

24. Jean Francoise Lyotard, *Libidinal Economy*, Iain Hamilton Grant (trans.), Bloomington, Indiana University Press, 1993, p1.

25. Gottfried
Wilhelm Leibniz,
Philosophical Writings,
Mary Morris and
G.H.R. Parkinson
(trans), Vermont,
Everyman, 1995,
p102.

can infer with certainty what the mind will choose'.[25] One's own incapacity for inference is included. And the vulva neither follows a predictable narrative of temporal 'choice' (what it will do) nor spatial 'choice' (what it will be).

Irigaray's model of the two lips shares much in common with Deleuze's work on Leibniz and Foucault. Through Leibniz, Deleuze elaborates the baroque as a physics of process over content, where any concept can only be apprehended from perspective, that is sensed, and that perspective offers folds which are believed to be present but are not 'visible' (knowable and so forth), which are visible but not able to be known - seeing in the dark - and the larger structure of which folds with the observer. The fold is a homogeneity made of heterogeneous expression which, at each reconfiguration unfolds and refolds (however not 'back' into an original plane). The unfold is a future and creates the conditions of possibility of the refold without knowing what the refolded concept will produce. If expression actualises content, then the fold is what actualises a thing, rather than a thing autonomously folding. The fold, like the möebian band, is made up of the sides of planes which, depending on the folded configuration, encounter each other in a particular expressive structure; thus elements which are not known to be commensurable are nonetheless possible and condition the possibilities of the next fold. The point of encounter also cuts across and between elements, traversing fold configurations and creating new trajectories between fold homogeneities. The organic and inorganic are not of the same matter yet activate folds with each other, emphasising the materiality of word and flesh as a sensuous continuum.

Deleuze lists six elements inherent in the baroque fold. Put very simply these are: 1. Fold as a problem not of completion but continuation. The vulva depends on the movement of the body to create new configurations, while only the still erect body can express the phallus. The phallus, truth and male sexuality seek completion. The feminine neither starts nor ends in space and time, and as a problem itself can neither be posited nor solved. 2. The line of inflection which does not reconcile or homogenise elements but harmonises them through their mobile relation. Women, lips, desires, speech are not the same between those of others or between themselves. Harmony is a question of relation without conversion to sameness. Harmony seeks not equilibrium but a connection which necessarily alters the nature of each element while maintaining its specificity - the hybrid moment of becoming. 3. Two elements: of and expressing the same world, but not in the same way. The problem which plagues phallologic is that things perceived as impossible or incommensurable are nonetheless present and express a world which does not agree with the phallic. The vulva is a schema of expression possible but not unifying. 4. The unfold as continuation, the temporality of the spatial event. The issue with any invocation of a schema, including becoming-vulva, is that it can be understood as a model into which one fits. Rather, in becoming-vulva, new positions open new ideas which could not have existed before - the elements are the model. There is no going back, so continuation is inevitable and, indeed, frightening, 'what opens up does not stop in any direction. No waymarkers in this total risk' (1992, p215). Irigaray sees risk as risk of life. Phallic life is equilibrium, stasis, atrophy, already dead. 5. The action-passion tension between elements - too taut and it breaks, not taut enough and it cannot attain harmony. Texture is dependent 'not on the parts themselves, but on the strata that determine its cohesion'.[26] The vulva is multiple strata, situating parts at places always crosses other places and creates particular conditions. Certain conditions will destroy the elements - Deleuze and Guattari's junkie and masochist risk death. Covertly when the subject becomes-woman understood as fetish the strata cannot continue until it leaves behind the masculine-active tautness. 6. The fold as inherently material, beyond an ideational-model. This is the most salient encounter with Irigaray and corporeal feminism in general, and why Lorraine claims Deleuze and Irigaray constitute a visceral philosophy. 'Unless it becomes the speech of the flesh, a gift and a message of the flesh, speech remains an outer skin that again and again exhausts, flays, that falls and covers without giving up its secret' (p111).

26. Deleuze, *The Fold: Leibniz and the Baroque*, op. cit, p37

In the fold, alterity is encountered within the self, through the other, and the other encounters the self in ways the self cannot autonomously express. Each element has aspects which are present to self and not present to self but to the other, and, simultaneously apprehends aspects of the other not present to themselves, all the while folds of shared indivisible presence are present to both. Deleuze and Irigaray both use a fold structure where the subject exists as folds and folds with the world to express a version of that world, necessarily therefore folding with other subjects. Both see desire as the driving force of the ways in which subjectivity unfolds and refolds, shifting paradigms and self as metamorphic, always and in spite of itself launching upon new becomings. The politico-ethical moment comes when the self seeks to fold with the unlike or inappropriate. Dialectic desire maintains distance and therefore subject and object do not involute, reducing the unfold-refold potential of the subject.

Becoming-vulva is splaying of self, becoming-indeterminate, palimpsest, the open and pure intensity of being a visceral, viscous and shuddering signification - stuttering, silence, folded, present but invisible, visible but not knowable, catalysing a structure and series of pleasure planes beyond and in excess of the phallus. It may include aspects of becoming-clitorised, variously penetrated and penetrating, onanistic and orgiastic, confusing dominance and submission and most importantly, becoming-manifold. Not knowing what will be-come of oneself as thought-materiality. Becoming-vulva is receptive and ravenous, desire as infinite and inevitable. 'It is defined by the number of dimensions it has; it is not divisible, it cannot lose or gain a dimension without changing its nature ... continually transforming itself ... according to its thresholds and doors' (Deleuze and Guattari, 1987, p249). The territory becoming-vulva reassembles the tensors and thresholds upon which it expresses (us as) force and by which force is expressed upon its various planes and dimensions. The self, the vulva and the world are labyrinthine threshold and their infinity relies only on our exploration.

Edinburgh
University Press

Deleuze Studies
Special Issue
Deleuze And Marx

Edited by Dhruv Jain

January 2010 • 96 pp Pb
978 0 7486 3893 2 • £16.99

▸ Offers new perspectives on Deleuze's early work

▸ Illuminates new connections between Deleuze's and
Marx's work

▸ Includes a critical re-reading of Deleuze's work

▸ Foregrounds a critique of Capitalism in
Deleuze's work

▸ Contributors include: Bruno Bosteels, Alberto
Toscano, Jason Read, Jeremy Gilbert, Simon Choat
and Aidan Tynan

www.euppublishing.com/book/978-0-7486-3893-2

Becoming-woman by *Breaking the Waves*

Chrysanthi Nigianni

To believe in realities, distinct from that which is perceived,
is above all to recognize that
the order of our perceptions depends on them,
and not on us.

H. Bergson

How is an essay on the Lars Von Trier's film *Breaking the Waves* (1996) related to an Issue on Deleuzean politics? If the phrase 'Deleuzean politics' sounds for many like an oxymoron, then the political character of a film like *Breaking the Waves* sounds even more problematic, and the whole story becomes even worse (or absurd?) with the claim that the film has indeed a political significance for feminist thinking and feminist politics. How can a film depicting woman as a victim, an object to be sacrificed, as the absolute idiot being stripped of any capacity for rationality, free determination and free will be a 'feminist' film, a film enhancing feminist politics? And how is it linked to Deleuzean politics?

Rather than starting by attempting a general evaluation of the political significance of Deleuze's work, as well as an overview of what constitutes a Deleuzean feminist politics (this is what this issue of *new formations* on the whole aims at demonstrating anyway), I will rather start by focusing on some specific links as they emerge from the cinematic event of *Breaking the Waves* - links which, as it will be argued later, challenge feminist thinking and bring into the fore some (often neglected) aspects of Deleuze's philosophy and thinking (a more 'mystical' Deleuze).

What are these links then? *Breaking the Waves* tells the story of Bess McNeill, who marries an outsider, a foreigner, who does not belong to the closed community of the small village Bess lives in; a community with deeply rooted fundamentalist Christian beliefs ruled by the elder men of the village, who determine the values of the social and personal lives of its members: according to these rules, life isn't for enjoyment; it is for serving God. Sex isn't for pleasure; it is for procreation. Outsiders aren't welcome. So Bess's decision to marry an outsider causes irritation to the community. But Bess is determined to marry Jan (an oil-rig worker), and the post-wedding scenes express the sexual awakening that signals also her happiness (personal sexual liberation is depicted as being positive for the subject's development). Nevertheless, Bess is somewhat simple and childlike, and has difficulty living without Jan when he is away on the oil platform. She prays for his return, and when he returns paralysed from the neck down after an accident in his workplace, she believes it is her fault. Being no longer able to make love,

DOI:10.3898/NEWF.68.07.2009

and mentally affected by the accident, Jan urges her to find and have sex with other men, and then tell him the details; a demand that becomes slowly in Bess's mind God's wish, and which leads her finally to her own death (a sacrificial death).

The theme of love is at the core of the film *Breaking the Waves;* however, love in Lars Von Trier's film escapes the clichés of an emotionality within a couple, and becomes instead a multifaceted event, a metamorphosising force that gives the film's narrative a multilayered, deep and complex character. *Breaking the Waves* is a film that brings together themes of love, religion (or better belief), spirituality, and difference, in a unique way that makes an urgent demand on us to rethink ethics outside the secularism-religion divide:

> It is highly spiritual yet anti-religious, triumphant yet tragic, and personal yet universal. Love forms the film's core, but rather than approaching the subject from a clichéd perspective, *Breaking the Waves* examines no less than six facets of the emotion: transformative love, sacrificial love, redemptive love, destructive love, romantic love, and sexual love.[1]

1. James Berdinalli, A Review of Breaking the Waves, 1996, found in http://www.reelviews. net/movies/b/ breaking.html

The film's plot is enacted by two main conceptual figures: that of the idiot (identified with a naïve believer, a faithful subject, the *ignoratnia amans*) and the sacrificial subject/object. Since the leading role is given to these two figures (incarnated both by the protagonist called Bess), we are given two options regarding a feminist reading of this film: either that we are presented with an(other) narrative, whose political force resides on speaking out, revealing, representing woman's social situation as victim within patriarchal society; or with a narrative that rules out our conventional definition of freedom as primarily being about self-determination and free will. In this case, we are either dealing with a deeply and perversely a-political and (un)consciously misogynistic film that simply perpetuates patriarchy's views on femininity; or we encounter a subversively political film that challenges received notions of freedom, and a whole complex of associated values (values which have always been tied into a monologic and monosexual culture, as commentators such as Luce Irigaray have argued). It is on the latter 'reading' that my argument of a new notion of agency, of an*other* feminist subjectivity as radically disrupting phallologocentric culture will develop. This agency is no longer an action but a passion, since it initiates other political forces like that of imagination, belief and affectivity. An active passivity then, which is no longer the activism of knowing and securing the known, but an act of problematising, raising questions (rather than giving answers); as well as the act of dreaming, hoping and praying over an 'absolute' future, opening up for the other to-come. This new conception of agency as it emerges from the film then is not a cogito but *an ignoratnia amans*, a lover's unknowing as a political position and an ethical attitude towards the other.

But what is the link between a Deleuzean politics and this new agency as suggested by the film? How does a theory of 'war machines', deterritorialisations, positive desire, nomadic movements, affirmative becomings(-minoritarian) and experimentation fit into the above image? In other words, how does Deleuze's theory come to read differently this new feminist agency? And reversely, how does this new feminist figuration come to 'write' the DeleuzoGuattarian concept of becoming-woman differently?

DELEUZE'S POLITICAL AGENCY

Deleuze's and Guattari's work provides us with several new images and figurations of new kinds of political agency that clearly break away from traditional notions of freedom (of the human subject) conceived of as self-determination and free will. These images range from machine metaphors that break away from anthropocentrism, like 'war machines', 'desiring machines', and 'sex machines', to animalistic figures like the pack animal, the werewolf, to finally, minoritarian, incomplete subjects like women, schizophrenics, children. All these figures come to undo the cornerstone of Western notions of politics and political agency: freedom and its related values. In the long history of political theory, freedom has been primarily conceived of as an attribute of the human: the human is defined by Aristotle as a 'political animal' and is thus differentiated from other species. Animals cannot be free in any political sense since they lack consciousness and rationality; hence, they are enslaved by their instincts and the laws of nature. Thus freedom is strongly linked to the notion of free will and the capacity for self-determination: a free subject is the subject who is capable of determining his/her own actions by making choices. Against this notion of freedom, indissociable from the idea of determination, Deleuze posits an ontological freedom as indeterminacy. Whereas determination is an act of negation - the Hegelian move of defining the self by what it is *not*, hence Being as the negation of nothingness - indeterminacy brings into the fore the positive and affirmative force of connectivity, so that the being is primarily a relational/interconnected being.

Following Spinoza and Nietzsche, Deleuze attempts to make freedom a purely positive force. Contrary to a 'free will' that presupposes an agent who can determine itself by separating himself from others (an ability that you acquire only if you have been fully determined in the first place and thus endowed with full subjectivity), Deleuze posits freedom as the undoing of such determination and the affirmation of the essential indeterminacy of all becomings. Hence, his notion of freedom no longer refers to a subjective, individualistic freedom that negates indeterminacy in order to affirm its being-free, but to the power of the a-subjective conceived of as ontological interconnection.

Deleuze thus writes:

We create grotesque representations of force and will, we separate force from what it can do, setting it up in ourselves as 'worthy' because it holds back what it cannot do, but as 'blameworthy' in the thing where it manifests precisely the force that it has. We split the will in two, inventing a neutral subject endowed with free will to which we give the capacity to act and refrain from action.[2]

2. Gilles Deleuze, *Nietzsche and Philosophy*, London, New York, Continuum, 2006, p21.

3. An interesting discussion of this point can be found in the essay 'Another always Thinks in Me' by Aden Evens, Mani Haghihi, Stacey Johnsosn, Karen Ocana, and Gordon Thompson, found in the collection *Deleuze and Guattari - New mappings in Politics, Philosophy, and Culture,* Eleanor Kaufman and Kevin John Heller (eds) University of Minnesota Press, 1998.

4. Gilles Deleuze, *Difference and Repetition*, London, New York, Continuum, 2006, p.199.

5. A. Evens, M. Haghihi, S. Johnsosn, K. Ocana, and G. Thompson, 'Another always Thinks in Me', op. cit., p277.

6. Gilles Deleuze, *Foucault,* New York and London, Continuum, 2006, p98.

Capturing freedom into notions of consciousness and 'free will' means inventing freedom on the level of representation,[3] separating it thus from the level of forces, energies and movement. For Deleuze, the elimination of the subject does not mean the elimination of agency, quite the opposite: he deconstructs freedom on the level of representation so as to restore it on the level of the force: a force which rather than fulfilling subjective goals and producing a self-determined 'I', affirms our singularity as the product of a 'fatal' connection/combination.

That we are infused with a power of decision does not mean that we select our imperatives or that our questions emanate from the I. We are not authors of our destiny. Even 'the gods themselves are subject to the … sky-chance'.[4]

Accordingly, the power of decision, the problems we pose, are not merely ours, there is an-other who 'writes' our destiny: not God, or any transcendent, vertical Being (any vertical transcendence is abruptly rejected by both Deleuze and Guattari as non-philosophy), but the other as potentiality and virtuality played out by chance, incarnated by the very possibility of having the dice thrown once more, thus affirming once again freedom as indeterminacy (any combination is possible), which precedes the social and subjective (hierarchical) determination of the self. Restricting the idea of freedom to the capacity for determination limits it to a subjective condition which ultimately impoverishes it rather than affirming and enhancing it. Freedom like thought is not ours; it is beyond and before us and we are constituted within it. Thus 'we must steal our freedom'.[5]

De-emphasising the image of the free subject means empowering another agency that breaks away from the illusions and traps of subjectivity. The Deleuzean other that comes to challenge and question the subject, the white Man Face, as the model of the only true and politically significant agent, is no longer a transcendent other, a divine extra-being. The other is always in the subject, precedes it and goes beyond it, a semi-divine being fully immanent to this world and this life.

> … it is a self that lives in me as the double of the other: I do not encounter myself on the outside, I find the other in me.[6]

'The Other *in* me' has nothing to do with views of subjectivity as interiority, or as a split subject, nor with psychoanalytic doubles. Deleuze's subjectivity is a pure and intensive surface, a folding and unfolding and there are many different ways in which bodies fold up to subjects. The other *inside* implies here the immanentist, anti-transcendent logic that traverses Deleuzean work: the other is not a structural impossibility, an outsider that haunts the structure and demonstrates its limits (as in Derrida's case), neither simply another structural possibility, but a virtuality that exists only as expression, and persists, informs and transforms the real:

> There is at some moment a calm and restful world. Suddenly a frightened face looms up that looks at something out of the field. The other person appears here as neither subject nor object but as something that is very different: a possible world. This possible world is not real, or not yet but it exists nonetheless: it is an expressed that exists only in its expression - the face or the equivalent of the face. To begin with the other person is this existence of the possible world.[7]

7. Gilles Deleuze and Félix Guattari, *What is Philosophy?*, London, New York, Verso, 1994, p17.

Consequently, Deleuze's political agency in all its forms and expressions is primarily related to this *other* vision and perception, the act of perceiving the other, the actualisation of the virtual other. It is thus related to a sense of possibility which is never purely ours, an ability to act which we can never fully own, an activity which requires a pause for the other-to-come, for the dice to be thrown once again and affirm another fatal combination/connection beyond our will or powers. The primary agency for Deleuze then is passion and not action: the passion of being affected by the other, being effectuated by it. Thus, the DeleuzoGuattarian work of reversing the hierarchy between activity-passivity, action-passion, vision-affection, clearly prioritises and emphasises characteristics that have been historically attributed to woman (as an incomplete and less human subject); hence, their privileging of the becoming-woman as the foundation of any conceivable political agency, able to initiate real change and transformation.

Nevertheless, far from constituting a mere reversal of the hierarchical dualism (an easy shift from knowledge to faith, from rationality to irrationality, from the self to the other, from man to woman, etc), Deleuze & Guattari's conception of 'becoming' posits political agency as an in-between movement, an intermezzo that brings together the majoritarian with the minoritarian, requiring from both however that they leave their position; becomings 'therefore imply two simultaneous movements, one by which a term (the subject) is withdrawn from the majority, and another by which a term (the medium or agent) rises up from minority,'[8] so that the dualistic structure as such (as the only possible way to connect) is challenged. Becoming then is not about separation or opposition but about proximities that effectuate changes in the way we think of binary terms and enact subjectivities accordingly.

8. Gilles Deleuze and Félix Guattari, *A Thousand Plateaus - Capitalism and Schizophrenia*, Continuum, London, New York, 2003, p291.

BECOMING-WOMAN DIFFERENTLY IN THE EVENT OF *BREAKING THE WAVES*

However, against an immanentist logic, which would define itself through a sterile opposition to transcendence, favouring matter at the expense of spirit, I would argue that Deleuze's transcendental empiricism risks becoming a closed system if we rush to cleanse the Deleuzean landscape of any trace of

9. 'Nomadic subjectivity as radical immanence implies a practice of spirituality of the non-theistic, post-humanist, non-Christian kind. This practice has to do with the ultimate phase of the process of becoming, namely the becoming-imperceptible'. R. Braidotti, *Transpositions*, Politiy Press, 2006, p258.

10. Deleuze, *Difference and Repetition*, op. cit., p2.

11. George Bataille, *Visions of Excess*, University Minnesota Press, 1985, p172.

12. Deleuze and Guattari, *A Thousand Plateaus*, op. cit., p213.

spirituality. Following Braidotti's argument[9] for a necessary spirituality that characterises Deleuzean radical immanence, this paper will move a step further by suggesting that such a spirituality can best be realised within a post-theistic framework (an atheistic religiosity as it emerges from the film) rather than according to the terms of a simple secularism. I would argue that in order to conceive of the Deleuzean sense of infinity - expressed in concepts like 'the plane of immanence' - and in order to understand the concept of 'becoming' as something which goes beyond any mere re-enactment of subjective identity - the movement of a horizontal and not vertical transcendence - we need to include the force of spirit in our materialist thinking.

It is in the cinematic event of the film *Breaking the Waves* directed by Lars Von Trier that this horizon of active passivity as the new form of horizontal transcendence will be traced and sketched out; a horizon inhabited and traversed by the figural becoming-woman-divine that embodies this spiritual vision, anOther perception that allows entry to this other, parallel and co-existing world. I argue that the cinematic persona of Bess incarnates successfully such a becoming as an agent of passive activity - the ignoratnia amans - who transforms action into passion by activating new political forces such as imagination, affectivity and belief.

Far from constituting a mere representation of the feminine - a proposition - the cinematic persona (of Bess) works as an expressive machine, a thought-event produced by a figure-image: an 'operative field'[10] of eventful connections between the virtual and the actual, the visible and the invisible, the real and the imaginary, passivity and activity, spirit and body; relations of a non-dialectic nature and thus with no effected resolutions, only with transformations produced by a sea-like movement, from 'a network of endless waves that renew themselves in all directions'.[11] The becoming-woman-divine as produced here signals thus the unfolding of a virtual femininity that leads to the a-subjective, the creation of an-*other* space, the appearance of a new economy as emerging after the 'death of (a masculine) God'; a death that does not lead to nihilism, cynicism or even atheism but to a new faith that another world exists under the impoverished world of an objective, discontinuous, materiality: that is, the sacred world of a lost intimacy and interconnectivity between the subject and the world, the self and the other, the subject and the object.

As has already been mentioned in the introduction, the lines of becoming-woman-divine pass through two Figures: the *idiot* as the deviation from the knower and representational thinking; and the *self-sacrificial subject* as resistance to the logic of appropriation, accumulation and utility that subsists in the economy of 'being'. Hence, the becoming-woman-divine runs through lines of stupidity and sacrifice, that is, molecular lines that reveal 'an entire world of unconscious micropercepts, unconscious affects';[12] an invisible world that simultaneously disrupts the real by restoring the symbolic and the spiritual into the material, while it destabilises the divine by challenging its transcendent nature and its hierarchical order. Therefore, the film *Breaking the Waves*, as the story of becoming-woman-divine through a zigzagging between the idiot and the sacrificial subject, works as an unorthodox story, which manages to reveal the power of an immanent spirituality that in turn may work as the exit from the human, into an all-too-human reality. Although the flight towards this all-too human destiny passes through various planes of intensities, this article will be specifically concerned with two: that of faith (as a religiosity without a religion) and sacrifice (as the affirmative negation of the economy of 'being').

REPEATING DIFFERENTLY

What will be attempted in the next section is a revisiting of this cinematic event not through analysis but through the process of a story (re-)telling: not the story of a subject but that of a becoming, and more precisely, the story of a becoming-woman-divine. I choose to think through a story, since as the protagonist of this film (Bess) says, stories are powerful: they give life to the lifeless, existence to the inexistent, image to the imageless. A story of a becoming is a story *in* becoming, which means it has neither beginning nor end. It is the kind of narrativity which, as Braidotti argues, contributes 'to the making of significant figurations of the kind of subjects we are in the process of becoming'.[13] Hence, 'my' (re)telling of the story will neither aim to a faithful[14] reproduction of the film's narrative, nor to precise analysis of its representations. Rather it will attempt to reveal the molecular lines of a narrativity that bubbles underneath the organism of the cinematic text: a counter-story as it is experienced/lived by the two figures of the Idiot and the self-sacrificial subject. Such a counter-narrative will map out the post-theistic framework as it has been suggested previously.

Constituting part of a wider project - a 'film-philosophy' project - this article attempts to reflect on, expand and actualise the DeleuzoGuattarian concept of becoming-woman within the event of film, and more specifically, within the cinematic event of *Breaking the Waves*. Being primarily a philosophical project that attempts to move beyond established semiological and linguistic structures that reduce language's forces to processes of signification and subjectification, this project leaves behind the more 'traditional' discourses of analysis that dominate the disciplines of film and cultural studies (e.g. the Lacanian, Saussurean and Althusserian approaches), since all of them reside on a structuralist premise of the constituting and determining role of language. However, language can account only for a negative, oppositional 'difference from', since it can only conceive of difference as signification and representation. Against this tendency and aiming at a more positive (and feminist) conception of difference-in-itself (as an ongoing differing), this article has attempted the experimental shift from 'films as representations' to 'films as cinematic events', approaching then films not as texts to be decoded but as events that open up problems; in the case of *Breaking the Waves*, the problem of ethics and politics. And perhaps this is what makes cinema and generally art deeply and inherently political for Deleuze: its ability to open up problems that require in turn a new thinking:

13. Rosi Braidotti, *Metamorphoses*, Polity Press, 2002, p21.

14. '"Faithfulness" here equates flat repetition', Braidotti, *Transpositions*, op. cit., p170.

15. G. Deleuze
in D. Frampton,
Filmosophy,
Wallflower Press,
2006, p10.

16. D. Frampton,
Filmosophy,
Wallflower Press,
2006, p9.

17. Daniel W. Smith,
'Introduction' in
Deleuze, *Critical and
Clinical*, University
of Minnesota Press,
1997, pxIiv.

18. 'So how can
we manage to
speak without
giving orders,
without claiming to
represent something
or someone, and
how can we get
people without the
right to speak … I
suppose that's what
it means to be like
a foreigner in one's
own language, to
trace a sort of line
of flight for words',
Deleuze, *Negotiations*,
New York, Columbia
University Press,
1995, p41.

19. All written parts
presented in the
middle of the page
are quotations taken
from the film.

I was able to write on cinema, not by right of reflection, but when philosophical problems led me to seek answers in cinema, which itself then relaunched other problems.[15]

Therefore, a Deleuzean problematics of films does not use the latter as illustrative examples of closed philosophical ideas, but wishes on the contrary to seek in them answers to given philosophical problems; in this case, how a re-thinking of an ethics of sexual difference can mobilise new political agencies, as well as, a re-definition of the political as such. Rather than being an application of philosophy to films, my film-philosophy approach follows Daniel Frampton's suggestion: that is, to work through the film philosophically. Hence, the question is no longer 'what can film do *for* philosophy?'[16] but 'how can film think on its own about given philosophical concepts and problems?', how might it produce a thinking from the outside.

Deleuze argues that as in the case of philosophy similarly in art, the artist creates his/her 'intercessors', that is, figurations that work as a 'thought-event' or better a 'figure-image' (the figure of the Idiot and the self sacrificial subject in our case), which embodies the concept that the cinematic image gives rise to, while providing the concept with an affective charge. Thus the intercessors in cinema move in-between a conceptual and an aesthetic level, creating an affective thinking: a deeply political (though impersonal) thinking of an absent/dead author, which addresses the 'people who are missing'. A thinking that can only emerge from conditions of impossibility (from what seems/feels impossible or intolerable and the event of *Breaking the Waves* indeed creates these conditions!) and which can only be articulated as a 'pure speech act', 'that is neither an impersonal myth nor a personal fiction, but a *collective utterance*'.[17]

Following from the argument (presented earlier), which holds for language's capacity to account only for a negative, oppositional 'difference from' (since it can only conceive of difference as signification and representation), my approach to the film-event *Breaking The Waves* will be the one proposed by Luce Irigaray as 'linguistics against linguistics'. An approach that aims at developing a new (cinematic) language, a rather political language, which, in our case, seeks to open up the problem of the interrelation between ethics and politics, and which wishes to speak differently: a foreign[18] language as embodied by the cinematic intercessor, Bess, who speaks the language of stupidity and belief. A minoritarian language, which addresses to the people-to-come, and which breathes out new possibilities of subjectiveness as primarily a/effectuation rather than as definitions and determinations.

THE IDIOT

I 've always been stupid.
But I am good at it.
I can believe·[19]

The concepts of faith and stupidity, as embodied by the figure of Bess, are bound together in a rather causal and inextricable relation. Bess is an idiot because she believes, and she can believe precisely because she is an Idiot. But how is stupidity related to faith, and faith to stupidity? How, in other words, do lines of stupidity meet lines of religiosity and delineate the lines of flight towards the 'woman-divine'?

As Deleuze argues in *Difference and Repetition*, being an Idiot is:

> a question of someone - if only one - with the necessary modesty not managing to know what everybody knows, and modestly denying what everybody is supposed to recognize ... Someone who neither allows himself to be represented nor wishes to represent anything.[20]

Consequently, Bess, as the Idiot, is incapable of representational thinking and the capacity for recognition, since her thinking 'lacks' a departure point, a pre-existing image of thought, that is, the 'semiological screen'[21] of equivalences that would enable her to work through resemblance, analogy, comparison and identity. Consequently, her mind fails to submit to the signifier and her faith fails to follow the Law (of the Father).

> ...the unconditional love for the Word that is written.
> I don't understand what you say.
> How can you love a word?
> ...the unconditional love for the Law.
> You can't be in love with a Word.
> ...
> Dear father, what's going on?
> Father where are you?

On the contrary, her thinking, or better, her faith starts from a zero ground and develops through encounters and connections from with*out* as well as from with*in*. Hence, her 'stupid' perception and thinking do not work through an appropriation of what already exists but as a creation of what is yet to come through exchange and connection. It is thus an epiphany or a revelation of the virtual. Far from being the faculty of a powerful subject exercised upon objects, the perception of the Idiot takes place in the interaction, the in-between space of the subject - object interaction. It is thus the result of the 'im*pressions*' the subject gives and receives in his/her connection with the others (both organic and inorganic ones).

For Bess, this in-between space of proximity and impressions, is love, as a zone of intimate communication, movement and becoming: the love for a personalised (feminine) God, or better, the love *to* God, the love *to* another human being, in this case, Jan.

You can't be in love with a Word.

20. Deleuze, *Difference and Repetition*, op. cit., p165.

21. Deleuze and Guattari, *A Thousand Plateaus - Capitalism and Schizophrenia*, Brian Massumi (trans), University of Minnesota Press, Minneapolis, 1987, p179.

You can be in love with another human being.

That's perfection.

22. Luce Irigaray,
I Love to You, New
York and London,
Routledge, 1996,
p110.

Her love is not the subjugation or consummation of the other, but a respect for its irreducibility. It thus constitutes a directional passion, a love *to* the other, with the 'to' guaranteeing proximity in distance, where actions (like 'to love') are empowered by becoming a force in themselves, and are not just referential/transitive activities.[22] Hence, the love to anOther requires a going outside the self and a simultaneous coming back (to self), a 'relating to' that does not lead to fusion and disappearance (since this would annihilate the act of relating as such), but to singularisation and transformation. Love to the other then is a movement away from a subjective molar perception towards (or backwards?) to a micro-perception, to a singular vision (a new perceptibility as deriving from a rhizomatic relatedness).

Therefore, it is not Bess who perceives, but Love that perceives on behalf of her, or better, it is out of love that Bess can see more; in fact, she can see too much: by being blind to what others see, or by seeing things a-new through a multiple, almost childish vision, she creates another (virtual) world to inhabit and exchange with. This other world is 'a world of make believe', a spiritual world of intimacy, continuity and expenditure in which dualisms like body-mind, material-spiritual, real-imaginary dissolve. Hence, in this world spiritual contacts are at the same time contacts of the flesh, which have material effects:

Jan and me have a spiritual contact (…)
I don't make love with them.
I make love with Jan and I save him from dying.

Her 'stupid' world is another economy: a world of intimate exchange and communication articulated on differences and not on equivalences of normality, where faith replaces thinking, belief surpasses logic, gift challenges isolation, intimacy overcomes community, rational acts give way to an activism of praying, hoping, dreaming, imagining; a world where miracles become possible and the virtual becomes effectuated.

23. Deleuze and
Guattari, *What is
Philosophy?*, London,
New York, Verso,
1994, p109.

Exchange is defined by Deleuze as the passing of something into the other; a process which results not in the disappearance of the terms, but in their transformation, and in the consequent 'becoming' of both terms[23] - hence exchange in Deleuzean terms is strongly linked to the notion of 'becoming', which is always two-directional. In her exchange with God (during her long personal talks to Him that we witness in many scenes of the film) God becomes Bess and Bess becomes God, so that both cease to be what they used to be: the faithful Idiot thus becomes powerful through her exchange with God. She acquires a dangerous, evil, almost ridiculous power that makes her a sinner by exclaiming 'I am the one who saved his life - I can save it again'; while God becomes less transcendent, more immanent, which means more intimate to her. She-the-God(dess) dares thus to ask:

> 'Why do we assume that God must always remain an inaccessible transcendence rather than a realisation - here and now - through the body?',[24] through my body?

God for her then ceases to name an outside, transcendent reality, an afterlife, but becomes instead a transformative force of a 'here and now', a verb ('to God'[25]) that effectuates changes, a promise for the absolute surprise, the unexpected (Jan's recovery), the opening up of the horizon of the possible to the impossible, an openness towards the other that is coming; a 'coming', which makes an urgent demand upon her and requires from her to act. Thus, God constitutes for her an invitation to explore her other self: to leave the self and go to the other, to leave the self so as to make the space for the other to come, so that she can start believing in her other (be)coming. God is the welcoming of the unknown.

> (Church people) : I don't know him.
> (Bess): His name is Jan.
> (Church people): We don't favour matrimony with *outsiders*.

Bess's God works as an act/demand of opening to the other, the foreigner; an invitation which only an idiot can respond to, since it is not a cognitive experience, a matter of knowing, but a matter of believing, a religious passion. Against meaningful, rational and 'proper' connections, the idiot chooses to connect with the unknown, the absolute foreigner, transforming thus herself little by little from a submissive religious subject to a post-theistic sinner. She thus asks:

> Am I going to go to hell?

Hence, her God has become an evil partner of exchange, her antagonistic double, who is both within and without her; something inside her that, however, she can neither master nor fully know, and which at the same time exceeds her and makes her realise that she is not a singular 'she' but a plural 'they', a subject in becoming.

Thus, the idiot's love is not the love within the (conjugal) couple but that *for/towards* the double, with the latter being neither the same, yet not an oppositional alterity, nor a mere deviation from the norm. It is instead pure heterogeneity, a doubling as the repetition of difference: it is 'a repetition, another layer, the return of the same, a catching on something else, an imperceptible difference, a coming apart and ineluctable tearing open'.[26] Bess' religiosity then is an unorthodox faith expressed as the love for her doubling: a line towards God without ever reaching it, her own Godding (becoming-God) as a line of escape from the repressive reality principle

24. Luce Irigaray, *An Ethics of Sexual Difference*, New York, Cornell University Press, 1993, p148.

25. "'God"- that is not only a name but an injunction, and invitation, a solicitation, to commend, to let all things be commended, to God', J. Caputo, *The Payers and Tears of J. Derrida - Religion without a Religion*, Indiana University Press, 2001, p141.

26. Michel Foucault cited in Deleuze, *Negotiations*, op. cit., p84.

defined by dichotomies and divisions that produce isolated subjectivities and restrictive identities. It is a journey towards continuity as connectivity and relationality. A long effort and (an) anguished quest: it is always a matter of detaching from the *real* order, from the order of *things*, and of restoring the *divine* order.[27]

Hence, Bess' prayers are an idiot's (and a sinner's) prayers that signify the loss of the (masculine) God.

Father where are you?
Why aren't you with me?

Bess prays to God to rid her of Truth: the medical truth that Jan is dying, the ultimate truth of the holy Word. She prays to God to rid her of Man: of the (male) God's word, as well as of her positioning by patriarchal discourse as a 'wife' that should not have sexual intercourse with others, and of her label as an idiot that lacks (man's) rationality. Finally, she prays to God to rid her of God:[28] the transcendent masculine God that comes to legitimate the patriarchal order, and her consequent restriction to a (feminine) subject position.

THE SACRIFICIAL SUBJECT

Every gift is a sacrifice
                    A. Tarkovski

It is time to abandon the world
of civilized men and its light.
It is necessary to become totally other,
or cease to be.
                    G. Bataille

First she dies, then she loves,[29] since the death of self and identity constitutes the condition of love, 'I have become capable of loving … by abandoning love and self'.[30] Bess' flight towards her own death, her self-sacrificial act, does not emerge from despair, weakness or victimisation but from a sovereign love for the other/her God, from a stupid faith that something other exists, which only exists elsewhere - a 'something other' that rationality forbids, reality excludes, thinking fails to grasp; a virtual other then, which always eludes the economy of being.

She thus exclaims: 'You my God, You my death!':[31] a call of the limits, a call beyond the limits … a call for life (Jan's recovery, another life for her), that is a simultaneous call for death (the death of her social self as well as God's death, the husband's death as the-Law-of-the-Father). Death then as a desire to lose the face,[32] to forget what she has been, what she ought to be so as to

27. George Bataille, *The Accursed Share*, Vol.1, Zone Books, 1991, p57.

28. Meister Eckhart: "I pray to God to rid me of God", found in Caputo, *The Prayers and Tears of J. Derrida*, op. cit., p4.

29. Hélène Cixous, '*Coming To Writing' and Other Essays*, Deborah Jenson (ed). Sarah Cornell, Deborah Jenson, Ann Liddle, Susan Sellers (trans), Massachusetts, Harvard UP, 1991, p36.

30. Deleuze and Guattari, *A Thousand Plateaus*, Brian Massumi (trans), op. cit., p199.

31. J. Derrida in Caputo, *The Payers and Tears of J. Derrida*, op. cit., p165.

32. 'The face is produced only when the head ceases to be part of the body, when it ceases to be coded by the body, when it ceases to have a multidimensional, polyvocal, corporeal code - when the body, head included, has been decoded and has to be *overcoded* by something we shall call the Face', Deleuze and Guattari, *A Thousand Plateaus*, p170.

meet her infinite becomings. Now she can clearly see, sense that intimacy means death,[33] giving up the self so as to fuse with the unknown, losing the face so as to meet the other ... taking off her clothes and making love with the-stranger, the newcomer, the arrivant, with the self that is to-come, with the other self she will always become; a communication at the limit of the possible, the moral, the normal. No, it's not her that desires after all, it is death that desires in her ... it is death that desires life, it is death that desires freedom, to free itself from an end, from a telos, a purpose.

So beyond the 'last man'[34] (*He* the God, the Husband, the Father[35]) there is still something going on, there is still Life, the 'monster of energy', the 'woman who wants to die'.[36] The woman who actively wants to destroy the face she was given, the image she was miming; the woman who denies being for the sake of becoming, who kills presence so as to free her absence, who sacrifices the individual self so as to dive into multiplicity, who hurts her body (Bess' conscious choice of being raped) so as to free the Body without Organs.[37]

She remembers pretty well that it was the ugliest of men, the higher man (the priest), the secular man of knowledge (the doctor), who killed his own God and then tried to take his place, become God himself, become the ultimate being by imposing his finitude to the infinite, his determination to indeterminacy. He couldn't realise that sooner or later, he would have to face his own limits, the limits *he* imposed on the world. He couldn't see that his reactive being, his negative critique, his negative, rational thinking, his tendency for over-determination would all turn back against himself ... and at this day, the day of the crisis, the Day of Judgement, *She* would be the one to cross the threshold, precisely because of her capacity to depropriate herself, to give the gift without return, to give her individual self for Life, to embrace indeterminacy by becoming imperceptible; while man would vanish into the last man, being unable to give up himself, his individual life for *a* Life that goes on independently of him, daring not to look beyond his narcissistic idol, his pre-determined and isolated image.

But thanks to this rupture (the husband's accident) the woman who wants to die emerges (Bess) and supersedes the last man: an active agent that affirms life, not her life anymore but *a* life - life as the very possibility of her singular existence.

Therefore, the idiot maps out a new territory, a new life experienced outside the threat of death: an economy of giving 'the gift without return' that supersedes the masculine economy of 'the gift-that-takes': a gift that demands the return to the self, to the 'white-man face', to the norm; giving as determining. However, for her-the-idiot, the gift has a meaning only as sacrifice; that is, the gift as the pure act of giving, a pure loss or an 'unconditional expenditure' without recovery, giving as falling back to indeterminacy (between the giver and given).

If there is a gift, the *given* of the gift ... must not come back to the giving. It must not circulate ... [or have it] exchanged ... the gift must remain *aneconomic*.[38]

33. George Bataille, *The Impossible*: 'I knew already that the intimacy of things is death ... and naturally, nakedness is death - and the more truly "death" the lovelier it is!', Bataille, *The Impossible,* City Lights Book, 1991, p54.

34. See Deleuze's discussion on Nietzsche in his work *Pure immanence*, Zone Books, 2001.

35. The term 'husband' is used to signify man as social position, the majoritarian subject, the dominant discourse, while the name Jan is used metonymically for God and signifies the absolute Other that stretches Bess' limits beyond the self.

36. A playful re-appropriation of Nietzsche's notion of the 'man who wants to die'.

37. A DeleuzoGuattarian term introduced in their work *A Thousand Plateaus*. A very good definition of the term is provided by Catherine Driscoll (2000:71): 'The body without organs is the body without hierarchised organs such as penis, phallus, vagina, even mouth; "opposed not to the organs but to the organisation of the organs"'.

38. Jacques Derrida, *Given Time: I. Counterfeit Money*, Peggy Kamuf (trans), Chicago, Chicago U P, 1992, p7.

The ultimate gift cannot be other than death, since death does not have an equivalent to be exchanged with and all the more, ruins even the expectation of a future return as it signals the end of empirical time. Therefore, sacrifice is the gift that violates the established order of things, the economy of accumulation and preservation, the economy of 'being' based on a linear conception of time, the morality of utility.

Thus, with her self-sacrifice (a conscious suicidal act), the figure of Bess creates her own ethics based on the total negation of the existing morality, which imprisons individual becomings (and especially minoritarian ones) under the notions of 'normality', 'sanity', 'rationality', 'reason'. Her ethics is not an ethics of life defined as self- preservation at any cost, but the ethics of death (of the Subject) as the active stepping back from the position of the subject for the Other to come. An ethics which affirms life through death, not the final physical death but these little deaths of selfhood as experienced in sexual orgasm, sacrificial love, intimate exchange.

Therefore, Bess' gift (her death) is more than just a reactive negation, a pure expenditure that leads to a nihilistic destruction of reality and Life. Bess gives for the other, dies for her other, dies for/with Jan, not as a good Christian that sacrifices her life with the expectation of a reward - the eternal life - neither as the victim that obeys the rules of her gender imposed by patriarchy (a wife that dies for her husband, for the Man). On the contrary, Bess dies as the sovereign subject, who 'risks to walk through the self toward the dark', based not on logic but on faith, as well as, on 'the desire to keep this other alive - hence some living feminine - some difference - and some love … "[39]

39. Cixous and Clement, 'Sorties: Our and Out: Attacks/Ways Out/ Forays' in *Feminisms: An Anthology of Literary Theory and Criticism*, Robyn Warhol and Diane Price Herndl (eds), New Brunswick, Rutgers, 1990, p97.

40. Cixous, '*Coming To Writing*' , op. cit., p38.

41. Cixous, 'The Author in Truth' in '*Coming To Writing*', ibid., p169.

It is within the economy of the gift that Bess' becoming-woman takes place, a primarily feminine economy, because 'she', as the positive absence, the creative lack, the minoritarian, can actually give without return, can actually lose without this being recognised, contrary to the masculine presence, which is a case of nonloss: 'if you want to lose, then there is *you* and *wanting* , there is nonloss'.[40] Bess' journey to death is a journey of exhaustion and expenditure, a reaching of the limits of womanhood up to the point of death both physically and symbolically, which does not signal a dead end but the opening up to a new world in which death is exchanged for life, morality for ethics, the self for the other, being for becoming; an economy of becoming-woman-divine that leads to the molecular feminine and is a consequent to imperceptibility, that is, to a 'pure "am", activity of being that does not lead back to the self … Woman does not stop at woman'.[41]

Thus, Bess's becoming expresses an anomalous force that activates life through death, that 'animates community while at the same time remaining separated from community in an infinite solitude that is both sovereignty and humiliation'. Being both a Loner and always in-relation-to, her becoming constitutes the paradox of immanence and transcendence, the paradox of being part of but also an outsider (a threshold), a paradox which consequently forces us to rethink community through the notions of intimacy, gift and indeterminacy, which means, as 'the spacing of the experience of the outside, of the outside-of-self'.[42]

Having taken her distance from the self, Bess now knows that *the god who remains unknown is of the earth*,[43] of the body, of her body.

I don't make love with them.
I make love with Jan and I save him from dying.

She-the-Goddess, the angel guard that makes sure the world is not reduced to its shell, and she to her gender. Hence, becoming-divine, approaching God, communicating with the other is living time in its openness, living life in its fullest up to the point of death, until the edge of the possible, where she meets the face of God, and she sees that God has no face … she tries to call God but she has no name to call her with …

What's her true name?
Bess:
An immature, unstable person?
A pervert? A sinner?
Or just good?

She will *know* it on the last day. It's promised.[44]

Yes, yes!
'A-dieu'.[45]
To-God

ANTI-LOGOS [46]

What Deleuze calls extra-Being is not a transcendence of,
or supplement to Being,
but denotes to becoming of 'Being in its very virtuality'
Keith Ansell Pearson

This essay has thus attempted to reveal the strong interrelation of politics and ethics suggesting that an 'ethics of becoming' cannot but correspond to (a) different definition(s) of politics. Deleuze's method of transcendental empiricism requires a shift in the way we conceptualise both 'ethics' and 'politics' and this shift has been examined in relation to the cinematic thinking of the film *Breaking the Waves*, since the latter problematises both what we call an ethics of (sexual) difference as well as well-established ideas about our sacred political values like freedom, free-determination, autonomy etc. The main argument of this article has been that the film manages to provide us with a so-called post-theistic framework that resonates but also pushes further Deleuze's transcendentalism, opening new paths for a

42. J.L. Nancy, *An Inoperative Community*, University Minnesota, 1991, p23.

43. K. Hart, *The Dark Gaze - Maurice Blanchot and the Sacred*, 2004, p99.

44. Cixous, 'Writing Blind' in *Stigmata*, 1998, p150.

45. Caputo, *The Payers and Tears of J. Derrida*, op. cit., p141.

46. It emphasises the nonliguistic approach of the film: the film is not a text to be decoded but a plane of pre- and post-signifying forces, hence, an anti-Logos. Contrary to feminist positions that argue for the reclamation of a woman's voice within the laws of the symbolic order, the aim of this article it to provide a de-territorialising analysis of the film, which aims at revealing the minoritarian language as it emerges from uncoded flows of desire. A deterritorialising analysis opposes an analytic machine of interpretation (that of psychoanalysis) that remains constant independently of the different body-texts, and which seems to hold the truth of the text (a *savoir*).

radicalisation of feminist materialism. *Breaking the Waves* provides us with a notion of (becoming-) woman in relation to Man that breaks away from the established discourses of difference, equality, reciprocity and respect that have traditionally informed the Self-Other relation, bringing in the themes of sacrifice, stupidity and belief. Departing from the film's thinking and its mobilisation of new political forces, and a new feminist agency, I have suggested a new framework so as to rethink 'an ethics of becoming-woman' that draws on an immanent post-theistic framework.

This post-theistic framework - a proposed new thinking plane - is not grounded on an easy and rather naïve reversal of the established hierarchical dualisms. Such a reversal would only end up producing another majoritarian model of politics, of mysticism and sacrifice this time, equally (if not more) exclusionary, repressive, conservative and life-diminishing. If the re-telling of the cinematic event *Breaking the Waves*, as has been attempted above, feels like risking this easy slippage, this is due to the fact that it adopts writing strategies that aim at making the reader primarily feel and live ideas (of new political forces), before picking these ideas discursively. In other words, it is a thought-experiment for the reader, so as to stimulate within him/her political forces of imagination, affectivity, sympathy. Forces that will reinvent the notion of freedom, not merely on the level of representation, but mainly on the level of forces, energies and movement, so that new political lines of flight will emerge and actualise an affective activism and a vitalist pragmatism, where subjective and non-subjective possibilities of agency enter into relations of mutual intensification.

Weatherman, the Militant Diagram, and the Problem of Political Passion

Nicholas Thoburn

'Mutant' workers in 'veritable *wars of subjectivity*'; for Félix Guattari, this is what constitutes the history of the workers' movement.[1] He has in mind the events of revolutionary upheaval, the Paris Commune, October 1917, May 1968. But the problematic of revolutionary subjectivity - in its affective, semiotic, organisational, and imaginary registers - is one that pervades modern socialist, communist and anarchist politics. This problematic is that of the 'militant', of 'militancy', a persistent marker - indeed, often the self-declared *guarantor* - of radical subjectivity across the spectrum of extra-parliamentary politics. One can think of militancy as a technology of the self, an expression of the working on the self in the service of revolutionary change. However, unlike the subjective correlates of the great revolutionary events, for Guattari this more prosaic aspect of radical practice is not altogether joyful.

1. Félix Guattari, *The Guattari Reader*, G. Genosko (ed.), London, Blackwell, 1996, p124.

This paper is a critique of the militant.[2] In particular it seeks to understand the ways militancy effectuates political passions and a certain unworking or deterritorialisation of the self in relation to political organisations and the wider social environment within which militants would enact change. To this end the paper traces a 'diagram' or 'abstract machine' of militancy, and considers a particular animation of this diagram in the Weatherman organisation in the United States at the turn of the 1970s. Returning to Marx's concept of the party, the paper then sketches the principle outlines of a counter figure - an 'a-militant diagram', or dispersive ecology of political composition - that suggests a rather different process of subjective unworking.

2. A different version of this essay has been published in Ian Buchanan and Nicholas Thoburn (eds), *Deleuze and Politics*, Edinburgh, Edinburgh University Press, 2008.

MILITANT PASSION

Guattari locates the emergence of the modern militant formation in what he calls the 'Leninist breakthrough' during the 1903 Second Congress of the All-Russian Social Democratic Labour Party, from where - following certain procedural and organisational disputes - emerged a set of affective, semiotic, tactical, and organisational traits that constitute a kind of Leninist diagram or abstract machine.[3] For Deleuze and Guattari, the diagram or abstract machine is that which governs the articulation and distribution of matter and function in concrete assemblages (where a concrete assemblage may be a carcereal institution, an aesthetic practice, a military technology, an architectural school, and so on). The diagram is not an ideal type, infrastructure or transcendent idea, but a non-unifying immanent cause that is coextensive

3. Félix Guattari, *Molecular Revolution: Psychiatry and Politics*, R. Sheed (trans.), Harmondsworth, Penguin, 1984, pp184-95.

with the concrete assemblages that express it. These assemblages, in their divergent manifestations and unexpected conjunctions, in turn feedback into the diagram, both consolidating and modifying its abstract imperatives. As such, even as one sees a regularity of function across its iterations, the diagram is in principle a force of undetermined change, and one existent in a state of disequilibrium.

As a tool of analysis, the concept of the diagram enables one to attend to continuities or resonances across superficially divergent phenomena, and to approach an understanding of the dynamic consistency of arrangements of heterogeneous materials (bodies, signs, images, technologies, affects …), whilst requiring attention to be paid both to abstract functions and to concrete manifestations as they exist in mutual presupposition. Insofar as the diagram is an abstract entity that is only perceivable through diverse concrete manifestations, the mapping of any diagram is an inexact, tentative, and experimental procedure. It is something like a 'working hypothesis that must be examined with care, re-worked, perhaps even ousted altogether',[4] and is useful only insofar as it brings an appreciation of consistencies, creative processes, points of tension, knots of power, lines of escape, that aid intervention in its field. Of course, any concrete assemblage - including a political grouping - will be governed by more than one diagram.[5]

As to the *militant* diagram (born in 1903 and consolidated in 'effects of repetition' largely secured by the place of Bolshevism in the 1917 revolution), Guattari argues that it is characterised by: the production of a field of inertia that restricts openness and encourages uncritical acceptance of slogans and doctrine; the hardening of situated statements into universal dogma; the attribution of a messianic vocation to the party; and a domineering and contemptuous attitude - 'that hateful "love" of the militant'- to those known as 'the masses'.[6] As any diagram, that of the militant draws together its substance in varying ways over time and place, but there is a noticeable regularity of functions upon which, as Guattari wrote in the 1970s, 'our thinking is still largely dependent today': 'From this fundamental breach, then, the Leninist machine was launched on its career; history was still to give it a face and a substance, but its fundamental encoding, so to say, was already determined'.[7] In discussing the post-'68 French groupuscule milieu Guattari thus contends that the range of groups from anarchist to Maoist may at once be 'radically opposed in their *style:* the definition of the leader, of propaganda, a conception of discipline, loyalty, modesty, and the asceticism of the militant', but they essentially perform the same militant function of 'stacking', 'sifting', and 'crushing' desiring energies.[8]

There is, however, a trait of the militant diagram that lacks full articulation in Guattari's presentation, that of *passional struggle* and its mode of subjective composition. This can be characterised in Deleuze and Guattari's terms as the constitutive 'line of flight' of militancy. Here we need to complicate Guattari's analysis, which chimes with what Deleuze and Guattari will later call the 'signifying regime of signs', with an appreciation of the place within militant formations of the 'passional' and 'subjective' 'postsignifying regime

4. Ibid., p190.

5. For a full elaboration of the concept of the diagram as it is used here, see Gilles Deleuze, *Foucault*, S. Hand (trans.), Minneapolis, University of Minnesota Press, 1988, pp23-44.

6. Ibid., p185, 190.

7. Ibid., p189, 190.

8. Félix Guattari, *Chaosophy*, S. Lotringer (ed.), New York, Semiotext(e), 1995, p59.

of signs'.[9] In the passional regime, one of a number of semiotic regimes that may be found in any concrete assemblage, the line of flight - the creative or exploratory aspect of an assemblage - takes a singular and dangerous value, operating as the vector upon which subjectivity is at once deterritorialised and intensified. Passional regimes are characterised by 'points of subjectification' that are constituted through the 'betrayal' of dominant social relations and semiotic codes - Deleuze and Guattari offer the example of food for the anorexic - and a certain 'monomania' that, like a 'black hole' of destruction, draws the assemblage through a series of finite linear proceedings, each overcoded by the pursuit of its end, an existence 'under reprieve'. The particular semiotic of the passional regime is composed of a subject of enunciation - a product of the mental reality determined by the point of subjectification - and a subject of the statement, where the latter is bound to the utterances of the former and acts - though the two poles can and do switch places and may be embodied in the same subject - in a 'reductive echolalia' as its respondent or guarantor.

To isolate this passional aspect of militancy requires a turn to an earlier period of Russian agitation, and Sergei Nechaev's 1869 *Catechism of the Revolutionist*. In the 48 principles that comprise the *Catechism*, Nechaev outlines an image of revolutionary action, operating through the closed cell of the political organisation, as a singular, all-encompassing passion. It is a cold, calculated passion that, beyond 'romanticism', 'rapture' or 'hatred', requires a dismantling of all relations to self and society that could be conceived of in any manner other than its own furtherance, even at the cost of death:

> The revolutionary is a dedicated man. He has no interests of his own, no affairs, no feelings, no attachments, no belongings, not even a name. Everything in him is absorbed by a single exclusive interest, a single thought, a single passion - the revolution ... All the tender and effeminate emotions of kinship, friendship, love, gratitude and even honour must be stifled in him by a cold and single-minded passion for the revolutionary cause ... Night and day he must have but one thought, one aim - merciless destruction. In cold-blooded and tireless pursuit of this aim, he must be prepared both to die himself and destroy with his own hands everything that stands in the way of its achievement ... If he is able to, he must face the annihilation of a situation, of a relationship or of any person who is part of this world - everything and everyone must be equally odious to him.[10]

Given the exemplary misanthropy of Nechaev's text, one might be surprised to find that it has had a persistent presence in radical cultures: Lenin expressed admiration for the tenets of the *Catechism*; it was until relatively recently accepted as part of the canon of revolutionary anarchism, as a work once thought to have been co-authored with Bakunin; and it was popular amongst, and published and distributed by, the Black Panther Party.[11] These direct appreciations of the text betray a sense in which its model of passional struggle articulates, albeit in exaggerated form, an enduring property of

9. Gilles Deleuze and Félix Guattari, *A Thousand Plateaus: Capitalism and Schizophrenia Volume 2*, B. Massumi (trans.), London, Athlone, Ch5.

10. Sergei Nechaev, *Catechism of the Revolutionist*, H. Sternberg and L. Bott (trans.), London, Violette Nozières Press, 1989, pp4-7.

11. Luther Blissett and Stuart Home, *Green Apocalypse*, London, Unpopular Books, n.d.; David Hilliard and Lewis Cole, *This Side of Glory: The Autobiography of David Hilliard and the Story of the Black Panther Party*, London, Little, Brown and Company, 1993.

the militant diagram. Its presence today, inflected through singular socio-historical conditions and amidst competing dynamics, is perhaps most apparent in jihadi approaches to struggle, but it can also be detected in left activist cultures,[12] and may even have some purchase on the popular imaginary - it would, for instance, seem to account for much of the seductive quality of the militant subjectivity constructed in the 2006 film *V for Vendetta*.

WEATHERMAN

In order to examine the tangle of militant matters and functions further it is instructive to consider the animation of the militant diagram in a particular political group, or concrete assemblage. The Weatherman organisation is a useful case because of the special emphasis the group placed on the militant transformation of subjectivity, and the way the diagram of militancy here mobilises and draws a consistency from diverse social fields and problematics, notably countercultural styles of living, Maoist approaches to collectivity and struggle, anti-racism, drug use, open sexuality and guerrilla ideology.[13] That Weatherman is currently the subject of some interest - with the publication since 2000 of a number of critical histories, a collection of communiqués and documents, the memoirs of two key figures, a novel, and an Academy Award-nominated feature documentary - also recommends it, especially since, as Jesse Lemisch notes, there are tendencies in the appreciation of the organisation that would fashion it within a critically unproductive, linear or generational narrative of a generic leftist resistance.[14] Rather than offering an icon of revolutionary struggle, Weatherman is more useful for the possibility it allows for an exploration of the sometimes highly problematic dynamics and affects that can pass for manifestations of communist subjectivity.

A core trait of the militant machine is the relation it draws between inclusion in the group and commitment to that which characterises the group's uniqueness. In both Guattari's account of the 'field of inertia' of Bolshevism and Nechaev's *Catechism*, the revolutionary organisation functions as a cut with the social, and as a means to consolidate and intensify its mode of activity, an activity that in turn secures the individual's subjective investment in, and formation through, the organisation. In the case of Weatherman, the mode of activity and the originality of the group was constituted through a particular conception of militant struggle. Framed as anti-imperialist action against the war in Vietnam and the repression of the black community in the US, militancy was characterised by two integrated aspects: the attempt to 'Bring the war home!' under the logic of opening up 'two, three, many Vietnams' in the fabric of US imperialism; and self-sacrifice or betrayal of the white-skin, bourgeois privilege that imperialism conferred on North American whites (including to a large extent the white working class). Militancy thus exhorted a flight away from bourgeois subjectivity toward a becoming with the Vietnamese and US blacks. Yet this was a strange becoming, one not constituted through the drawing of situated relations and projects, but through the mimicry of

12. Nina Pelikan Straus, 'From Dostoevsky to Al-Qaeda: What Fiction Says to Social Science', *Common Knowledge* 12, 2 (2006), pp197-213; Sian Sullivan, '"Viva Nihilism!" On Militancy and Machismo in (Anti-)Globalisation Protest', *CSGR Working Papers* no. 158/05, 2005, www2. warwick.ac.uk/fac/ soc/csgr/research/ workingpapers/2005/ wp15805.pdf

13. Weatherman emerged from the 1969 position paper 'You Don't Need a Weatherman to Know Which Way the Wind Blows' (a title famously taken from Bob Dylan's 'Subterranean Homesick Blues') as the most militant wing of the anti-Vietnam war movement, initially as a faction within the mass organisation Students for a Democratic Society but soon as an independent and then underground group, when it came to be known as the Weatherman Underground and, later, the gender-neutral Weather Underground Organisation, effectively disbanding in 1976. This paper is focused on the brief, pre-underground period of Weatherman.

14. Jesse Lemisch, 'Weather Underground Rises

a particular military practice (in what was clearly a very different context to the war situation of Vietnam) and the resultant experience of repression. In discussing Weatherman's 'Days of Rage', Shin'ya Ono expresses something of the kernel of this approach: 'We began to feel the Vietnamese in ourselves. Some of us, at moments, felt we were ready to die'.[15]

Framed in Deleuze and Guattari's terms, this militant sacrifice of the bourgeois self was Weatherman's passional point of subjectification, and offered the vector of its line of flight: 'If you believed something, the proof of that belief was to act on it. It wasn't to espouse it with the right treatises or manifestos. We were militants ... *Militancy was the standard by which we measured our aliveness*'.[16] This vector was characterised by the impossible limit of truly becoming Americong, of experiencing the full weight of the repression of the US black working class, of fully escaping white subjectivity through militarisation. Militancy thus posed not only a moral standard against which revolutionary vitality and commitment would be assessed, but a kind of 'quasi-spiritual test' (as one pro-situationist critique of Weatherman put it), a test premised on the purification of subjectivity that could only be found through an ever-renewed and -intensified struggle whose limit was constituted ultimately by a preparedness for death.[17] Such was the force of this vector of militancy that it could be affirmed by Weatherman - in a striking resemblance to Nechaev's image of revolutionary passion, and exemplifying Deleuze and Guattari's understanding of the characteristic delusion of the passional regime - as a monomania.[18] As Mark Rudd declared at the 1969 Flint 'War Council', the last and somewhat frenzied public gathering of Weatherman before its move underground: 'I'm monomaniacal like Captain Ahab in *Moby Dick*. He was possessed by one thought: destroying the great white whale. We should be like Captain Ahab and possess one thought - destruction of the mother country'.[19]

What becomes clear in this articulation is that the efficacy of struggle, the possibility of situated and effective intervention in the social field, is subordinated to, or equated with, the militant construction of subjectivity. Through a betrayal or sacrifice of the bourgeois self, Weatherman came to constitute precisely the self (bolstered through the group subject of the organisation) on its passional line of flight as the locus and guarantor of political truth. This truth was manifest through a set of techniques by which the passion of struggle was played out across the body of the militant.

Most pronounced was the activity, transposed from Chinese Maoism, of collective 'criticism/self-criticism'. In criticism sessions that might last for hours or days, Weather collectives would challenge and confess weaknesses in individual commitments to struggle, tactical mistakes, emotional investments, preparedness for violence, racist inclinations, sexual orientations, aesthetic preferences and so on. Blunt though it could be, criticism was a technology of collective access to, and modulation of, the psychic, cognitive, and affective territories and refrains of the self; put another way, it generated an open field of points of passional betrayal. Sessions could be directed at a particular problem

from the Ashes: They're Baack!', *New Politics* 11, 1 (2006), www.wpunj.edu/newpol/issue41/Lemisch41.htm

15. Shin'ya Ono, in Harold Jacobs (ed.), *Weatherman*, Berkeley, Ramparts Press, 1970, p241. Weatherman's 'Days of Rage' action in Chicago in October 1969 aimed at direct physical confrontation with the police and the destruction of property in order to encourage the subjective 'breakthrough' necessary for the establishment of a white revolutionary force.

16. Bill Ayers cited in Jeremy Varon, *Bringing the War Home: The Weather Underground, the Red Army Faction, and Revolutionary Violence in the Sixties and Seventies*, London, University of California Press, 2004, p87.

17. Point-Blank!, 'The Storms of Youth', *Point-Blank!*, 1 (1972), 30-41, p36. Weatherman's integration of purity, struggle and sacrifice is especially apparent, and critically attended to, in the autobiography of Cathy Wilkerson, *Flying Close to the Sun: My Life and Times as a Weatherman*, London, Seven Stories Press, 2007, where she writes: 'The purity of total dedication scraped away many of the complexities of life and promised ultimate gratification.

Besides, the competitive part of me wanted to be on the best team, the most passionate, the most sacrificing, the most uncompromising, and the most willing to follow each position to the extreme'. Ibid., p293.

18. Weatherman did of course operate in a particular socio-historical environment. If militancy had its own momentum, the horror of the war in Indochina and the brutalisation of black North Americans, most publicly the police assassination of the Black Panther Party's Fred Hampton and Mark Clark, fed Weatherman's passion (in the 2002 documentary film *The Weather Underground*, Mark Rudd talks of the knowledge of the war as having been 'too great to handle' and something he was aware of 'every second of my life') and was to a considerable extent the guarantor against its consummation.

19. Cited in Ron Jacobs, *The Way the Wind Blew: A History of the Weather Underground*, London, Verso, 1997, p85.

20. Lowell Dittmer, 'The Structural Evolution of "Criticism and Self-Criticism"', *The China Quarterly*, 56 (1973), 708-729.

21. Susan Stern, *With the Weathermen:*

for the group, but would tend to focus on an individual member, each of whom - important for the weaving of a passional bond - would at different times experience the subject positions of accuser and confessor. Whilst for the Chinese Communist Party, at least in the period before the Cultural Revolution, criticism or 'inner-Party struggle' was primarily a formal procedure for externalising offending acts and developing a redemptive integration of individuals with the organisation,[20] in Weatherman criticism took subjectivity directly as its object. The core purpose, as Susan Stern makes clear in her autobiographical account of the Seattle Weather collective, was to break-down and remake the self:

> The key to the hours of criticism was struggle ... To purge ourselves of the taint of some twenty-odd years of American indoctrination, we had to tear ourselves apart mentally ... With an enthusiasm born of total commitment we began the impossible task of overhauling our brains ... Turn ourselves inside out and start all over again ... The process of criticism, self-criticism, transformation was the tool by which we would forge ourselves into new human beings.[21]

In accord with the impossible standard of militancy, even the most ferocious criticism could be justified as part of the process of self-transformation. Indeed, as is very clear from Stern's account, a readiness both to enact brutal critique against another and to offer-up in cathartic confession one's worst character traits were markers of revolutionary *vitality*, a preparedness to live the necessary betrayals of subjectivity and personal attachment that militancy required. Ayers thus describes the process as a 'purifying ceremony involving confession, sacrifice, rebirth, and gratitude'.[22] The net effect of these sessions was of course that further commitment to struggle and investment in Weatherman was a means to absolve or defer the ever-returning failings of subjectivity that criticism/self-criticism revealed.

This manner of constituting the collective body of the militant had a corresponding mode of sexuality, one characterised by an enforced anti-monogamy, the rotation of sexual partners, and group sex, apparently known as 'wargasm'. Whilst anti-monogamy had an important role in feminist and countercultural critique of patriarchal relations and domestic structures, its expression in Weatherman's militancy was such that its dominant function was to counteract the detrimental effects that monogamy could present to the intensification of collectivity.[23] 'If monogamy was smashed, so the theory went, everyone would love each other equally, and not love some people more than others. If everyone loved each other equally, then they could trust everyone more completely'.[24] Stern frames collectivity here in terms of 'love', but she is especially attentive to the way that monogamy was seen as an obstacle to the full pursuit of criticism/self-criticism - the principle constitutive field of Weatherman's desire - such that the critique of monogamy was a common focus for these sessions; Stern recounts an occasion where a monogamous couple were subject to two days of criticism after having been encouraged to ingest LSD.[25]

Other techniques for the self-constitution of militant investment in action included the 'gut check', the practice of psyching-up oneself and others in a readiness to face or commit violence as an overcoming of perceived cowardice, racism, privilege, or lack of revolutionary commitment in the face of the continued oppression and death of US black peoples and the Vietnamese. It was in such moments of subjective 'breakthrough', experienced as an immanence with the foundational violence of capitalist society, that Weatherman found a kind of revelatory truth, one that marked the 'exemplary' position of the organisation in pushing beyond what they saw as the left's fear-bound and half-hearted opposition that served to pre-empt its own defeat.[26] Something of the orientation of the gut check - or its extreme variant, the 'death trip' - is evident in Ono's account of the Days of Rage:

> We frankly told people that, while a massacre was highly unlikely, we expected the actions to be very, very heavy, that hundreds of people might well be arrested and/or hurt, and, finally, that a few people might get killed. We argued that twenty white people (one per cent of the projected minimum) getting killed while fighting hard against imperialist targets would not be a defeat, but a political victory …[27]

Militancy also plays out through linguistic and symbolic form. As I noted above, for Guattari the signifying regime of Bolshevism is characterised by the transformation of the situated statements of central figures and organisational bodies into dogma and stereotypical formulae, whose repetition as refrains of the organisation function as dominant utterances to construct a field of authority and police divergence. It is a phenomenon clearly evident in Ayers's assessment: 'We began to speak mostly in proverbs from Che or Ho. Soon all we heard in the collectives was an echo'.[28] The reduction of political language to dogma is aided by, and contributes to, the relation that the militant diagram draws between theory and action. It is on this axis that the passional semiotic can take hold, a semiotic that is 'active rather than ideational', functioning 'more as effort or action than imagination'.[29] Rather than critical reflection and conceptual production being seen as a constitutive part of practical engagement with the world, struggle tends to be presented in a dichotomous relation to thought - 'Mere words … mere ideas'.[30] The possibility of struggle informed by and inflected through thought is thus passed by in favour of an affirmation of the importance of 'doing something'. But once this division is established, language and theory (in the mode of cliché and dogma) can now flip over to the other side of the dichotomy to circulate in a reductive echolalia as so many postulates or 'concise formulae' in the intensification of struggle.[31]

Deleuze and Guattari are attentive here to the place of the word and a certain monotheism of the book - 'the strangest cult' - in the postsignifying regime of signs, as the book becomes the body of passion, extracted from its outside, elevated from critique, and entwined with subjective flight.[32] This militant trait is most apparent in the Cultural Revolution, where 'Mao Zedong

the Personal Journal of a Revolutionary Woman, Garden City NY, Doubleday and Company, 1975, pp94, 96.

22. Bill Ayers, Fugitive Days: A Memoir, Boston, Beacon Press, 2001, p154.

23. It is clear that feminism had a complex and important presence in the organisation and that the 1970s guerrilla more widely had a strong feminist component - fascinating on this point are the interviews with female members of the Red Brigades conducted by Alison Jamieson, 'Mafiosi and Terrorists: Italian Women in Violent Organizations', SAIS Review, 20, 2 (2000), pp51-64. My argument is that the militant diagram articulates feminist and other political and cultural elements in a manner that tends to further its own imperatives, albeit that these elements so articulated will also have progressive effects for women in militant groups and on the margins of core militant functions.

24. Stern op. cit., p114.

25. Ibid., p197.

26. Ono op. cit., p254.

27. Ibid., p251

28. Ayers, op.cit., p156.

MAO ZHU XI SHI WO MEN XIN ZHONG DE HONG TAI YANG

Figure 1. 'Chairman Mao is the Red Sun of Our Hearts', 1966 Chinese poster

Thought' - articulated as a cosmic truth and embodied most characteristically in the 'Little Red Book' of quotations - had a clear function as immortal substance, nourishment, and energiser of a passional struggle that was to transcend individual mortality. In the words of a 1966 People's Liberation Army newspaper, 'The thought of Mao Tse-tung is the sun in our heart, is the root of our life, is the source of all our strength. Through this, man becomes unselfish, daring, intelligent, able to do everything; he is not conquered by any difficulty and can conquer every enemy' (see Figure 1).[33]

Weatherman was of course a rather different entity from the Cultural Revolution, and constructed little of the latter's highly complex vectoral semiotic components. Nonetheless, the organisation was keenly aware of the militant power of words, even if the language now seems only shrill and bombastic. Jeremy Varon draws attention to this aspect of Weatherman, suggesting that: 'Its crude talk of vilifying "pig Amerika", triumphant slogans, and speeches like those made at the Days of Rage all aimed at strengthening the resolve of its members to use militant action to accomplish what words alone could not'.[34] Moreover, he argues that Weatherman text and image - in particular its aesthetic forms of collage and cartoon - worked to 'de-realize', and so accelerate, the group's confrontation with the state.

This mode of militant semiotics, then, is not confined to words, but subtends gesture, tone and image. As Guattari argues, 'It's a whole axiomatics, down to the phonological level - the way of articulating certain words, the gesture that accompanies them'.[35] It is thus possible to perceive the militant semiotic of Weatherman in operation not only within, for instance, Bernardine Dohrn's infamous invocation of the Tate-LaBianca murders by the Manson gang - 'Dig it; first they killed those pigs, then they ate dinner in the room with them, then they shoved a fork into pig Tate's stomach. Wild!'[36] - but also in the deployment of images of Ho Chi Minh and the North Vietnamese flag, the posture held at the rostrum, the hard-hat worn at militant actions and disseminated as an iconic image of Weatherman's extremism - even, if one allows for unintended co-production with the

29. Deleuze and Guattari op. cit., pp124, 120.

30. Ono, cited in Varon op. cit., p89.

31. Deleuze and Guattari op. cit., p120.

32. Op. cit., p127.

33. Cited in Robert Jay Lifton, *Revolutionary Immortality: Mao Tse-tung and the Chinese*

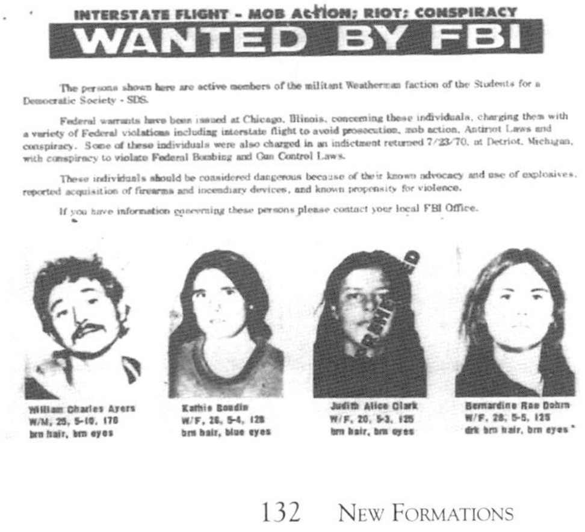

INTERSTATE FLIGHT - MOB ACTION; RIOT; CONSPIRACY

WANTED BY FBI

The persons shown here are active members of the militant Weatherman faction of the Students for a Democratic Society - SDS.

Federal warrants have been issued at Chicago, Illinois, concerning these individuals, charging them with a variety of Federal violations including interstate flight to avoid prosecution, mob action, Antiriot Laws and conspiracy. Some of these individuals were also charged in an indictment returned 7/23/70, at Detroit, Michigan, with conspiracy to violate Federal Bombing and Gun Control Laws.

These individuals should be considered dangerous because of their known advocacy and use of explosives, reported acquisition of firearms and incendiary devices, and known propensity for violence.

If you have information concerning these persons please contact your local FBI Office.

William Charles Ayers
W/M, 25, 5-10, 170
brn hair, brn eyes

Kathie Boudin
W/F, 26, 5-4, 125
brn hair, blue eyes

Judith Alice Clark
W/F, 26, 5-3, 125
brn hair, brn eyes

Bernardine Rae Dohrn
W/F, 28, 5-5, 125
drk brn hair, brn eyes

Figure 2. Quarter section of an FBI Weatherman poster

FBI, in the faciality (the field of eyes like so many passional black holes[37]) of the widely distributed 'Wanted' posters (see Figure 2).

It is on this plane of sign and image that the seductive aspect of a militant group like Weatherman is most manifest in wider environments. The composition and circulation of images, styles, sentiments and gestures is certainly a key element in the affective texture of all political milieux. In this context, and drawing a relation to the US group that was most influential on Weatherman and its self-representation, Guattari's comments on Genet's account in *Prisoner of Love* of the 'image function' of the Black Panther Party are instructive.[38] In Guattari's reading, the style and comportment of the Panthers created a rich enunciative texture and psychic formation that had especial generative power for black communities in politicising cultural and phenotypical traits, and in developing an experimental image and practice - myths as 'collective operators' - of black resistance and cultural expression, whilst simultaneously haunting and disquieting majority Whiteness (Figure 3). Though of considerably less significance than the BPP, and working with a rather different repertoire of styles and stratifications, the image function of Weatherman (the 'Weather-myth' as it was known) also worked to compose an imaginary and affective field of resistance to US imperialism - and one patterned and inflected by a wider pop- and counter-cultural set of forms and vocabularies - that could have been constitutive of progressive political effects beyond those determined by Weatherman's particular practice.

Cultural Revolution, Harmondsworth, Penguin Books, 1970, p72.

34. Op. cit., p89.

35. Op. cit. 1995, p58.

36. Dohrn, cited in Varon op. cit., p160.

37. Deleuze and Guattari, op. cit., pp167-91.

38. Op. cit., 1996, pp218-30.

Figure 3. Kathleen Cleaver and other Black Panthers in the office of the Prosecution against Huey P. Newton, 1968 © Bancroft Library, University of California.

In raising this possibility, however, it is important to be attentive to the way such images can produce a spectacle of revolution that is easily commodified by - or co-produced with - news media and culture industries, and consumed in the politically unproductive manner of an imaginary identification with an icon of resistance. This would seem to have been a prominent feature of the cultural appreciation of the 1970s guerrilla, whether as an alienable unit of consumer style in the 'Prada-Meinhof' mode or, as Bruce LaBruce irreverently dramatises in the queer porn film *The Raspberry Reich*, a repertoire of radical postures (Figure 4). Whilst it is possible to unsettle or exceed spectacular forms of circulation and consumption - media modulation is certainly more complex than a simple game of resistance and recuperation - one still needs to be careful that the affective charge that may emerge from engagement with these images does not reproduce the militant moods and functions latent in them; even in the existential richness and political intensity of the Panthers' iconography there was interwoven a rather suspect militarised and patriarchal image of militancy.[39]

39. James Carr, *BAD: The Autobiography of James Carr*, London, Pelagian Press, 1975; Erika Doss "'Revolutionary Art Is a Tool for Liberation": Emory Douglas and Protest Aesthetics at the *Black Panther*', in Kathleen Cleaver and George Katsiaficas (eds), *Liberation, Imagination, and the Black Panther Party*, London, Routledge, 2001.

Figure 4. Bruce LaBruce, The Raspberry Reich, *2004 © Peccadillo Pictures/Jürgen*

Bruning Filmproduktion

It is a central paradox of militancy that as an organisation constitutes itself as a unified body it tends to become closed to the outside, to the non-militant, those who would be the basis of any mass movement. Indeed, to the degree that the militant body conceives of itself as having discovered the correct revolutionary principle and establishes its centre of activity on adherence to this principle, it has a tendency to develop hostility to those who fall short of its standard. Weatherman resolved this paradox by investing revolutionary agency in the anti-imperialist struggles of the global South, most prominently that of the Vietcong, and the movements of black revolutionary struggle in 'the internal colony', especially the Black Panther Party. In this arena of agency, the substitution of Weatherman's own exemplary action for a domestic white working-class movement freed it up to exist in splendid isolation and in contempt for the mass of white America.[40]

Ultimately cut off from the possibility of engaging with wider social strata by these techniques, Weatherman was driven into the logical extension of an intensified militancy closed in upon itself, and developed 'the politics of full alienation' (as one member put it to Stern, in the affirmative) in the movement to a clandestine, underground organisation: 'Going underground was not just a wild gambit for me. It was all that was left before death'.[41] Ayers characterises the build up to this phase of the organisation in a fashion that foregrounds the self-devouring tendencies of militant passion (albeit in a reflection coloured by the New York townhouse bombing[42] that was to act as something of a break in Weatherman's militant line of flight):

> It was fanatical obedience, we militant nonconformists suddenly tripping over one another to be exactly alike, following the sticky rules of congealed idealism. I cannot reproduce the stifling atmosphere that overpowered us. Events came together with the gentleness of an impending train wreck, and there was the sad sensation of waiting for impact.[43]

CONTOURS OF AN A-MILITANT DIAGRAM

In order to approach the possibility of a political practice beyond militancy I want in the remainder of this paper to consider some initial contours of an a-militant diagram, or dispersive ecology of composition. To do this I will confine the discussion to the relation between the political group and that which lies outside it, what might be known by militant assemblages as 'the masses' - as Guattari implies, it is on this axis that the question of an 'other machine' beyond that of the militant should be posed.[44] It is instructive to address this question through Marx's problematic of the party.

Given the dominant twentieth-century image of political Marxism, *The Manifesto of the Communist Party* has very little to do with the kind of party one might expect. It sets up a 'Manifesto of the party itself' to counter the bourgeois 'nursery tale of the Spectre of Communism', but the party is not announced as a distinct (much less, timeless) organisational entity:

> The Communists do not form a separate party opposed to other working-class parties.
> They have no interests separate and apart from those of the proletariat as a whole.
> They do not set up any sectarian principles of their own, by which to shape and mould the proletarian movement.

40. Varon op. cit., pp93, 166.

41. Stern op. cit., p240.

42. Three members of Weatherman were killed in March 1970 when bombs they were preparing accidentally detonated, completely destroying a town house in Greenwich Village. These were the only deaths caused by Weatherman, though the devices being constructed included nail bombs intended for a noncommissioned officers' dance. A compelling first hand account of the explosion and the build-up to it can be found in Wilkerson op. cit., p336-348.

43. Op. cit., p154.

44. Op. cit., 1984, p190.

The Communists are distinguished from the other working-class parties by this only:

1. In the national struggles of the proletarians of the different countries, they point out and bring to the front the common interests of the entire proletariat, independently of all nationality.

2. In the various stages of development which the struggle of the working class against the bourgeoisie has to pass through, they always and everywhere represent the interests of the movement as a whole.[45]

45. Karl Marx and Friedrich Engels, *The Revolutions of 1848: Political Writings Volume 1*, ed. D. Fernbach, Harmondsworth, Penguin, 1973, pp79, 98.

If not an organisational entity, the party instead suggests a *diagram* of composition, a virtual set of parameters and orientations, and one that is immanent to 'the proletariat as a whole'. Though the party seeks to forward certain modes of thought and community - notably, internationalism and the critique of capital - Marx is at pains to stress that it is not a concentrative articulation, but a dispersive one. The party is stretched across the social, dependent upon social forces and struggles for its existence or its substance, and, in an anticipatory and precarious fashion, oriented toward social contingencies and events. As Alain Badiou argues - if to use his work in this context is not to deform it too far - not only is it the case that 'For the Marx of 1848, that which is named "party" has no form of bond even in the institutional sense', but 'the real characteristic of the party is not its firmness, but its porosity to the event, its dispersive flexibility in the face of unforeseeable circumstances'.[46] To this should be added that, inasmuch as the party is immanent to the manifold arrangements of capitalist social production, a production that is fully machinic ('this automaton consisting of numerous mechanical and intellectual organs'), it poses a terrain of alliance and event that exceeds an abstract humanity.[47]

46. Alain Badiou, 'Politics Unbound', in *Metapolitics*, J. Barker (trans.), London, Verso, 2005, pp74, 75.

47. Karl Marx, *Grundrisse: Foundations of the Critique of Political Economy (Rough Draft)*, M. Nicolaus (trans.), Harmondsworth, Penguin, 1973, p692.

Given the precarious and anticipatory orientation of the party, there is considerable insight in Jacques Rancière's argument that Marx's party - for all its universality - is directed not toward unity but *division*, that 'first of all the purpose of a party is not to unite but divide'.[48] In Rancière's reading of Marx, this division names the communist disruption of the modes of identity and security associated with the workers' movement; one could say that it is the effect of the proletariat as its own overcoming on the workers' movement as identity.[49] Yet Rancière reduces this process of disruption to a mechanism of interminable deferral on Marx's part, a mechanism that induces Marx's dissolution of the Communist League and thereafter sets up the science of capital, and the writing of its book, as the proxy of the proletariat forever postponed. In making 'division' function in Marx as a self-separation from politics, Rancière both elides the fundamental innovation of Marx's dispersive understanding of the party and ignores the dynamic and intensive facets of its division in the practical critique of authoritarian and anti-proletarian organisational practice - vis-à-vis, for instance, the persistence of Freemasonry and the secret society in the workers' movement, Jacobin models of dictatorship by enlightened minority, utopian efforts to bypass

48. Jacques Rancière, *The Philosopher and His Poor*, J. Drury, C. Oster, and A. Parker (trans.), London, Duke University Press, 2003, p86.

49. Nicholas Thoburn, *Deleuze, Marx and Politics*, London, Routledge, 2003, Ch3.

the working class, Bakuninist 'invisible dictatorship', and so on.

Jacques Camatte and Gianni Collu's 1969 open letter 'On Organization' (which marked the withdrawal of the group around the journal *Invariance* from the post-'68 groupuscule milieu and their dissolution as an organised body) approaches Marx's party in a more productive fashion than Rancière.[50] In the left communist tradition with which Camatte is associated, the variable nature of struggle over time and the complexity of forces and problems that make up any historical conjuncture are such that there is no necessary continuity of a 'formal' party.[51] Indeed, in times when agitation is on the wane, attempts to constitute revolutionary organisations become counterproductive, not least because they substitute organisational coherence and continuity for diffuse social struggle as the object of communist politics (this, as part of maintaining global conditions conducive for the survival of the Soviet economy, having been a key effect of the Communist Party on the international stage). As such, in François Martin's assessment, 'The dissolution of the organizational forms which are created by the movement, and which disappear when the movement ends, does not reflect the weakness of the movement, but rather its strength'.[52]

Camatte and Collu extend this position to argue that all radical organisations tend toward a counter-revolutionary, 'racket' form, functioning as anti-inventive points of attraction and solidification in social environments. In a critique that bears comparison with Guattari's account of Bolshevism, Camatte and Collu argue that the radical group is the political correlate of the modern business organisation, orchestrating patterns of identity and investment appropriate to a capitalism that - in what is an early use of the concept of 'real subsumption' - has disarticulated sociality from traditional forms of community and identity and incorporated the workers' movement in its own dynamic. Operating through a foundational and ever-renewed demarcation between interior and exterior, the group coheres through the attraction points of theoretical or activist standpoint and key members (themselves constituted as such through intellectual sophistication, militant commitment or charismatic personality), and the motive forces of membership prestige, competition for recognition and fear of exclusion. The effect is to reproduce in militants the psychological dependencies, hierarchies and competitive traits of the wider society, constitute an homogeneous formation based on the equivalence of its members to the particular element that defines it, and mark a delimiting separation from - and, ultimately, a hostility to - the open manifold of social relations and struggles, precisely that which should be the milieu of inventive communist politics. Importantly, the problem is not at all one of the relative formality of the group; these tendencies may well be found at the extreme in 'unstructured' aggregations or 'disorganisations', where informal inter-subjective relations take primacy.[53]

Some of these aspects of militant group-formation have been seen above in Weatherman, but the pertinent point here is the way Camatte and Collu seek to develop a way out from the organisation. In opposition to the centripetal dynamics of the group-form and its militant subjective correlate, Camatte and

50. Jacques Camatte and Gianni Collu, 'On Organization', Edizioni International (trans.), in Jacques Camatte, *This World We Must Leave and Other Essays*, A. Trotter (ed.), New York, Autonomedia, 1995, pp19-38.

51. See Karl Marx, 'Marx to Ferdinand Freiligrath, February 29 1860', n.d., www.marxists.org/archive/marx/works/1860/letters/60_02_29.htm, where against the accusation of 'inactivity' and 'doctrinaire indifference' he positively evaluates his non-involvement in political associations in the period after the collapse of the Communist League; and Jacques Camatte, *Origin and Function of the Party Form*, n.d., www.geocities.com/Cordobakaf/camatte_origins.html

52. In Gilles Dauvé and François Martin, *The Eclipse and Re-emergence of the Communist Movement* (revised edition), London, Antagonism Press, n.d., p57.

53. Jo Freeman, *The Tyranny of Structurelessness*, London, Anarchist Workers Association, n.d.;, Andrew X, 'Give Up Activism', *Reflections on June 18*, no publisher given, 1999; J. J. King, 'The Packet Gang', *Mute* 27, 2004, www.metamute.com/look/article.tpl?IdLanguage=1&IdPublication=1&NrIssue=27&NrSection=10&NrArticle=962

Collu assert that communist practice is necessarily characterised by a refusal of all group activity, a kind of warding-off of the dominant social tendency toward group formation. This critique of the group is not followed with an assertion of individual subjectivity - a locus of composition no less able to accrue prestige and authority in opposition to dispersive social struggle. Indeed, the critique of the group has a corresponding *subjective* unworking in the 'revolutionary anonymity' that Camatte and Collu borrow from Amadeo Bordiga, as signalled by their text's epigraph from Marx: 'Both of us scoff at being popular. Among other things our disgust at any personality cult is evidence of this ... When Engels and I first joined the secret society of communists, we did it on the condition *sine qua non* that they repeal all statutes that would be favourable to a cult of authority.'[54] In place of the group and the individual, the basis of composition instead becomes an immanence with social forces: 'The revolutionary must not identify himself [sic] with a group but recognize himself in a theory that does not depend on a group or on a review, because it is the expression of an existing class struggle.'[55]

Camatte and Collu's anti-voluntarist subtraction of agency from communist minorities is an intriguing and important articulation of Marx's dispersive and disruptive party. But as it plays out in line with a common dilemma for left communist groupings - whose opposition to the Leninist party can result in a reluctance to engage in any form of intervention for fear of directly or indirectly introducing anti-inventive dynamics and leadership models into proletarian formations[56] - it offers only a partial solution to the problem of militancy. Outside a period of agitation, Camatte and Collu leave communist minorities in a rather anaemic position, without a positive conception of the field of political composition other than the development of theory and the maintenance of a small network of informal relations between those engaged in similar work.

Deleuze and Guattari's approach to the question of the group and its outside shares much with that of Camatte and Collu, not least in their own 'involuntarism' - a crucial mechanism in opening a breach with received political practice, identity and authority, and orienting toward the event.[57] But out of this shared problematic emerges a more productive sense of the terrain of a-militant composition. In his preface to *Anti-Oedipus* Foucault rightly draws attention to the way the book invited a practical critique of militant organisations and subjectivities:

I would say that *Anti-Oedipus* (may its authors forgive me) is a book of ethics, the first book of ethics to be written in France in quite a long time (perhaps that explains why its success was not limited to a particular 'readership': being anti-oedipal has become a life style, a way of thinking and living). How does one keep from being fascist, even (especially) when one believes oneself to be a revolutionary militant?[58]

Unlike Camatte and Collu, however, this practical critique of militancy is characterised not by a withdrawal from groups as such. It initially takes the

54. Cited in Camatte and Collu op. cit., p20.

55. Ibid., pp32-3.

56. Dauvé and Martin, op. cit., p63-76.

57. Jérémie Valentin, 'Gilles Deleuze's Political Posture', C. V. Boundas and S. Lamble (trans.), in C. V. Boundas (ed.), *Deleuze and Philosophy*, Edinburgh, Edinburgh University Press, 2006; Ian Buchanan and Nicholas Thoburn, 'Introduction', op. cit.

58. In Gilles Deleuze and Félix Guattari, *Anti-Oedipus: Capitalism and Schizophrenia Volume 1*, R. Hurley, M. Seem and H. R. Lane (trans.), London, Athlone, 1983, pxii.

form of an analytic of groups and a certain affirmation of the 'subject group' as a mode of political composition oriented toward innovative collective composition and enunciation, and open to its outside and the possibility of its own death - in contrast to the 'subjected group', cut off from the world and fixated on its own self-preservation.[59] Yet this formulation, useful though it is in the analysis of group dynamics, is perhaps still too caught up with activist patterns of collectivity and voluntarism. As Deleuze and Guattari's project unfolds, the model of the subject group thus loses prominence in favour of an opening of perception to, and critical engagement with, the multiplicity of groups - or, in Deleuze and Guattari's terms, assemblages or arrangements - which compose any situation, following their notion that 'we are all groupuscules'. Guattari thus states in a 1980 interview:

> At one time I came up with the idea of the 'subject-group'. I contrasted these with 'subjected groups' in an attempt to define modes of intervention which I described as micro-political. I've changed my mind: there are no subject-groups, but arrangements of enunciation, of subjectivization, pragmatic arrangements which do not coincide with circumscribed groups. These arrangements can involve individuals but also ways of seeing the world, emotional systems, conceptual machines, memory devices, economic, social components, elements of all kinds.[60]

In this conception there is a clear disarticulation of political practice from the construction of coherent collective subjectivity, or a strong critique of groups, but in a fashion that bypasses the anti-group position with an orientation toward the discontinuous and multi-layered arrangements that traverse and compose social - or, indeed, planetary - life. Crucially, the associated political articulations - 'cartographies' or 'ecologies' in Guattari's later writings - are machinic in nature. They include, and may be instigated by, material and immaterial objects - technological apparatus, medias, city-environments, images, economic instruments, sonorous fields, landscapes, aesthetic artefacts - as much as human bodies, subjective dispositions and cognitive and affective refrains. As such, they are open to political analysis, intervention and modulation through tactical, sensual, linguistic, technical, organisational, architectural and conceptual repertoires. It would certainly be a mistake to see this ecological orientation as a retreat from a passional practice - if *Anti-Oedipus* suggests an antifascist ethics, *A Thousand Plateaus* is precisely concerned with the exploration of modes and techniques of passional composition, often of a most experimental and liminal kind. This is a passion, however, that arises not in a subjective monomania carved off from its outside, but from situated problematics that are characterised by a deferral of subjective interiority and a dispersive opening to the social multiplicity and its virtual potential. This is how one can understand Deleuze and Guattari's affirmation of 'becoming imperceptible' - of drawing the world on oneself and oneself on the world - as a political figure; it is not a sublime end-point of spiritual inaction, but the immanent kernel of a-militant political composition.[61]

59. Gilles Deleuze, 'Three Group-Related Problems', in *Desert Islands and Other Texts 1953-1974*, D. Lapoujade (ed.), M. Taormina (trans.), New York, Semiotext(e), 2004, pp193-203.

60. Félix Guattari, *Soft Subversions*, S. Lotringer (ed.), D. L. Sweet and C. Wiener (trans.), New York, Semiotext(e), 1996, pp227-8.

61. I have approached some of the many subsequent questions about the nature of such composition - not least with regard to the place of capital - through the figure of 'minor politics' in Nicholas Thoburn, op. cit., 2003, and 'The Hobo Anomalous: Class, Minorities and Political Invention in the Industrial Workers of the World', *Social Movement Studies* 2, 1 (2003), 61-84.

62. Yann Moulier, 'Introduction', P. Hurd (trans.), in Antoinio Negri, *The Politics of Subversion: A Manifesto for the Twenty-First Century*, Cambridge, Polity Press, 1989; Bureau d'Études, 'Resymbolising Machines: Art after Oyvind Fahlström', B. Holmes (trans.), *Third Text* 18, 6 (2004), pp609-16.

63. Colectivo Situaciones, 'Something More on Research Militancy', S. Touza and N. Holdren (trans.), *Ephemera: Theory and Politics in Organization* 5, 4 (2005), pp602-14.

Given the prominence in twentieth-century political culture of visual images of the heroic militant, it is important to note that aspects of this ecological or cartographic approach can also be seen in the aesthetic expressions of political bodies - from the anecdote that the orientations of Italian *Operaismo* were such that the bedroom walls of activists saw the substitution of diagrammatic maps of the FIAT Mirafiori plant for the iconic images of Mao and Che Guevara, to Bureau d'Études who, mindful of the dangers of the conventional signs of militant aggregation such as the flag and the raised fist, symmetrical with the images of national sovereignty as they can be, have developed a political and pedagogical ecology routed through the aesthetic and cognitive object of the map (Figure 5).[62]

The exploration of some of these themes is also evident in contemporary problematisation of activist practice. A most striking instance is the Argentinean grouping Colectivo Situaciones, whose figure of 'militant research' evokes a knowledge/practice that works without subject or object through an immanent appreciation of encounters, problems and situations, and in a fashion that is particularly attentive to the dangers of transcendent models of political subjectivity and communication.[63] The problematic of a dispersive political practice is raised too in the Luther Blissett and Wu Ming projects, concerned as these experiments in the 'multiple name' have been with a disarticulation of

Figure 5. Bureau d'Études 'Infowar/psychic war', utangente.free.fr

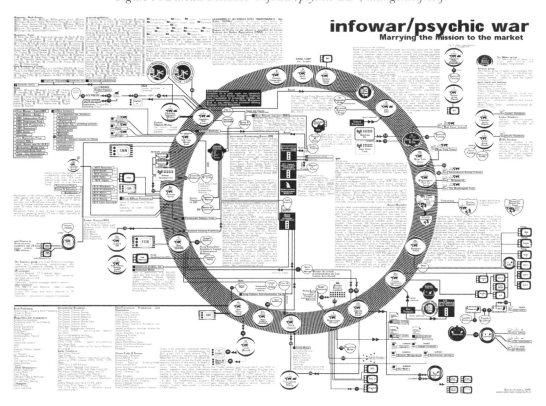

seduction, style and mythopoesis from the author-function and its associated regimes of property and authority - something of a left communist erasure of militant faciality (Figure 6). But these formations lead to questions of composition that are best approached through an appreciation of their particularity, and that move beyond the specific focus of this paper, the critique of the militant.

Figure 6. Wu Ming's 'official portrait' 2001-2008, Creative Commons License, en.wikipedia.org/wiki/Wu_Ming

CONCLUSION

One can discern in Deleuze and Guattari's work an identification of, and a response to, the problem of militant subjectivity. This response posits a deterritorialisation of the self that develops not from a concentration in militant passion (as one finds in Weatherman) or a surrender to revolutionary inaction (the danger that haunts Camatte's critique of organisation), but from the condition of being stretched across the social in a diffusion and critical involution in the technical, aesthetic, semiotic, economic, affective relations of the world. In resonance with Marx's understanding of the party, this suggests not a serene unanimity but a complex, intensive, and open plane of composition. The party here is a field of intervention in social relations that undoes identity, not an identity carved off against social relations.

This is not, of course, an actualised politics or programme; it is better seen as the first principle of an a-militant, communist diagram. The interventions, aggregations, functions and expressions that animate and enrich this diagram may well configure environments of a directly insurrectionary nature, but

64. Karl Marx and Friedrich Engels, *Collected Works Volume 10: 1849-1951*, London, Lawrence and Wishart, 1978, p318.

they would be so as the collective and manifold problematisation of social relations and events, not as the invention of militant organisations acting like 'alchemists of the revolution'.[64] For it is in the multiple and diffuse social arrangements and lines of flight that political change emerges and with which political formations - in their 'dispersive flexibility' - need to maintain an intimate and subtle relation if they are not to fall into the calcified self-assurance of militant subjectivity. Deleuze's warning about the danger of marginality has pertinence here too:

> It is not the marginals who create the lines; they install themselves on these lines and make them their property, and this is fine when they have that strange modesty of men [sic] of the line, the prudence of the experimenter, but it is a disaster when they slip into the black hole from which they no longer utter anything but the micro-fascist speech of their dependency and their giddiness: 'We are the avant-garde', 'We are the marginals.'[65]

65. In Gilles Deleuze and Claire Parnet, *Dialogues*, H. Tomlinson and B. Habberjam (trans.), London, Athlone, 1987, p139.

Deleuzian Politics?
A Roundtable Discussion

Éric Alliez, Claire Colebrook, Peter Hallward, Nicholas Thoburn, Jeremy Gilbert (chair)

Nick and Jeremy circulated some general questions to think about before the discussion, which particularly focused on the surprising fact that many casual commentators, and indeed, some self-styled 'Deleuzians', seemed to regard Deleuzian philosophy as wholly compatible with an embrace of market capitalism and its tendency to celebrate the ephemeral, the individual, the hyper-mobile, the infantile; while others seemed to think of Deleuze as a wholly apolitical or even anti-political thinker, mired in Nietzschean aristocratic elitism, ineffectual mysticism, or old-fashioned individualism. As such, the first question touched on the relationship of Deleuze and Guattari to Marx.

VIRTUAL MARXISM?

Jeremy: So - our first question. One of the big questions we want to discuss is 'what do we make of Manuel DeLanda's assessment that Marxism is Deleuze's and Guattari's "little Oedipus"?' Nick - you don't agree with that, I think.

Nick: There are interesting questions about why Deleuze and Guattari declare themselves to be Marxists: it's not straightforward, and I think this declaration has a number of functions in their work. Some of these would seem to amount to a deliberate provocation in the face of neoliberal consensus, 'Marx' being a contentious name to invoke at what was a time of general unpopularity for Marxism. But it is very clear to me that the relationship to Marxism is a point of creative tension, an opening, a disruption in their work rather than a limiting, 'Oedipal' factor (which is DeLanda's claim). So I see their Marxism as dynamic - a kind of 'virtual Marx', as Éric has put it - which propels rather than constrains their system.

And certainly whilst they declared themselves to be Marxists they also problematise Marxism quite regularly, as a narrative of development and as a potentially constraining identity-form. Nonetheless, what seems to me really clear is that *Anti-Oedipus*, at least, is completely traversed by Marx and Marxism. The conjunction of free labour and undetermined wealth; the engineering of social relations through money; the tendency of the rate of profit to fall; the Asiatic mode of production: these are all fundamentally important concepts to their work. So it would be very difficult to just extract Marxism from Deleuze and Guattari, as DeLanda suggests one can do. It appears that the problem with capitalism for DeLanda is simply one of monopoly: so 'small is beautiful', and all one needs to do is to abstract labour relations from monopoly formations, and that solves the problem that Deleuze and Guattari call 'capital'.

Jeremy: DeLanda's formulation is based on Braudel's distinction between 'markets' and 'anti-markets', and the consequent claim that capitalism is only defined by 'anti-market' monopoly institutions, rather than by the market as such.

Nick: Yes, so the whole analysis of abstract labour or the commodity form just vanishes.

Peter: The way you've put it - describing the reference to Marxism as a kind of disruptive, liberating, opening-up kind of dynamic in their work - is already for me an indication of the problem. That there are Marxist elements in *Anti-Oedipus*, or in fact in much of Deleuze's work and Deleuze's and Guattari's work, is clear. But if you think about the usual, conventional way of using Marx, in someone like Sartre for instance - one of the last philosophers who was able to talk meaningfully about politics in a way that exceeded the limits of academic philosophy - he talks about Marxism in the 1950s as a way to 'get a grip on history', and it informed the work that he was doing on Algeria, and a few other places, at the time. A text like Sartre's 'Colonialism is a System' is designed precisely to get a grip on the issue, to analyse it strategically. Such analysis can enable something like a collective determination to take shape in a such a way that it can have a strategic impact and change that situation. It's all about unifying, solidifying, strengthening, focusing - themes opposed to the general logic of *Anti-Oedipus*. In that book the emphasis, it seems to me, is on escape, deterritorialisation, disruption, breaking apart, getting out, scrambling the codes. The distinctive contribution of schizoanalysis to a logic of capital concerns how to get out of it, to reach this point where the body without organs is presented as a kind of apocalyptic explosion of any form of limit, where the decoded flows free to the end of the world, etc. There I think people who take some more conventional point of reference from Marx would be confused. They would think: 'what is this for?'

Nick: The proletariat is itself the party of its own abolition, according to Marx, so these processes of deterritorialisation and destruction are immanent to his own concepts - they're not a Deleuzian anomaly. I think there's a danger of presenting Marx as offering an *identity* to the proletariat, facing-off with the bourgeoisie, when that's not what is going on in this concept that is intimately concerned with deterritorialisation. But, also, it seems to me that Deleuze and Guattari's real importance is in talking about *composition*. *A Thousand Plateaus* is full of descriptions of processes and techniques of expression, composition, consistency. So deterritorialisation is certainly part of that, but it's not affirmed *in itself*: that would be chaos, and that isn't what they're about.

Peter: I think it *is* affirmed in there …

Claire: The key point that you make there is in your reference to 'expression', because if you look at that remark of DeLanda's when he says that Marx is their 'little Oedipus', I am assuming he means that that's the point of unthinking fixation in their work: that that's the thing that they didn't think through, that that's the bit which they swallowed as dogma.

Now, he has to see it that way because he wants a simple materialism with a simple positivism of relations, instead of thinking about the fact that one of the ways of thinking about Marx philosophically is through the idea of the generation of the immaterial from the material, which is what you're talking about if you're talking about 'expression'. Part of what you're talking about if you are talking about collectives and collectives of bodies and so on, is the question of how one thinks of oneself as a member, or how one thinks of oneself as an individual.

I think that one way of looking at Deleuze and Guattari's language of 'smashing codes', liberation, 'making oneself imperceptible', is as negative, as just ruining big categories. But the positive way of reading them, in line with the legacy that comes from Marxism, is to think about these issues in terms of a logic of expression; which is to say, in terms of the emergence of the immaterial from the material and in terms of processes of individuation. This is the whole question of how one thinks of oneself as a being, without identity politics, or without individualist politics. It's about how one individuates.

So I think one way to think about the positive Marxist legacy, not just in the *Anti-Oedipus* project but in everything they do, is to think of it in terms of the emergence of the immaterial, the emergence of sense, the emergence of the virtual: which, they say, for good or for ill, is directly political. And that's Marxist isn't it? Marxism is about the material emergence of the immaterial, the material conditions of expression. I think they do have little Oedipuses; I think there are bits in the corpus that are unthought through and that are swallowed rather religiously: but possibly the Marxism is the *least* indigested.

Éric: I think that this quotation from Manuel Delanda is a perfect shifter, because it immediately shows the condition not only for a 'neoliberal Deleuze' but for an apolitical (i.e. social-democrat) or anti-political (out of this world) Deleuze as a short-circuit which attacks and denies the hard political core of the ontological project affirmed with Guattari, i.e. a *revolutionary* (in all the possible senses of the word) political ontology.

Coming back to *Anti-Oedipus*, let me read this statement of Deleuze about Marx because it goes right to the point and expresses the whole economy of this book provocatively conceived as a book of 'political philosophy' *because construction commands expression*: 'What is very interesting in Marx is his analysis of capitalism as an imminent system that is constantly overcoming its own limitations and then coming up against them once more in a broader form, because its fundamental limit is capital itself.'

I don't want to comment on it against DeLanda (where machinic constructions are reduced to the latest expressions of the theory of complexity), but rather, forgetting DeLanda for a moment, to use it to underline the paradoxical situation with which we are apparently confronted in the UK, and more generally in the anglo-american world, where a philosophy that has been one of the very few that took seriously the question of politics *after the break of '68* - and through an effective historical analysis of the mutations of capitalism developed in a (spinozist) 'Marx beyond Marx' *avant la lettre* - is suspected of being apolitical or, worse, anti-political. This is quite odd coming from these currently extremely powerful philosophies that affirm themselves politically in a systematic anti-Deleuzianism, which is used to assert the most generic 'communism' (un *communisme de principe*), through a commitment to universal of equality that just brackets off any kind of close analysis of the mutations of capitalism.

The second point I want to make comes back to the provisional end of Deleuze and Guattari's trajectory. In *What is philosophy?*, the chapter on 'Geophilosophy' is extremely important because this is where they are synthesising a final materialist definition of philosophy as such. Their idea is, brutally formulated: philosophy is political, it involves a politics of being, to the extent that *it carries the movement of relative deterritorialisations to infinity - but an infinity that takes over from a relative deterritorialisation in a given field.* And it is in this materialist (or wordly) connection that philosophy is able to make absolute the relative deterritorialisation of capital ... In other words, philosophy, philosophy *qua* materialist practice of the concepts inscribing thought into the liberation of the world from its capitalistic regulation, is able to go through, to break through what had been the Marxist correlation between the analysis of capitalism and the anti-Hegelian denial of any internal necessity for philosophy to grasp the real (its 'onanistic' monopoly of thought) ... Following Marx's critique, there is no internal necessity to philosophy for Deleuze (to answer to Peter's Sartrian statement), but (in a Deleuzian Marx beyond Marx) a *contingent* one which *necessarily* poses revolution as the plane of immanence of a thought that opens, critically and affirmatively, the 'Now-here' to the movement of the infinite. At this point, Deleuze and Guattari refer to the construction of the *concept* of capitalism by Marx, and posit that philosophy is this abstract-real thought that can't affirm the materiality of its movement without *being* political philosophy. This is an extraordinarily radical statement that *de facto* retrojects (another Marxian movement!) *this* philosophy *qua* ontology back onto the break with the 'traditional', i.e. classical image of thought accomplished by Deleuze in *Difference and Repetition*. That's why he declares that all he has done since with Guattari is connected with the 'Image of thought' chapter; with the break with this philosophy of truth that supposes that the true concerns solutions in the form of *philosophical propositions capable of serving as answers*. It is this break that relates the liberation of/in the world from its capitalistic reduction/limitation/normativity to the liberation of thought itself: depending on the *direct impulse* produced by what forces us to think, on these problematic encounters which escape 'recognition' and give philosophy the possibility of a *real confrontation* with its true enemies, 'which are quite different from thought'…

Talking about 'Deleuzian politics' involves necessarily this *deterritorialisation of philosophy* which constitutively and 'politically' opens it to the Outside, in the substitution of problematic agencies for theorematic answers: a substitution into which Deleuze and Guattari, in their Geophilosophical chapter, don't hesitate to include Adorno's Negative Dialectic … At this point, it is not surprising, for me and *tout court*, that Peter brings back, *contra Deleuze*, a more *classical* image of thought, which inevitably reasserts the previously-denied centrality of philosophy 'itself'. This *classical* image of thought - maintained in its communicational scope based on a common argumentative sense - is accompanied by a political *bad conscience*, whereas by contrast Marxism is, after all, invested as a war machine against Philosophy, against the limits of philosophy itself …

CAPITALISM and DETERRITORIALISATION

Jeremy: I suppose one of the questions which comes up, with regards to what you guys have just said, is 'how celebratory do we understand Deleuze and Guattari's account of the mutations of capitalism to be?' Because one of the readings - both for and against Deleuze and Guattari - that gets circulated is the one that reads them as essentially celebrating the deterritorialising power of capitalism.

I think this touches on Peter's point in so far as it relates to the question of how far there is a normative dimension to this emphasis on deterritorialisation, the emphasis on freedom, etc. There is one reading of Deleuze and Guattari which argues that there is no normative claim here, and that their emphasis on this deterritorialising dimension of capitalism is merely a *correction* of the philosophical tradition's obsession with stasis. Alternatively, there's another reading which says 'well, at the end of the day, Deleuze and Guattari *are* just celebrating deterritorialisation; and because they celebrate deterritorialisation they must celebrate capitalism, because capitalism is the great deterritorialiser …'

Éric: Well, this 'celebrative' position is just kind of a joke, because you could then say exactly the same thing about Marx. You could say that Marx celebrated capitalist deterrorialisation because in his analysis communism is coming from/out of the deterritorialisation produced by capitalism's decoding of labour and wealth, the antagonism of the productive forces *versus* relations of production, etc. I think that it would not be impossible to show that Deleuze and Guattari's very notion of deterritorialisation as it emerges in *Anti-Oedipus* is really coming directly from a reading of Marx - since it firstly supports a 'universal history' whose contingent movements can only be understood from the new decoding and cooperative necessities of capitalism.

Claire: It comes before that though. The emphasis on deterritorialisation *is* normative to an extent because they see deterritorialisation as immanent not just to capitalism but to life itself. This means that capitalism isn't just an accident that befell us, such that if we had been smarter or better it wouldn't have happened. There is a tendency towards both territorialisation and deterritorialisation in life itself, which is always a positively marked term for Deleuze and Guattari. That means I think the emphasis on deterritorialisation *is* strictly normative. According to their model, biological life only proceeds by differentiating itself and making connections that, as it were, do away with identity; but in order to create new identities. This process is going to create certain political formations.

So then, from this perspective, the problem with capitalism is that it's not 'capitalist' enough, it is not deterritorialising enough, and that's why that quotation about how it comes against its own limit is so important. That's where we find the possibility for analysis. For example, this framework would enable us to consider the political ambivalence of the situation wherein a capitalist organisation moves into an Aboriginal community in outback Australia. The people are completely destitute, and then there is this massive influx of benefit and material goods. But at the same time we see the complete evacuation of anything indigenous that would resist the system. At those points then you don't need a stupid, reactive, anti-capitalism, which would say 'it's capitalism and therefore it's bad'. You don't need a distinction between good and evil. You need a very fine-tuned analysis of the relation between deterritorialisation and reterritorialisation and the ways in which, under conditions of accumulation, it all gets turned back into an axiom of profit, or capital.

Nick: I do think that there are dangers in that notion of pushing capital beyond its limits: which, I agree, is their position at times. The danger is that you then start affirming the market against the state, the market being the deterritorialising pole of capital, and the state being its constraint or limit, its reterritorialisation. That position is evident to some extent in *Anti-Oedipus*, but it drops out of *Thousand Plateaus*, and in *What is Philosophy?* it's gone completely. And you find that the speed of capital in *What is Philosophy?* is actually associated with the banalisation of promotional culture: with a kind of universal equivalence generated by the speeds of communication, which they have no sympathy with at all. So deterritorialisation becomes a much more complex figure: sometimes a kind of stillness, sometimes the speed of thought, and so on. And the specific political articulations of deterritorialisation become much less positively alloyed with the general movement of capital.

Claire: But that's because capitalism is an instance, an example of deterritorialisation, of which it is a tendency: so it exemplifies something, but it's not responsible for it and it doesn't exhaust it. That's the whole point of *A Thousand Plateaus* as different from the *Anti-Oedipus*, because in *Anti-Oedipus*, the historical and political analysis is made in traditionally Marxist terms, telling a story about society and social bodies; whereas in *A Thousand Plateaus* you get on to the stuff about organisms, works of art, cellular systems, and so forth. It all becomes more complicated, and we get to the idea that deterritorialisation *is* in life, which can help us to explain capital but which also means that we can't reduce deterritorialisation as such to the rhythm of capital.

Peter: Just going back a bit to what you said, Éric. It's absolutely true that Marx and Engels are fascinated by the deterritorialising thrust of capitalism: 'all that is solid melts into air', etc. There is a real point of similarity there. The thing is, though, that having made that assessment, what distinguishes the communist movement in the nineteenth century from, say, the anarchist movement, which would agree on that point, is precisely the strategic conclusion that they draw. The communist conclusion is that we need, in response to this situation, an institution, an organisation, direction, and so on: precisely so that the proletariat can indeed dissolve itself as a *class* (within the historical constraints of a class-bound situation) but not as social existence, not as 'emancipated labour'. What is required, from this perspective, is the construction of a disciplined working-class political organisation that would be capable of *winning* the class struggle that takes shape around this time. Later, people will make roughly the same sort of argument in defence of the mobilisation of national liberation movements, for example. Both sorts of organisation emphasise things like discipline, unity, strategic purpose: certainly at the risk of problematic consequences, but the risk is unavoidable. This is the political legacy of Marxism, if you ask me. It's the combination of these two things: an assessment of historical tendencies and economic logics, articulated together with the formulation of political strategy.

What is original and distinctive about Deleuze and Guattari, on the other hand, is that they substitute for something like the mobilisation of the working class, or national liberation movements, things like schizo and nomad. They *do* privilege the movement of 'absolute deterritorialisation', however much they might seem to qualify it by adding that all deterritorialisation is accompanied by forms of reterritorialisation. Their political alternative, if that's the right word, is precisely something that unfolds in what they call infinite speed. It is something like a politics of the nomad which they identify with the deterritorialised *par excellence*, a deterritorialised movement which only reterritorialises on the movement of deterritorialisation itself. That, it seems to me, is what is distinctive and strong in their position. It's not presented as one of several strategic options to choose from, as if here we should do one thing, there we should do another. There *is* a strong teological moment in their thought. They say: this *is* the movement of becomings, for example. They say that the thrust of deterritorialisation goes in a particular direction and that we should follow it, basically. And that I think is politically and strategically problematic.

Éric: Ok - trying to get to the core of the question - I do think that what Peter has just described as the political organisation of the working class corresponds, for me at least, and to a certain extent, to what Foucault calls 'the disciplinary society', wherein one is necessarily caught up in this particular figure of the classic-modern conflict, struggle and war. In this context, historically, forms of political organisation have to follow the social form of organisation of society as such in the most dialectical figure of the class struggle. Now, in brief, if *Anti-Oedipus* tried to answer to the necessity for a new conception of politics which was called for, on the one hand, by 68's world-event, and on the other, already, by the immediate post-68 counter-revolution (which is not at all a 'Restoration'), it is *A Thousand Plateaus* which confronts itself with the emergence of what Deleuze would later call the 'control society' (we can find Foucauldian equivalents from his Collège de France lectures on Neoliberalism). And this is the real explanation for its caution with regard to deterritorialisation - with the way capitalism reterritorialises itself on the most deterritorialised ... Conclusion: *Never believe that a smooth space will suffice to save us*.

In the control society, power no longer operates through enclosure, as in the disciplinary society, but through processes of what Deleuze calls 'modulation' that give an entirely new dynamic to exploitation. So to position oneself as 'Deleuzian' (but I avoid doing this for myself, preferring to think with and from ...) is always to remember, without becoming historicist, the importance of this kind of historical frame and framework for a political ontology of the present. From this perspective, we can't just carry on with the same old forms of political institution, the same modes of working class social organisation, because they no longer correspond to the actual and contemporary form of capitalism and the rising subjectivities that accompany and/or contest it. That's where I come back to the importance of the systematic enquiry into the mutations of capitalism, which is, fundamentally, through the 'machinic' dystopia which they enact, Deleuze and Guattari's central project. For sure, Deleuze and Guattari suggest that we should 'schizophrenise' Marx; but, my gosh, Marx was writing mid-nineteenth century and look at what is going on since then, and above all since 1968!

COLLECTIVITY AND IDENTITY: *BECOMING-X* VS COLLECTIVE SELF-DETERMINATION

Claire: If you think about contemporary politics: all we have to do is move from talking about national liberation movements and workers' movements to looking at some of the most tortured and vexed political situations, such as the relationship between indigenous Australian communities and European settled communities, and we can see that as long as we have a notion of collectivity that's founded on the traditional notion of labour and its organisation, then we will always be necessarily disenfranchising and robbing those people of a potential form of individuation.

This is what this is all about. The key question is how you can take part in some form of collective action without necessarily being identified as or appealing to 'classes' in the old sense. So the 'molecularisation' of politics which Deleuze and Guattari propose is about how to get beyond a situation in which, within a given context of communication, there are things that can't be heard. The question is: how can you have some maximum degree of inclusion with a minimal degree of identification? This is a crucial question if you want a global politics which can allow for notions of contamination, and which can get beyond the limitations of models of politics modelled on opposed pairs of identities: workers vs. capitalists, national liberation struggles vs globalist struggles. You can't have that anymore: you can only have these extremely molecular, local, individuating political gestures.

Peter: Well it depends on the situation. There are contexts where something like an indigenous mobilisation verging on identity politics, grounded in an indigenous tradition - as in parts of Bolivia and parts of Guatemala, and other places - has been politically significant and is today politically significant. The same applies to contemporary forms of class struggle. Of course things are changing all the time, but the basic logic of class struggle hasn't changed that much over time: the dynamics of exploitation and domination at issue today are all too familiar, and remain a major factor in most if not all contemporary political situations.

Claire: That's why the model of political engagement needs to be re-thought, why in a Deleuzian register one always refers to a '*becoming-x*'. Because yes, there is a strategic need for molar or identifiable movements. But if they start to think 'OK - this is our movement, this is what we are identified as, and this is the only way it's going to work', then apart from the philosophical problems of identity that run there, such a movement is also going to destroy itself precisely by being identified and stable. The only way a transformatory political project is going to work is if it has a notion of redefinition that is inbuilt.

Peter: It's not a matter of identity, it's about collective self-determination, or what Gramsci used to call 'collective will', a tradition that goes back to Rousseau and the Jacobins. The question here is: what kind of social body or 'social organism' (this is Gramsci's phrase from 'The Modern Prince') is capable of a militant collective will that is grounded in a dialectical understanding of the situation as it actually is (and not in some kind of abstract ideal of sufficiency), and that is able to intervene and to act effectively?

Claire: But the 'dialectical' is the becoming. The collectivity can only act and intervene to the extent that it realises that it is itself constantly in a process of redefinition: that's what the molecular is.

Peter: Becoming and dialectic aren't the same thing. Molecular becoming isn't a dialectical process, and it isn't concerned with the consolidation of strength. It is, on the contrary, non-dialectical, rejecting any broad dialectical conception of historical negation and historical determination that makes sense to me, and placing an emphasis precisely, one way or another, on the *dissolution* of specific political groups.

Jeremy: Forgive me for intervening. In relation to Gramsci, who you mentioned, Peter: for me one of the most important ideas in Gramsci is that the key point in the hegemonic struggle is that moment when the class or political grouping transcends what he calls its 'corporate' character, when it begins to take on a different political role: you could say 'when it enters into a process of becoming', because, at this moment it necessarily transforms itself and puts at risk its established identity. That's Gramsci's re-working of Lenin's account of the shift from trade union consciousness to revolutionary consciousness.

Claire: It becomes virtual. It's not staying in the same body, with just *this* body of collective will, which we all decide to become part of; it has the potential to become *any body whatever*. It's displaced from the present to some possible body.

Peter: But you have that in Rousseau already, in the sense that you already have a movement from the particular to the universal: what would be gained by substituting the universal for the virtual there?

Claire: The important notion here is potentiality: one doesn't just speak of 'any man whatever', 'any subject whatever', or 'any individual' whatever, but of a pure *potentiality*.

THE PARTY, THE UNIVERSAL, AND REVOLUTION

Nick: It seems to me that what is at stake here is precisely the problem of *composition* that Peter has raised in relation to the problem of class struggle. I would say, Peter, that Deleuze and Guattari are with you on that: they also see that as a key issue, but they're addressing the problem of the party form after the failure of the vanguard party and after the experience of the authoritarian state form of the Soviet Union. They are just as much concerned as Peter with questions of the composition and organisation of groups, and out of that interest they produce a very variegated sense of the different dynamics - consistencies, expressions, modes of appearance - of political formations.
  Some such formations are completely immanent to social relations, and

would take the form of becoming-imperceptible, of modes of sabotage, of certain types of literary production, all having almost no apparent political identity. Others would be *consolidations* of social forces engaging in precisely the kind of frontal manoeuvre that might actually lead to a revolution. It's just that there is a variegated field here, in relation to which the Leninist party signifies a dogmatic and anti-inventive contraction of possibility. So I think that this is where the tension between, for instance, Peter's position and Deleuze and Guattari's might lie. But it's not that Deleuze and Guattari are unconcerned with organisation; organisation - in all its tactical, semiotic, libidinal registers - is one of their principle concerns.

Peter: I agree that that is the best way to work within this tradition. If you aim to use Deleuze politically then this is the best way to do it: to think about what kind of resources he and Guattari give us for understanding how political composition works, how capitalism works, how political organisations might become more supple and inventive, and so on. All I would say is that for me it's an extremely mixed picture: what they contribute is, in my opinion, undercut by the things that they undermine. Certainly it's important, for example, to politicise issues such as the Stalinisation of the Leninist legacy, but *everybody* was doing that.

Éric: Ah, the Maoist destalinisation of the Leninist party ...

Peter: Right, the Maoist project is precisely that, entirely so, explicitly, from the beginning.

Nick: But Deleuze and Guattari's critique isn't Maoist *at all*.

Peter: No, it's not.

Éric: I have to agree on this point.

Jeremy: Let's try to specify the difference between their position and the Maoist position as you understand it.

Peter: The Maoist position maintains that the work of avoiding something like bureaucratisation and Stalinisation has to come from within the party structure, using its own forms of discipline: the instrument of radical political change shouldn't be thrown away or destroyed, but has to develop its own capability to renovate itself, renew itself and avoid this kind of bureaucratisation. That's what the Cultural Revolution was designed to do, whether or not you think it succeeded.

Nick: But in the Chinese case that you hold up, Peter, renovation is complicit with economic development and the intensive exploitation of labour, which is far from a revolutionary project. And it develops into its own kind of mania, in the case of the Cultural Revolution.

Peter: I don't think it's now a matter of going back to the Cultural Revolution as such, or even of going back to party in the strict Leninist sense. So of course there is work to be done, of inventing new political forms, of discovering what might be, in Gramsci's terms, our political 'organisms', our organisational forms which are capable, to some extent, of sustaining a collective determination or a collective will to force through political change, in the circumstances in which we now find ourselves. And I think that's what people have been trying to do in places like South Africa or Bolivia, or Haiti, or whatever example you want to pick. And it's also what people have been trying to do, mostly unsuccessfully, in what's left of organised labour in countries like the UK or the US. But if that's your criterion, if that's what you're looking for, then in my opinion, Deleuze and Guattari don't add very much.

Claire: But if Deleuze and Guattari's direct equation is 'desire = revolution', that means it *can't* have the kind of framework that you're talking about, as in the idea that revolution needs to occur within some sort of institution and programme. Your problem with them seems to be due to the fact that their idea of revolution has in it something that's absolutely extra-institutional, absolutely extra-collective.

The molar, for Deleuze and Guattari, might be required as some sort of passing stage through which to achieve revolution, but the criteria for its success ultimately has not just to lie outside of molar formations, but to be defined against them, even if not negatively; they have to be working in some way to mutate. The 'desire is revolutionary' requirement seems to me to mean that there *is* something *prima facie* desirable and normative in mutation, which means that it's not just slightly different from what Peter is describing as the Maoist position: it has to be absolutely opposed to the idea that revolution has to occur through some collective organism. Actually, 'organism' is an interesting phrase, because that's a body. But for good or for ill it seems to me that Deleuze and Guattari's conception answers well to our historical situation, in which no *one* revolutionary organism or body is ever going to do any work. It's going to belie the actual political conditions and also not be suitable to them.

Éric: I would like to briefly return to the important question of the universal, not least because I think it is sustaining substantial 'cultural' differences around this square table. If we think about the political tradition that asserts the exclusive value of universal equality: nobody, absolutely nobody, is denying the importance of the fight for equality which has been so important to struggles such as the women's liberation movement. That importance is absolutely obvious. Now, the question is: if you don't think about equality only in formal terms, in terms of formal democracy, but in terms of the processes of the real immanence of the social and the political, then what are all the material and mutant composites of this so-called 'equality'? And this is where we can see that the fight for equality, the determination to fight for equality, implies necessarily a certain kind of becoming, of singularisation, etc, that cannot anymore recognise itself in a unitary figure. And this is true historically and ontologically of the women's liberation movement, for example, when it affirms a 'post-identary' becoming. The same could be differently affirmed of the 'sans papiers' mobilisations: in France, they want less and less a pure and simple integration to the republican order!

So for me it's really based on a caricature, this critique which reads Deleuze and Guattari as only interested in escape, deterritorialisation, getting 'out of this world' [the title of Hallward's critical book on Deleuze], and which asserts that if you problematise the universal as such you cannot engage in any fight for equality and in politics *tout court*. That's not the way it works and the way 'differences' are at work in the creation of new worlds: it's a defiguration that tries to 'escape' the real political questions for today. *A Thousand Plateaus* is still important precisely because it is constantly problematising the relationships between the molar and the molecular, between deterritorialisation and reterritorialisation, and trying to make a very precise social and historical analysis the key for any revolutionary praxis that refuses the constituted disjunction between the social and the political.

Peter: I don't think that Deleuze and Guattari are much interested in equality. You seem to take that as a given.

Éric: It is rather that equality can't work *for real* as any kind of given universal, beyond a strategic point of departure …

Claire: If you take Deleuze's books on Bergson and on Hume, which would at first glance seem to be his least political gestures, the book on Hume is actually all about the production of social sympathy. That is: it's about the idea that I can feel close to those bodies that are next to me because there's some form of self-interest and partial affection involved, but that the real notion of politics is to have sympathy for a body that is not directly before me. That's Bergson's two sources of morality and religion, isn't it? The idea being that you move beyond morality to the spiritual when you free movements of social control and organisation, beyond self-interest, towards some notion that 'any body whatever, any subject whatever, any life whatever' has an individuating power. That formulation might not use the word 'equality', but that's because it doesn't mean equality in the 'equal-to' sense; it means equal potentiality. So I think, actually, it's interesting that Deleuze and Guattari don't use the word, because they're anti-equalisation, but their thought is actually more equalitarian or egalitarian insofar as it's about equal potentiality. What Éric was saying about the women's movement was right because that movement is partly about liberation from notions of humanism; it starts off with the assertion 'we're as human as you', but it has to develop to the point where it doesn't want to have to answer to that standard. So I think this approach is *more* equalitarian.

Nick: I'd support that completely, and I'd also say that it's almost a kind of *provocation* not to use the word 'equality', because as soon as you do, you're back on the terrain of formal equality and social democratic consensus, and I'd argue that they're actually radically opposed to all of that.

Éric: 'Liberté, Égalité, Fraternité' - even Sarkozy uses that language ... And Hobbes' Leviathan, this Liberalism's Monstruous Father, proposes a kind of equalitarian model too ...

Peter: Well here we really do disagree, but it's an interesting disagreement. The kind of equality that I'm talking about is not the equality of liberal democracy. It's the equality that is implicit in something like the constitution of a general will or something like a Jacobin conception of politics - which takes shape in a very specific kind of conjuncture - or the equality that's implicit in a generic set, which is in my opinion a far more coherent way of talking about 'anyone at all', because it provides a very clear conceptual analysis of what exactly that involves, and is *exactly* antithetical to a tradition which comes out of, say, Hume and Bergson (a slightly obscene combination), and which is based on 'sympathy' and ultimately on a kind of mysticism. Who are they, these people who are capable of having sympathy for the people who are not part of their immediate situation? It's the Great Souls, the rare Great Souls - the elite. Much the same thing applies to Spinoza and in Nietzsche, two other key philosophical sources for Deleuze.

Claire: I agree with you - in Bergson it's the saint, and in Hume it's the good polity that creates the right social fictions: but I think you have to address the question of why one would *not* want to refer to a 'universal will' or a 'collective will'. That vocabulary still implies, as the concept of the generic set does, *a* collection that will then have a clear identity, which will become the standard for equality; which is very different from a perspective that recognises that even equalisation/equalitarianism/egalitarianism has continually to change itself.

Éric: ... in the lived and multiple temporalities of the event as production of subjectivity in-becoming. The question, then, is no longer necessarily to start from a kind of standard common humankind as a transcendental-real support for a Jacobin general will, assumed to express politically the unitary excess of the 'people' with regards to the mere bourgeois foundation of individual rights. There is no organic unity that the revolution restores 'in a generic set', by subtraction of the real social movement in its largest objective and subjective amplitude. And it is from the starting point of the constructivist 'schizoanalysis' of capitalism in *Anti-Oedipus* that Guattari can reassert, with Negri, the Marxian breakthrough : 'We call Communism the real movement which abolishes the present state of things. The conditions of this movement result from the premises now in existence' ... Premises that identify the development of the productive forces with the affective and cognitive development of humankind as a kind of cyborg, which is the real plane of social forces unthinkable in terms of the fixed identities of 'citizenship'. It is this development that prevents the integration of equality into identity and unity, at the very same time as it makes possible and necessary its non-totalisable realisation.

Peter: I'm not talking about *fixed* or specified identities, but you still need some criterion for individuation: even Deleuze still talks about *a* life, *a* line of flight etc.

Claire: In those cases, it's not a question of having a criterion *for* individuation: individuation *is* the criterion.

Peter: But on that score, *a* general will has the same kind of individuality, except that it includes its own self-determination. And likewise I would say, coming out of the Hegelian tradition (Hegel basically adopts this from Rousseau at the beginning of the *Elements of the Philosophy of Right*), that it's a collective individuation which includes something like a conscious self-determination. And that's the part that's missing in Deleuze, and that can be understood (along neo-Jacobin lines) as egalitarian, as opposed to the Deleuzian metaphysical points of reference, which are all explicitly *anti-egalitarian*. So is his ontology. His ontology is a differential, anti-egalitarian ontology: everything is in univocal being and *unequally* so, right?

Claire: That's anti-egalitarian if you only understand egalitarianism in terms which require something like *a* political organism, *a* representative body or *a* collective will. You're right that that is one form of individuation, but it neither should be nor is *the* politically-focussed notion of individuation. Deleuze's *is* a form of politics which, for good or for ill, is trying to get away from homogenising collective forms of individuation, to ask whether you could have a politics that wouldn't be about *a* general will or *a* people. And I think about that not only in terms of the collapse of the validity of a notion of something like humanity: one has to think in terms of non-human kinds as well.

Peter: Okay, so what do you mean by all this? Can you give an example?

Claire: For me the most tortured situation I face as a white Australian is this: we have an indigenous people, and actually it would be an act of violence for them to form a collective body because it is only a fiction of the West that there is something like an 'Aboriginal community'. It would be like them referring to

Japan and the UK as 'the West': it has about as much individuation as that.

So on the one hand you have a body of people trying to enter the political debate, but the condition for them doing that at the moment is to remove all of their capacity for collective individuation, and I think this just goes back to one of the questions which was on the value of communication and consensus in politics. Either you say 'this is great because there's a *differend*', or you have to find means of political communication that don't rely on the formation of a 'collective will'. I think that is the only way that it's going to work because otherwise one is imposing *a* model of individuation - i.e. the collective political body - on other forms of individuation that I think have as much political purchase and right as Rousseauist traditions of *a* general will.

Peter: My own country Canada has a roughly similar history, as you know, but still in some sense when you talk about something like the relationship between white Australia and the indigenous, however multiple and fragmented that term 'indigenous' is (and it's equally so in Canada, perhaps even more so), you can still say, I think, that there is enough of a structured conflict between these two general groups to make sense of it as *a* conflict.

Claire: You can't remove the molar: that's why for a certain point in the political debate, you're always going to have a gathering together for a body, but that also has to remain completely provisional and completely open to the multiple forms of individuation which might constitute it.

Peter: *Completely* open and completely provisional - who has an interest in that? In my experience, if you talk to people who are engaged in labour struggles - for example trying to organise a group of immigrant workers in California - or to people who are fighting to strengthen the social movements in Haiti or Bolivia, what they constantly say is: 'we are too weak and what we need is some form of continuity and strength, and our enemies are constantly trying to bust it up, to break it up, to fragment it, to divide us, to make it provisional, to reject any kind of consolidation of the instruments that we need to strengthen our hand.'

Nick: But even then there are variable articulations. It's complex, isn't it? Such collectivities don't derive from a general notion of their specific coherence - they emerge in response to a particular problem or a particular event - so I don't see how your examples are at all in opposition to a Deleuzian understanding of the formation of collectivity as imminent to its situation.

Éric: I think that an important question at this point is the question of minority as it superimposes itself onto exploitation in a non Marxist way. The usual criticism is to say: 'these minorities are fighting in a necessarily identitarian way, for the recognition of their particularities'. I think it is important to note a key aspect of the Deleuzo-Guattarian schema (and this is where the Badiouian treatment of this question, in *Saint Paul* for example, is really out of focus since it reduces the production of connective singularities to mere identitarian particularities): of course you have the majority, a redundant majority, and you have minorities, but Deleuze and Guattari write explicitly that the minorities regress to *subsets* as soon as they lose their quality of nondenumerable and cancerous flow. There is then a third term which is '*becoming-minoritarian*', and which redefines politically the minorities as open multiplicities-in-becoming, through the molecular revolutions which they develop and spread, before and beyond the antagonistic struggles they become engaged in. This means that the minorities are a kind of middle-ground, where constantly the question, the negotiation, the tension, is between the aspiration towards a kind of will (and social necessity) to become 'recognised' through the majoritarian rules ('to be counted among the majority') and something else, which brings the creation of new liberatory and experimental agencies at a time when the proletariat does not offer any longer a form of universal consciousness of the history of struggles. Deleuze puts the matter brutally: 'the question for minorities is to destroy capitalism'. So it is clearly not, for Deleuze, a question of giving to the minorities a kind of multicultural status as respected subsets of the market society.

Peter: But who's talking about that?

Éric: I'm afraid you know perfectly the answer, *mon cher*: Old Marxists yesterday, and Badiou today in his henceforth constituent *contra Deleuze*! But beyond this point, I think this is one of the major political questions at stake in our discussion. It would oblige us to come back to the question of the universal: is it possible to explore alternatives to the notion of the universal as transcendental category constitutive of political philosophy? The investigator of 'Deleuzian Politics' could then interestingly explore Deleuze's works before 1968, before what he presents as his passage to politics, in his work with Guattari, before the moment of constitution of what he presents simultaneously as 'My Philosophy', philosophy, political philosophy in his own *double* name; because this later work marked by the passage from a biophilosophy to a biopolitics doesn't come from nowhere. We would have to understand what Deleuze did before, from his *perverse* early studies of other philosophers, subtracted from the History of philosophy, to the synthesis of *Difference and repetition*, as constituting an inquiry into the non-representative determination of ontology as such, and into an ontology which was being precisely defined against the philosophy of representation through the concepts of difference and multiplicity as a global alternative to a dialectical philosophy.

Peter: I'd love to talk about that, but as we're leaving the question of identity behind, I want to make clear that the tradition of politics that I'm talking about is nothing to do with an identitarian attempt to get respect for hitherto under-appreciated or marginalised minorities inside of an existing society. This tradition coming out of Rousseau, Robespierre, and then later Fanon, Sartre and Badiou, all in their own way, is completely indifferent to that. It's not about 'given this identity, how do we then get better representation for ourselves within the existing system?' For Fanon, yes, the constitution of a national liberation movement is at stake, but precisely at a distance from anything like a bourgeois investment in the particular history of a place (Algeria, for example) or tradition or essence. The question is precisely: 'how can something come together, something whose identity emerges, if it has one, through its self-determination, not through some existing predicates or existing particularities, that is then able actively and forcibly to engage with the things that oppress it and dominate it. The civil rights movement, the UDF in South Africa, Lavalas in Haiti: these are the sort of movements I have in mind. The general question is what can and *will* actually undermine the domination of a ruling elite, or a form of capitalist exploitation, or of discrimination: what will do that? Something like a discourse of minority, which is to say a force of becoming? Or will that merely tend towards the dissolution of any kind of strategic grip on the situation?

DESIRE AND THE DECISION

Claire: All the language you use, Peter, is a language of decision, will, self-formation which seems to imply a sort of voluntarist notion of politics.

Peter: That's right: absolutely.

Claire: Well *maybe* this voluntaristic form of will and human intentionality would be good, but this account of politics doesn't seem to take account of all the affective and even suicidal tendencies in collective behaviour. Nothing is more obvious than that people often do not act in their own best interests. So any notion of politics has to take into account movements, desires, etc: factors beyond intentionality, decision, will-making and self-formation. This seems to me to be, again, what these broader notions of political analysis are for; they're for dealing with the question of why political movements do *not* form themselves properly, why they form themselves rigidly, why they become, to use Deleuze and Guattari's metaphor, 'cancerous'. How does something which starts to act in terms of self-identity and self-formation also start to rigidify itself and to form itself in such a way that it undoes itself?

Nick: I entirely agree, and that seems to be precisely Deleuze and Guattari's question: how to prevent those cancerous bodies emerging out of progressive organisational formations, *and* how to affirm distributed processes of composition against authoritarian models that would separate the function of leadership from the mass political body.

But they also provide very interesting analysis of specific revolutionary modes of organisation. I'm thinking of the 22 March movement in 1968: Guattari has a lovely analysis of its forms of libidinal transference, as a collective organisation that remained part of the wider uprising - it didn't solidify into a separate movement - whilst also functioning as a point of transference in the political body, allowing distributed and self-critical struggles to emerge. Or there's his work on the party, asking what exactly was the Leninist break, what kind of semiotics did it have, what affects did it create, how did it work to effect ruptures and continuities in the social formation of the time?

Claire: And that's why desire, which looks like a de-politicising term (as soon as you talk about 'desire' rather than 'power', it looks de-politicising) is actually part of a politicising problematic. It's a way of looking at what used to be called 'interests' - but that term is still to voluntarist and too cognitivist. We're supposed to be going through an 'affective turn' in cultural theory at the moment, which again looks depoliticising at first glance, but it shouldn't be: it should be about how bodies desire their own complicity, and it's about the production of political formations against the manifest aims of power. I think the problem is the use of the word 'decision', as though to see something as a politically 'good thing', to know that one wants this, could ever be enough in itself; as though the decision these days would be enough either for oneself or for a collective body. We all know that that's not how political movements work or could work these days.

Jeremy: You're referring to the elevation of the decision as the defining act of a democratic process?

Claire: Yes.

Peter: Any kind of will is of course preoccupied with all the things that weaken it, divide it, defer it, undermine it. Much of Rousseau's work on the general will is concerned with the issue of how to engage with the factions, with private, particularising interests. The mobilisation of an actively and sustainably general will is a rare thing.

Claire: Isn't that why, following Deleuze, one refers to a *passive* vitalism? In *What is Philosophy?* we see two traditions of vitalism. There's an active, voluntarist vitalism which goes back to Kant and then there's a passive vitalism which runs from Liebniz to Deleuze and Guattari, according to which there might be the will and there might be the decision, but then there are all those other factors that aren't decided, within one's own body or within the social world or wherever.

Peter: It doesn't disprove this voluntarist tradition, just to say that there all these other factors to consider. First of all, will isn't primary - it emerges - and decision is never primary either. Needless to say, in many or most situations it makes no sense to talk about collective decision. But there are some situations in which something like a decision can crystallise, if people are determined to make it. In August 1792, after enduring years of repression and betrayal, the people of Paris force a decision about the king and about the way the French revolution has to go; after which you are either for or against this decision and there is no more middle ground. It wasn't like that before and later it won't always be like that, but in that moment, and in the immediate future it opens up, that *is* the case.

Claire: But these are threshold points to which a thousand decisions have contributed. Of course you're right, and the same was true of the English revolution, when they beheaded a king; of course it's got a date, it's got a time and it could have happened otherwise. But there's a thousand indecisions which lead up to that which have to do with completely material versions of contingency and stupidity.

Peter: That's one side of it: but there are also principles, there are reasons, there is a sort of political logic. The emergence of something like the UDF in South Africa in the 1980s is no doubt a hugely complicated thing. You could have described it, I suppose, in some ways, as a sort of rhizomatic complex of assemblages. But it was also animated by very clear decisions, and commitments, and principles: one man, one vote, the freedom charter, etc - and there is an element of straight decision and engagement, just as there could have been around the prescription to stop the war that we're waging today.

Claire: That's true, and Deleuze and Guattari's position is that philosophy will, at the end of the day, create a concept; and there's something active in that idea and in the idea that philosophy, and its concepts, can *do* something. But we also have to take into account their rich analysis, according to which the condition of possibility of that emergence is completely dispersed, and not within the scope of one's intentionality.

Peter: I don't see it in those terms at all. People fighting for these things see it straightforwardly and immediately as a matter of principle that they have been fighting for, often for as long as they can remember, and there's something very clear about these kinds of engagements.

Éric: This reveals one of the difficulties with our discussion, because effectively we are all motivated by a 'cultural' background which involves certain kinds of philosophical and political 'decisions'; for you, Peter, there is no escape from a rationalist philosophy of the Subject (that you re-embody 'humanistically' beyond Badiou) and a pre- and overdetermined definition of politics from this 'universal-subjective' theory of foundation. You know what a subject is and must be, and you know what politics is when it is - a motivated *purification* of the social guided by a general will - and between the two there is that which you and your post-cartesian tradition call Decision. That's fine, absolutely coherent, but personally I feel closer to another tradition, more 'objectively' problematic and less 'subjectively' axiomatic, believing more in *transversal multiplications* than in *voluntarist unifications* as reality conditions under which something new can be created. But let me simply add this: it is fifty years of contemporary philosophy that disappear in your neo-sartrian 'engagement'. And when I say fifty years of contemporary philosophy, I mean also a whole alternative tradition, a whole counter-history of philosophy that disappears (from Spinoza to Nietzsche, and so on …). You can insist that 'everybody', with you, simply *know* what politics is when it *happens* in its evental rarity, but the real problem, ultimately, is that we are confronted with an intensive 'de-definition' of politics with regard to its formalist as well as its decisionist definition - invalidated by the 'real subsumption' of the entire social world under the biopower of capital. And the new kinds of antagonisms and divergent subjectivities that emerged/escaped from it have been less inspired by the Rousseauist legacy of the French Revolution which they would radicalise than they have been determined by the very mutations of capitalism; along with the radical democracy experimented-with by the mobilisations and 'coordinations' of those social forces which it cannot stop, and which continually shatter the deadly conditions of reproduction of capital.

LIFE ON EARTH

Claire: It's not just about the last fifty years of philosophy - we're looking at humans facing extinction at the moment. There might be self-conscious political movements that want to save themselves, but it's also the case that we're destroying ourselves precisely through the constant re-taking of the decision to survive: we want to survive and we've got these resources so we'll use them, and in the process we're destroying the ecosystem. It's the straightforward fact of the ecological future, isn't it? Contemporary capitalism functions such that the condition of the possibility for individual survival is destruction at a much broader level. This means that one has to go beyond the mere immediate question of one group's or individual's self-constitution and survival: even if, as you say, these movements don't see themselves as problematic in those terms. There I agree with you: you enter a women's collective and they don't see themselves as molar aggregations. But the condition for the survival of all such groups and the bodies which compose them is *not* to see themselves that way, precisely because we're in a historical phase of self-destruction, and our hopes for emerging from it can't rely on things like the subject and decision.

Jeremy: I'm glad you've raised this, Claire, because it brings us to an interesting question. Although I'm probably more broadly in sympathy with your perspective, I think that Peter's tradition is entitled to ask of the Deleuzian perspective: on what grounds do you even recognise it as a problem that the human species might destroy itself? I have actually had people say to me, claiming Deleuze (and, admittedly, Delanda) as authorities: 'who cares? who cares about the destruction of the human race? why should we care? let the capitalist movement of deterritorialisation carry on to its logical conclusion ...'

Peter: 'Let the desert grow ...'

Éric: Do we have to answer this Pseudo-Deleuzianism? It's a patently hallucinated and pathologically *interested* interpretation. Politically absurd, and philosophically so weak, so ignorant of what it is supposed to know! An *Embedded Deleuzianism*!

Claire: I think this is a problem with taking some of Deleuze and Guattari's language in a literalist manner - which is always the problem with DeLanda. When you talk about becoming-imperceptible, if you take it absolutely literally, then this does strictly follow, and it follows that if there is a tendency in life towards deterritorialisation then *prima facie* that deterritorialisation is a good thing, so the human being can deterritorialise itself, life goes on, and that's okay.

But there's also a fold-back movement in their thought. If you look at *What is Philosophy?*, you can see that they are fascinated by the fact that from the production of material processes something immaterial can emerge, which is philosophy. And there seems to me to be a normative *prima facie* value attached to *that* as well, because it's a higher deterritorialisation - it's an example of life creating something which somehow has gone beyond life. From this normative perspective, insofar as humanity is a subject, if humanity can create a virtual body beyond itself, like the philosophical archive, then it ought to. And it seems to me that there's no stronger defence of human life than that because everything else *is* probably dissolved by such a perspective.

Nick: To follow on from that: if labour is the metabolism between the human and nature - and Marx talks about the 'inorganic body' of the Earth here in terms that resonate strongly with Deleuze - then you can start to think about the possibility of a certain denigration of the human that is actually an *affirmation* of the capacities of human life. So I don't see the critique of the human as a nihilistic position. Rather, it's necessary to make it, in favour of a much richer understanding of the life of the planet.

HOW DO WE FIGHT?

Éric: Coming back to our political agenda, I think we cannot indefinitely delay the questions: 'how do we fight'?, 'what are the new social forms of conflict?', i.e. against/*within* the neoliberal subsumption of society, where the so-called 'society of control' means, after all, a total managerial monitoring of the social. Is it possible to resist, in an efficient and not *regressive* way, the capitalistic new codification of all relations of work, of all human relations whatsoever in an 'enterprise/company-society', without calling *exclusively* for a revival of capitalism's historic compromise: the deceased welfare state? Even if there is no objection to playing strategically this game of 'socialist capital' as well, the problem with the political and unionist left is that they don't know any other game at all! And today, Bernard Stiegler proposes a political programme based on the separation of healthy industrial capitalism from perverse financial capitalism ... With the help of the credit crunch, *on vit décidément une époque formidable!*

But how is it possible to engage ourselves with these questions without a deep problematisation of the very idea of labour as it is put to work in the current workfare-state, and of the very idea of life which is involved in the currently dominant terminology of 'biopolitics'? For sure, for example in France, the so-called 'coordinations' are practical and radical alternatives to unions on the one hand and to the party-form on the other.[1] Coordination of nurses, coordination of students, coordination of 'intermittents du spectacle', unemployed or workers with precarious status, of railwayworkers or researchers, of immigrants 'sans papiers' or of 'mal-logés' and squatters, coordination of alternative media activists and developers of a network culture, alterglobal mobilisations ... they are all dealing with this life/labour problematic through the affirmation of an extensive/intensive common (public services, social rights, social property, equality of rights, intellectual production, right to culture, etc) and through a process of autonomous subjectivation experimenting with forms of collective open self-valorisation that break with the capitalist management of life ... Without necessarily focussing on the 'coordination des Intermittents du spectacle et Précaires d'Ile de France', in which *Multitudes*, and more particularly Maurizio Lazzarato invested a lot of energy and time, these are the real questions that *we* need to investigate. But to describe these movements in Peter's 'decisionist' terms seems to me quite regressive with regard to the new forms of militancy they embody. May I add that I perceive the presence and the importance of Foucault, Deleuze and Guattari, not to mention Negri, in these problematics which are conflictually contemporary to the rise of neoliberal governmentality: but not at all that of Badiou's 'platonic' ideation of communism ...

Jeremy: Peter - Éric has raised the question, which is of course the urgent one, of *how we can fight* against capitalism, neoliberalism, etc, in the current conjuncture. I would say that one of the reasons for the popularity of Deleuze and Guattari, at least insofar as they offer analytical resources for a lot of us in the West, is this: in a country like Britain today, the problem with the tradition that you identify and identify with, is that it simply doesn't work. This is always my final argument against people who appeal to the Leninist

1. 'Coordinations' has been the name used in France by self-organised networks of workers. Amongst the most significant conflicts that have appeared in these last years in France, there has been the 'Coordination des intermittents du spectacle', struggling against a new organisation of the professions through a more restrictive and 'controlled' unemployment insurance, presented as a pioneering (i.e. neoliberal) 'social refoundation'. Commentators such as Lazzarato have seen these as typical of the new forms of mobilisation characteristic of the global 'anticapitalist' movement in the age of post-industrial capitalism.

tradition of proletarian struggle: it just isn't working. It's been decades since any significant numbers of people could be mobilised by appeal to that tradition and its rhetorics. Appealing to people in terms of those identities and those forms of organisation hasn't really achieved anything in this country since the 1930s. So I wonder what you think the purchase of that tradition is in a context like, say, Britain or France today.

Peter: I think it's far too early to tell!

In my opinion the implication of what you're saying, Éric, and the implication of the way that certain people use Deleuze, is to try to make a virtue of defeat. It's largely a philosophical attempt to appropriate and re-value the last thirty-plus years of counterrevolution. We've lived through this extremely reactionary period which is described in broadly similar ways by people from, say, Chomsky across to Badiou, or whoever you want. The fact is that (as a result of a very aggressive set of measures taken by the ruling class in this country and others) the kinds of political responses that did achieve certain things in the 1930s or back in the nineteenth century, around issues of labour and so on, aren't there, and we can't reproduce that sort of political situation now - that's true.

But think about the period in between, the Paris Commune of 1871 and the Soviet revolution. At the beginning of 1917 the situation was hardly very encouraging. Yet you would have been foolish simply to abandon the tradition that to some extent did enable certain things to happen, for example during the Paris Commune. Lenin was obsessed with that example and what its limits were, but also with what it made possible.

Personally I wouldn't want to abandon the Cuban experiment, with all its limitations. As to your precise question as to how we can engage with capitalism, how we can engage with questions of work, and justice and race and various other things: I would say that I think Cuba gives you a set of limited but nevertheless innovative and inspiring answers to that question. I think, likewise, of the mobilisations that people are undertaking, with extraordinary courage, in certain parts of the world. The example that's in my head right now is Haiti but there are certainly other examples: Bolivia is perhaps especially interesting, in terms of forms of organisation. What's happening in Venezuela, again with limitations, is a point of reference which opens up certain possibilities, but it also establishes continuities with the past as well: it's not called the 'Bolivarian' revolution for nothing ...

In the case of Britain, and France, one thing that will have to happen is that the forms of isolation which lock us into, for example, a completely vacuous notion like 'the West' - which is a term which should be erased from political vocabulary - need to be overcome. That'll happen in part through issues around immigration and globalisation, but it also has to happen much more forcefully and, I would say, deliberately, and ultimately through deliberate acts of self-determination, such that we actively rethink our relationship with the countries that we currently exploit and dominate. We have to rethink the relation that the EU has with Africa, which is obscene, and which is something that we could start to change through a deliberate series of decisions about trade and immigration and 'aid', and so on, if we chose to do it. We have to rethink our relationship to these wars that we are fighting, as we speak, in different parts of the world, and that we've effectively decided that we cannot change. That's ridiculous. We could decide collectively to change it. It doesn't mean that you just snap your fingers and things change, but we could initiate a process of organisation and mobilisation - which would be laborious and slow and inventive - that would bring these criminal wars to an end.

Claire: You use the word 'we', but that 'we' doesn't exist, does it?

Peter: No it doesn't, just like the general will doesn't, before we constitute ourselves as the subject of *this* decision that we have to arrive at. But we have enough to go on: we know that this is the right thing to do; a principled collective 'hunch' is good enough as a point of departure.

Claire: That's true. But then the problem is exactly that expressed by Deleuze and Guattari's call for 'a people to come' and their remark that 'the people are missing': these thoughts express precisely the problem that the 'we' doesn't exist. So the problem then becomes: what forms of analysis would allow you to get there? One would be affirmatory, saying 'we have the means to make the decision already there'.

Another would be to face up to political reality, which I think is what the analytic tools of the two volumes of *Capitalism and Schizophrenia* make possible, by asking: '*why* is it that the "we" doesn't exist? And what is it about life that makes the "we" difficult to find?' I mean, the discussion of deterritorialisation isn't *necessarily* an affirmation: deterritorialisation isn't a moral good *per se* because there are also processes of the dissolution of desire and its capture in which deterritorialisation can play a part.

Jeremy: It's very interesting that you say that Claire, because that does seem to be a slight revision of your answer to my earlier question about normativity. I think there is a bit of a tension here, insofar as the strongest defence of Deleuze that has been made - and it was being made by Éric right from the start - is around the value of the analysis, around the *analytic* strength of the work, as offering a way of understanding the mutations of contemporary capitalism, and of the things which limit the possibilities for effective struggle. Whereas what Peter has reacted to most strongly has been a certain normativity which seems to *valorise* a kind of politics of disillusionment and an aesthetic of disorganisation, above everything else. I'd like us to speak to that, and I'd like to know, Peter, if you dispute the analytic power of Deleuze and Guattari's work as well as its normative value.

Peter: Well, yes I do - although I have *more* sympathy for the analytical side of things because of course I do think that Deleuze and Guattari help to illuminate some important issues. For example, the question of why it is that people desire their own repression; they pose that question, and they weren't the first to pose it, but they posed that question in ways that I admit are productive and useful.

However, I think that for me the question - and it's more like a standard Chomsky-type question - is: if you ask why it is that - for lack of a better phrase -'the will of the people', or our capacity for collective self-determination, or whatever you want to call it, has been weakened, then you would answer it better by, for example, analysing some of the things that Naomi Klein talks about very usefully in her *Shock Doctrine* book. Klein is able to show - and I think it's convincing - that some of the political strategies, such as 'shock therapy', are designed precisely to weaken this form of collective will, and it is in fact easy to see how: you isolate people, you break them up, you demoralise them, you deprive them of information or you overload them with information. All these techniques are designed essentially to soften up people, make them passive, make them willing to go along with what happens and abandon things that they might otherwise have defended. Foucault made a similar point, with reference to the development of 'psychiatric power' in the wake of the French Revolution.

Claire: But then it's a question about desire. I mean if you look at 'the West' - and I agree with you that that's a disastrous collective notion - you don't even have to be Naomi Klein. You just have to look at the mass-production of anti-depressants and artificial stimulants, at the drugs that are coursing through and deadening the population: and you've got to look at this at the level of bodies, which is why I think that notions of 'the Subject', 'the decision', 'will' and 'collective self-formation' are of limited use. What you need analytically is a philosophical apparatus which will show you why these thresholds or moments of decisions occur or don't occur, which is precisely the question asked by a molecular politics: what weakens individual bodies to the point where they don't act?

STOP THE WAR

Nick: Molecular politics is also interested in the crucial question concerning why it is that even when such collective acts of self-determination *do* occur, the act of decision in itself isn't enough. Take the example of the massive demonstration against the last invasion of Iraq. In February 2003: clearly there was a decision by a hell of a lot of people to show up, to vent their opposition, to defy the media, Bush and Tony Blair: a very clear *decision*. But then it was completely ineffectual and actually rather apolitical. I personally felt rather disempowered, compared to having been at many much smaller, more dynamic direct-action events - this act of decision just wasn't enough.

Claire: Because it was pious - it was 'not in my name'.

Peter: Because it wasn't a clear decision! In my opinion this was the perfect paradigm of a decision that was *unclear* and thus indecisive - no decision at all. 'Not in my name' is a disastrous slogan, which says 'go ahead with your stupid ugly war if you must, but I'd prefer to keep my hands clean'. A clear decision would have been 'No - we will stop the war, and we will do whatever it takes to stop it.' Which means inventing something, I agree.

The voluntarist tradition I'm referring to would focus on what *we* can do, and although the doing is not reducible to willing, I would say that it's a mistake to think you can or should get rid of the *deliberate* element: what can we do, to engage with this or that injustice or this or that project or cause or whatever it is? Deleuze and Guattari give you some instruments, I admit. I'm not claiming that the issue of desire or the body is irrelevant but I am questioning the value of what I think is most distinctive about them, given that even someone like Rousseau would say that those things aren't irrelevant (don't forget the emphasis he puts on the cultivation of sympathies, on virtue, which is not just some abstract moral category - there's a whole investigation of technologies of political will in the broad sense in Rousseau). I don't think Deleuze and Guattari do much to help illuminate these problems or help think about why these forms of collective agency don't emerge; they effectively dissolve them. There's really no place for effective collective action in their thought.

Nick: I'm sorry but I still don't get this at all: books like *Kafka: Toward a Minor Literature* and *A Thousand Plateaus* are intimately concerned with techniques of composition.

Claire: But the process of composition and recomposition - of singularisation, in other words - has to keep going, and avoid becoming fixed. *That's* the normative value of deterritorialisation; it's not just some attempt to dissolve perception into nothing.

Éric: I don't feel very comfortable with the 'normative' vocabulary proposed by Claire, but I think it would be a simple question of semantics. This is obviously not the case with my disagreement with Peter. First, nobody is denying the post-68 counterrevolution. I already mentioned it, Guattari used to refer to it as the 'Years of Winter', and Deleuze contextualised in this way the political meaning of the *Nouveaux philosophes*. But counterrevolution means that there has been an on-going revolution, that 68 existed as an opening of new radical possibilities (which don't exactly *fit* with your analysis) - and we know that in Italy '68 lasted ten years, until the uprisings of '77 ... It may have been an event (nobody planned it) but it did not exactly come from nowhere, and the social mutations it embodied have been repressed as much as depotentialised in the process of their capture by an extended capitalistic valorisation that did not put an end to the crisis. And the fact is that high and massive conflictuality remerges in Europe in the mid-1990s, before inventing this new global political dynamic that crystallised at Seattle, and with the multiplication of World Social Forums that directly addressed the realities of trans-national capitalism and the *post-68* organisational question of the 'movement of the movements' ... You can criticise, show that this anti-model reached its limits to explain its *reflux*, etc - but, first, it reveals that '68 never completely ended; and, second, the fact remains that it existed in a way, dear Peter, *globally*: a clear alternative to your own neo-cuban model.

I'm being deliberately provocative, of course, but it is only so as to, more seriously, mark my distance from Peter's comments about Cuba, etc, in new directions. I think that once you have admitted - thank God! - the limits of that model (but I suspect they are for you only 'historical' limits), then there is still something that we have to analyse not only geopolitically - which is, you're right, extremely important - but biopolitically too, at least with regard to the 'South'. In South America today, in the globalised South America of today, perhaps for the very first time, there is a dynamic and conflictual *continental* autonomisation against American power in this area. This cannot be underestimated on any terms, but it must be completed for example by a racial analysis of the social stratification of these countries that largely contradicts the long-term tradition of their leftist nationalism (Gilberto Freyre's racial democracy is still the reference for a large part of the Brazilian left!) - leftist nationalism which, moreover, is not exactly 'naturally' supportive of environmentalist fights, women's movements, homosexuals' rights, etc ... But these biopolitical questions are the privileged ground for the revolutionary crossbreeding *(metissage)* of a radical democracy in the Global South. It does not obey/concede to the defeated European (post-)Robespierrist-Leninist tradition of the 'people' and its Unitarian model of 'general will', but it participates in the general contemporary human condition where resistance is not only a struggle-form but a figure of existence, a dispositif of life-power *(potentia)*, re-qualifying life as whole *in this world* ...

Peter: What does that mean, though? I mean, take a case like Bolivia, the site of some of the most interesting and inventive forms of political organisation in South America. The mobilisations in Cochobamba in 2000 and the various other really quite extraordinary and remarkable popular mobilisations were grounded (often in keeping with the tradition of the *ayllu*) in forms of forceful collective deliberation, which then apply to their members, so that once a decision has been taken - and often such decisions might take weeks to formulate - there is a form of collective responsibility for that decision which is implemented and enforced in a way that someone like Robespierre might have admired. So what does the Deleuzean approach have to add about this? These are people who are working in the world as it is: it's true that they're not calling for the abolition of private property, and they're not calling for a kind of absolute utopian vision; they're calling for specific, forceful, very significant change that would turn their country upside down. What does your Deleuzian analysis add to this? All right, so we analyse it in depth: what do we get?

Éric: Well, at least in South America, we should never forget that the question of the State - and its power to enable social inclusion in the market as the reality condition of economic 'development' - *clashes* with the question of the relations of power, which are constantly at stake amongst the struggles as soon as they break with the classic-modern equation of economic development *qua* political democratisation: because they involve *de facto* the totality of the material bases for a real-alternative citizenship. I don't know about Bolivia as well as you do, but I could mention the movements of young black people in the Brazilian peripheries and *favelas*, which, after all, reveal non-standard and quite 'wild' processes of collective subjectivation and cultural radicalisation; or the self-organisation of the *bairros* after the Argentinean collapse, which largely escaped from the deliberative *assembleias* because of their infiltration by the 'professional' militants, and their superior 'general will'- without falling into any utopian spontaneism!; or the Zapatista Indian insurrection which developed movements of global action based on the reactualisation of pre-colonial commons ... But I could mention also the question of the status of women in Venezuelan society. This question today is really something which is producing some kind of molecular destabilisation of many features of that society (against a gendered Bolivarian justice ...).[2] Beyond your insistence on an exclusive and constituent 'decision', which is supposed to reintroduce Rousseau-Robespierre contra Deleuze as the politico-philosophical frame of any deliberative moment, I think it's quite symptomatic that all your examples seem, on the one hand, cut off from any micropolitical analysis of power (to speak Foucauldian and not Deleuzian ...), and, on the other hand, absolutely non determined by the sequence 1968-1989 ... Sorry, Peter, but after 1989, the Cuban form of island-socialism is definitively pre- and post-historical!

2. See http://www. opendemocracy. net/article/gender-advance-in-venezuela-a-two-pronged-affair.

Claire: Peter you made that point earlier about 'the West', and said 'look at all this stuff that's going on that we should object to'. But the point is that there probably is a widespread objection and sense of outrage which remains completely dormant. These are indeed the bigger global political issues, struggle around which could really make an impact. And yet so far, such struggles have proved ineffective.

In a sense this comes to the question of what counts as a decision, because the decision *was* that nobody wants this war, and yet it went ahead anyway. I mean, you said that that's not really a decision, but then that just seems to me that you're saying that when it works it's a decision, when it doesn't work it's not a decision. So then you need the analytical tools to understand the difference, to understand why this demonstration became completely pious and sanctimonious.

Peter: The answer to that is that you need to have a *stronger* politics of the decision - not a weaker one! It took a very long time for parts of the United States to decide to abolish slavery - sixty years longer than it took in Haiti - and it took people like John Brown and others to make it happen.

Claire: But doesn't it have to do with affective investments of the body?

Peter: Why?

Claire: Well, for example you can look at the examples of things like racism and sexism - they often today take the form of people saying explicitly: 'I completely acknowledge equality, I completely acknowledge the rights of all these people', but on a day-to-day level and at the level of political mobilisation, there's still a kind of affective repulsion which is racist in character. Racism is a non-cognitive issue, which means it has to be dealt with not at the level of decision, but at the level of affective investments. These are mobilised in really politically clear ways in election campaigns, where you can see the way that hatred is stirred up at an affective level.

Peter: That's one approach; but the approach taken by Toussaint L'Ouverture, by Robespierre and by John Brown is exactly the opposite, which is to say that this is a matter of self-evident justice: it has to do with equality and justice, it has nothing do with colour, it has nothing to do with affect.

Jeremy: Well Peter you're talking about the level at which one makes the decision that something is wrong. But then one has to look at the level at which this decision can be politically *effectuated*, the level of political *strategy*. This for me is the value of the Deleuzian approach - it forces attention to dimensions of politics which have to be thought through if one is going to understand why, for example, the Stop the War campaign didn't get anywhere.

Now I know that you wouldn't disagree with a lot of this: the problem with the Stop The War campaign was that it was predicated on the assumption that we are still operating within this mid-twentieth-century mode of representative politics, according to which if you have a million people demonstrating against a war, a government has to listen, because you just can't pursue a war under those conditions. Personally I think - and this is just my analysis - that what goes wrong with the campaign after the war is that it remains a moralistic campaign about the war rather than one which tries to address the broader question of the *inability* of people collectively to exercise their desire in such a way as to prevent it.

But that precisely *was* the tactic of the Leninist Socialist Workers Party, and the Stop the War Coalition which they dominated. They refused any call to broaden the campaign out to address questions of democracy and participation; this was precisely the moment in 2003 when the SWP was actively trying to prevent the formation of local social forums in the UK, insisting that the only focus for radical activity had to be the war. The result was a failure. Now, to some extent, the Deleuzian approach allows me to think, precisely, about the broader processes of affectivity that would be involved in the creation of what you, Peter, call a general will: which is exactly what the politics of the SWP was predicated on not thinking about.

NOT IN MY NAME?

Éric: It would have been possible to make an entirely different analysis of that famous slogan 'not in my name', in terms of a politics of collective secession in relation to this imperial war made in the name of democracy; in relation to the absolute reduction of democracy (our supposed common name) into this global capitalistic earth which internalises (security society) and externalises (post-modern imperialism) war as affirmation of a global sovereignty. Now, effectively, *after* the demonstration, there has been thorough *rhetoricisation* of the most moralistic dimensions because of a non collective problematisation and appropriation of these questions. But let's not forget that in the UK, this was the biggest demonstration ever. This in itself is something extraordinarily interesting, and has to some extent given rise to an unexpected process of emotional interaction through the whole society: just because it existed in immediate opposition to the war figure of neoliberalism from a deep 'ethical' engagement that exceeds the 'politico-political' sphere.

That's why it's an extremely difficult phenomenon to analyse, before and beyond its supposed political failure. The easiest, being to criticise, from a narrow political point of view, the *clean* slogan 'not in my name'. But I really think that there are other potentialities inherent to this gesture of ethical refusal; and in the world that we live in, we have to be extraordinarily attentive to such potentialities, because they can produce strong and unpredictable effects.

Claire: So the declaration 'not in my name' could be a gesture of non-inclusion - 'don't include me' - or one of refusal.

Éric: Global refusal, immediate secession, whatever, at least on this war question, which is not marginal …

Jeremy: I don't think we should fetishise that slogan - it's been much criticised, and on the demonstration most people were carrying banners which read 'Don't Attack Iraq' - it wasn't all 'Not in My Name'.

Peter: I think it's also possible that we can imagine a history in which that moment will figure more positively than it does now, and that it will have contributed to something which went beyond it and exceeded it. But the question now certainly is: why was it so ineffectual so far? And all I would say is that if you compare it to something like the anti-apartheid movement, which was extremely laborious, as I'm sure you all remember, and took place year after year in the face of very strong opposition from much of the establishment: it happened because, laboriously, groups of people in schools and on campuses and in workplaces and so on made it stick and forced it through. And all I would say is that that's what has to happen with the stop the war campaign.

Éric: Fine, we agree on this last point. But, Peter, sorry to come back to my dissatisfaction with all of your examples which are, in my terms, quite generic in their intention - the generic affirmation of the egalitarian idea you embody subjectively in your constituent decision used as the marker for a no less generic political organisation. Regarding the South African example, if it is supposed to be paradigmatic of your general statement, you would have to confront yourself with the moral strategy of the 'Truth and Justice' Commission that extended the equality parameter to produce a kind of *tabula rasa* of the past, totally disconnected from the next foreseeable step: a private/public modernisation of capitalism under the formal-real leadership of a new black bourgeoisie which does not consider the redistribution of wealth as a national priority. We don't need to be Hegelian to know that slavery, apartheid, etc, are quite counter-productive from an effective capitalistic point of view: they inhibit capitalist development and are contradictory with its modern articulation with the 'democratic State'. What is actually going on in South Africa, with the terrible situation in the townships, confirms, if necessary, this statement. But the actual violent struggles in-between factories and townships are projecting the question of the *realisation* of equality onto a totally new terrain, involving a social break with the political space and a patchwork of non-totalising experiences of struggles and everyday life that may *empower* a black post-apartheid multitude. Now, coming back once more, and for the last time, to the importance that you still attribute to Cuba: it's hardly representative of the post-68 and post-socialist movements we live in (and not only in the 'West') ...

Peter: The Cuban Revolution took place in the 1950s and it's limited in certain senses by its context and the constraints of its situation, like anything is. But I would not at all be prepared to consign it to the past or to say that there's nothing that can be learned from it; or that the model, for example, of Cuban intervention over issues of health in various parts of the world isn't a far more useful model than the one we tend to use here of intervention through NGOs like *Medecins Sans Frontières* or Oxfam or whatever.

Part of the reason, if you ask me, why this demonstration against the war was not successful - one of the many factors - was that we have become used to delegating our political commitments to ideological state apparatuses like NGOs or their equivalents. And Cuba is an interesting example of a refusal of that logic from top to bottom. When Cuba helps a country like Haiti they send direct support to its government in the form of the immediate provision of services, and they keep relatively quiet about it. The contribution that they make compares extremely well with things like NGOs or more network-friendly type initiatives which are often trumpeted in the language that we're using here, as in 'this is more adapted to contemporary situations, more fluid'. Advocates of these latter models could well draw upon a bit of Latour, they might quote a bit of Deleuze for that matter, and they'll say 'this model of intervention is more adapted to a mobile contemporary capitalism'.

Claire: But surely the political problem here is the mobilisation of desire. You say that we palm these things off onto MSF or Oxfam, but then the question is - how would you have it otherwise? And then you need to go back and analyse formations of desire and the *absence* of decisions. We all agree that a decision would be a good thing, that an event or a change would be a good thing, that if what you see as good in Cuba could occur elsewhere then that would be a good thing. But then you have to ask *why* it doesn't occur elsewhere. It doesn't occur because decisions don't occur elsewhere, and those decisions don't occur because the *desire* isn't there. It's not that we're mistaken, or deluded. You can't just *refer* to 'will': you have to have some condition for analysing it. And isn't that what micropolitics is about?

Peter: Well, that's one way of reading it, but you could also read it as effectively collusion with the same processes at work which weaken those processes that can lead to the formation of a collective will.

Claire: But even if we *were* to accept the point that some of this corpus of French philosophy is partly collusive, but also to observe that there is an element of it that can be liberated: then even then wouldn't it be precisely the legacy of those who read it and use it to take the bit that's not collusive with a straightforward capitalist model of deterritorialisation, and take it beyond that potential complicity. And that goes back to the question of forms of Deleuzian scholarship which are anti-political. Of course the *potential* exists in the corpus for such an anti-political deployment ...

Peter: It's not just potential.

Nick: I see *nothing* in Deleuze and Guattari that links to a kind of abstracted, social-democratic, NGO model. Their politics is immanent to the machinic processes of life, and social democracy is a sort of abstract universal way of configuring equality in opposition to the political assessment of such processes.

Peter: Well, that's precisely how a lot of NGOs describe themselves. But I wasn't accusing Deleuze and Guattari directly of that, I was just giving an example of one of the reasons why our forms of collective determination are so weak - that's all.

Peter: Let's take two things that Deleuze says: one about the subject, one about the object.

So on the subject - this is from *Foucault* - 'there never remains anything of the subject, since he is to be created on each occasion': the subject is always the effect of a process, there is no subject of desire, for instance, let alone of any process we might describe in terms of a collective or popular will.

And on the other hand, constituting an object - this is from *Difference and Repetition*: 'the object must be in no way identical, but torn asunder in a difference in which the identity of the object, as seen by a seeing subject vanishes. Difference itself becoming the element, the ultimate unity', etc. So, given any object, the basic operation is to find or invent the ways of understanding it as a pure instance of differing, a radical self-differentiating or ultimately purely-differentiating thing, in a kind of fractal dispersal of the object. But if your object is something like a mechanism of oppression or domination, and if your subject is something like the mobilisation of people fighting against that oppression, what does this philosophy, which develops a metaphysics on this basis, offer? Why should we turn to this philosophy?

Claire: But that's like saying that if you get rid of God, there's no justice. So much the worse for a fiction! Yes - there are subjects and there are objects, and the world would be great if we were all completely rational subjects capable of making decisions: but reality, and the past fifty years of history, proves that not to be the case. Under conditions of late monopoly capitalism, subjects *are* just ephemeral. You pick and you choose. Look at party politics - there's no longer an ideology at that level, it is completely ephemeral. Either you admit that or you're lost.

Peter: I don't agree. You said, Claire, that the history of the last fifty years show that subjects are basically ephemeral. But if you ask me, the last fifty years show - and not just the last fifty years, but many more - that every time there's something like an instance of subversive collective self-determination, the powers-that-be squash it, for reasons that are very clear: because it sets a terribly bad example, which is what Chomsky has spent his life analysing.

So it's not just as if, in the situation as it is, people aren't interested in pursuing things like more militant trade-unionism or national liberation movements. What happens is that if they *do* pursue such projects, they pay a huge price for it. In the case of Nicaragua or Vietnam it was very clear: Westmoreland et al basically said, 'we are going to make sure that no-one does this again, that nobody in their right minds is going to launch a guerilla war against us, because they're going to pay such a price', and that's exactly what they did, and they were largely successful. So no wonder there aren't too many liberation movements on the Vietnamese model: guess why? But it's not because people aren't interested.

Éric: On this issue of the subject and the object, the point is not to be 'against' the subject for I-don't-know-what ideological reason. The point, in Deleuze, from the beginning, from his empiricist beginning conceived as the projection of a new 'philosophy of experience', is to think in terms of processes of subjectivation, in terms according to which the subject is not a given, not a point of departure for a neo-Hegelian teleology of self-consciousness, but the always provisionary terminal of a movement, a 'heterogenesis' between all the possible levels of pathic and social existence. It is in this sense that the subject is a kind of unstable, ephemeral, in-becoming historical process or relation of crystallisation, etc. That's the first point.

Now, second point, you can't just say 'let's take the object to be relations of oppression' because - and this is exactly what is meant by a philosophy of immanence, as Deleuze designates his philosophy - the relations of power in general are by definition involved in this process of subjectivation - or, if you prefer, in the Subject. *Capital is a point of subjectivation par excellence ...* That's why, philosophically and politically, I don't see how you can say: 'let's take relations of oppression as an object'. And if you *do* so, it is to better reproduce the cliché of so-called anti-humanism etc. But I really think that the question is not at all 'subject or not subject'. This is the very pragmatic dimension of Deleuzian philosophy, radicalised by the collaboration with Guattari: to look at subjects and to see how they work and are put to work, how they are *constituted* and *subjected*; to ask what might be alternative and collective processes of 'molecular revolution' which could open onto new possible worlds from inside our hypercapitalist world; to figure out how to dismantle the semiotics of Modern White Man, etc. So I really can't go along with your account of subject and object. Subjects are not only dependent on social agencies, they are 'assemblages' *(agencements)* involving an engineering of desire, just as much as 'Mechanisms of oppression' that are definitively not objects, even in a transcendental sense ...

Peter: A philosophy that's interested in the self-determination of a collective subject, to go back to that phrase, accepts that it's not originary, that it's something that emerges precisely through the course of its self-determination, and you have resources for understanding that, I think, from Rousseau, Hegel, Sartre and various others.

Éric: But it is precisely from the Sartrean opposition between subject-group and subjected-group that Guattari *resets* the question - with regard to the capitalistic management of life and subjectivity ...

Jeremy: It would seem to me that one of the points of not just the Deleuzian, but also several other 'anti-essentialist' critiques of the revolutionary tradition, is that the problem with that tradition is precisely that it takes the self-constitution of a collective subject as its *aim*. So, for example, the aim of revolution is the coming to itself of the class-for-itself, the realisation of class consciousness. In this tradition, class-consciousness is not consciousness of a *potentiality*, for a 'New earth and a new people', in Deleuze's terms - but is about the realisation of the *true*, essential identity of the proletariat. Peter, I wonder if you wouldn't agree that this way of thinking is problematic because it always tends to lead to a fetishisation of an identity, whether it's the identity of the party, the identity of the class, the identity of the nation: would you accept that this is ever even problematic, ever a danger?

Peter: It's a danger, yes, but it's not a fundamental or prohibitive danger. Just because there's a risk doesn't mean we shouldn't ask. You can easily take the position, as Sartre did, of saying that people generally speaking want to have some kind of grip on their own destiny or their own project. To some extent they want - and Lacan has his own version of this - to *assume* what they're saying or doing. Does that mean they have to assume an identity? No. Lacan and Sartre don't have a theory of identity. They both have a theory of a subject without interiority, without essence, without identity. But they do have a concept of a project, that to some extent you participate in its determination, and I think it's crucial to insist that people *do* generally want that, yes. It seems obvious to me that people, generally speaking, given the chance, do want to have some sense that they are, at the very least, participating in the determination of their lives; people generally seek to become active and not merely passive in relation to what happens to them, and I think we can all agree on that ...

All: Yes

Peter: So perhaps the disagreement is just a matter of emphases and so on ... (smiling)

Éric: Not at all! (laughing)

WHAT CAN A BODY DO?

Claire: Isn't the difference between us a matter of rationalism - the question being one of the degree to which that can take the form of some kind of cognitive, calculating, rational and effective decision, or whether it's distributed? The key thing about Deleuzian politics is that it's less about the conscious will, the decision, the rational, the calculation, the recognition of injustice and the attempt to put that right. It's more about questions such as: at what point do people get hungry enough to resist? How much can a body bear? How much suffering can it take? And these are calculations which are made by capitalism itself, aren't they? How much we can take, how much we can extract from this body before it starts to rebel. And those are calculations that capitalism has always been making, but anti-capitalist rhetorics have worked less in this register because they've relied far more on that rationalist subjective model.

Peter: And do you propose to compete on that terrain? Because if you do, you'll lose.

Claire: I think that if you look at why it is that a decision can't be made, what would be the conditions of possibility for that decision, and then relate that to questions of desire … one of the reasons why Deleuze and Guattari are sometimes seen as anti-political is the huge investment they make in aesthetics, which can be seen as a form of aestheticism, a naive celebration of the aesthetic, but it can also be seen to have a much more critical dimension, in that as long as we deal with the domain of cognition, we'll never know at what point a body's pleasures or powers become diminished or mobilised. And yes I think that maybe it's hard to compete on the terrain of managerial and capitalist organisations in calculating how much a body can bear, but unless a political movement looks to that, it won't understand or overcome large swathes of acquiescence: which is the problem, isn't it?

Nick: Isn't there also a problem in that capital tries to *induce* subject-formation? That's what I read into your earlier question about the political dangers of identity, Jeremy. The problem would be that maybe there's a sort of *inducement* of subject-formation amongst radical movements, such that, for example, a diffuse anti-capitalist communism ends up becoming an affirmation of labour and its identities. In the 1880s Marx's son-in-law is already having to say 'hey - hold on - we should be *against* work, not championing the right to it': and this is only ten years after the First International has broken up.

We also get the emergence of forms of workers' political subjectivity that are highly exclusionary: early trade union movements had a strong nationalist bent, many still do, and were often explicitly racist, in the US at least. And workers' organisations have had a persistent tendency to enforce the gendered division of labour. Against these tendencies, the basis of a properly generative praxis becomes one that *fights against* the emergence of certain kinds of subjectivity. And there have certainly been many communist movements that have insisted on this - problematising unity as a constraint on grass-roots practice, problematising trade-unionism as a form of corporatist organisation, problematising the centrality of the *white* working class. So it's not that capital always holds back the formation of subjectivity - sometimes it *induces* it in very dangerous ways that are destructive of much more inventive and effective forms of politics.

Claire: Like forming representative bodies, for example.

Peter: The history of capitalism's relation to genuinely threatening subjects that challenge its hegemony, however, is not generally one of tolerance. I know what you mean, though.

Nick: The two things are not in opposition.

Peter: Sure. So again, if we agree that the whole thing boils down to the question of what can we do, what is to be done, and some kind of collective agency that includes different kinds of components: what is that we want to emphasise? Do we want to emphasise dissipation or distribution or multiplicity of decentralisation and complexity, or do we want to emphasise strategic unity, concentration of power, etc. To my mind, emphasising the latter runs up against the danger - and it is an inevitable danger that you have to confront directly - of over-centralisation, and with it the danger of coercive unity, a concern for identity or uniformity. Sartre is right to be obsessed with this question, isn't he? Half of the *Critique of Dialectical Reason* explores what some of the consequences of such problems might be. But for me, in the situation that we're in now, in the situation of actual ongoing struggles that are not archaic but just don't happen to be based in France or Britain, these issues of strategic unity are the crucial ones.

Claire: These struggles which you refer to are not archaic just because they are not in the West: it's because they're not ecological. They're to do with the formation of a body, in relation to its own furtherance and striving. But they're not to do with the relation between that body and all the others, which might have paid a price for that self-formation. It's true that you might get a workers' movement that's incredibly mobilised and achieves a lot for itself, but the question then would be: what other bodies have to suffer as the cost for that self-formation? The environment, for example - the environment suffers.

Nick: And I'm suggesting that the workers' movement even oppresses *itself* if it accepts that formation; if it consolidates around its affirmation of labour, for instance.

Claire: Yes - it subjects itself to what defines it: 'I am working, and don't define me by anything else ...'

WINNING THE ARGUMENT

Peter: In the case of the indigenous movements that I'm thinking about, in Bolivia and so on, there are processes which address these kinds of issues of ecology, of internationalism, of avoiding essentialism and imposed uniformity. You raised the question of ecological disaster: what is going to deal with this in a meaningful way if it's not some kind of slow, collective determination to do something about it?

Claire: Yes, but that would have to take into account the massive levels of irrationalism and denial which (a) has got us up to this point in the first place and (b) prevents us getting out of it. What is central here is the promotion of a very narrow, limited and subjective notion of self-interest, which says: 'I'll only deal with what perturbs me, and as long as my environment and milieu maintains itself and I'm in the process of self-formation, well and good'. Such a conception of self-interest lacks any notion of other durations, or it doesn't have a strong notion of the virtual that takes it beyond the types of collective bodies we know and that we recognise. It seems to me a *post*-subjective politics is about recognising the limits of that approach.

Peter: But the goal of a more enlightened attitude to ecological interdependence cannot be achieved by deferring, or complicating or disrupting or dispersing our awareness. It can only be achieved by saying to people 'look, you live on the same planet as the people who are paying an extremely high price for your refrigerator and two cars and who happen to live in Sudan: and here are the consequences, in the end you cannot evade them, you will have to take responsibility for this, one way or another'.

Claire: Doesn't that mean we have to encounter the difference between knowing and not-knowing? Don't we have to think about the condition wherein one can say to oneself 'I know that we're on a path towards planetary self-extinction, I know it, but …

Peter: 'I know very well, but …' Yes, well, in part that's true. But this is also about a straight political fight, and if we can clarify the issue then that's the first step. And you do that in part through things like the demonstration of a clear argument, with a solid basis. It's a matter of winning that argument, and overcoming the things that have every interest in weakening it and disrupting it and dividing it. And so on a question like that, the *distinctive* contribution of a Deleuzian philosophy - not just the things that it shares with, broadly speaking, anybody with an interest in something like progressive politics - works, in my opinion, against what has to be done.

Éric: Your 'argumentative' argument seems to me quite ingenuously rationalist when the whole point is to make it understood that American cars are *really* making the desert grow in Sudan … Ecologists all over the world have been explaining it for forty years now - and the argumentation is working reasonably well since Al Gore got the Nobel Prize, and the new American administration will have, sooner or later, to sign the Kyoto agreement before 'electrifying' the car industry … I'm joking, but not so much. More seriously, is it not quite obvious that environmental ecology depends more than ever on a global social ecology which is not only locally and globally geopolitical but which calls too for existential mutations, reconstructing human relations and experimenting with new solidarities at every level of the socius? From geopolitical to micropolitical, the link is not utopian but intensively hyperrealist! This is what Guattari used to call an anti-capitalist 'generalised ecology'; not forgetting, in its transversality, the importance of a mental ecology which exceeds discursive logic when it locates itself before the subject-object relationship, focussing on a-signifying ruptures that determine real subjective and collective breaks in a constructive, processual fashion.

Jeremy: It seems to me that the consistent disagreement here between the Deleuzian and the non-Deleuzian positions is not so much around the actualities of political practice or objectives but around the question of whether or not the Deleuzian perspective actually adds something valuable to the analysis, and Peter's position is that the only things that it brings to the table that other positions don't bring to the table are things that are destructive and unhelpful.

Claire: And that criterion is there in the Deleuzian corpus itself - philosophy should be there to further, enable and maximise life, and if it doesn't do that then it's not a good philosophy.

Jeremy: But Peter I would like to ask you what you think about the situation where we are now, today in Britain. You didn't use this term, but I took you to be saying that the precondition for a progressive politics in Britain would be a kind of popular internationalism, and I wonder how you would imagine the mechanisms for disseminating that or generating such a thing, or what they would be, because it seems to me clear enough that they would have to involve some kind of cultural politics, an affective politics, rather than just a set of rational arguments.

Peter: Yes: you would have to address issues such as how the media is controlled and why it serves certain interests and not others, why it is that education is being turned into a corporate business, etc. All these struggles have to be fought on the terrain on which we are.

Let me give you one small example of the sort of struggle I mean, and the way it connects with various forms of power. It's not going to change overnight, it's going to be a long process, but it's certainly too early to say that there's no possibility of success. Take the issue of Britain's relation to Haiti, which on one level is a trivial political issue because Britain doesn't have much at stake. Nevertheless in May 2007, the Turks and Caicos Islands (a British colony) intercepted a group of Haitian migrants, as it regularly does, and killed many if not most of them in the middle of the night by towing their boat in heavy sees, which was grotesquely negligent; everyone involved, including the US coastguard, admitted that to tow the boat like that was virtually guaranteed to capsize it. So the boat goes under and eighty people die in the middle of the night at the hands of what is effectively the British coastguard. But there is no response from the British press. The *Guardian*, for example, never mentions it. It's as if it never happened. The *Telegraph* never mentioned it. The *Times* has a 35-word extract from the associated press. That's it. It took place the day after Madeleine McCann disappears, which attracted a certain amount of media interest, as you might know.

I think it would be possible to build a popular internationalism, and hence a world in which that would be a front-page story, an immediate outrage, and some discussion would take place of what is going on here - about why these people are leaving Haiti in the first place, why they want to go to the Turks and Caicos Islands, about who's working for whom and under what conditions, and so on. It could be done, but you would need to change the media, you would need to assert some popular control over the public sphere. It would be a long process, but I can at least understand what that might mean, in terms of a series of steps that we could take, more than I understand the meaning of 'we need to engage in a politics of desire that in some sense isn't really going to fight against capitalism but maybe people could *desire* slightly differently …' I still really don't know what that *means* …

Éric: This persistent caricature has more to do with the flattest Anglo-American reception of Deleuze and Guattari (a postmodern humanism) than with their published work and their political interventions (Deleuze actively supported Guattari's activism and political theorisations as an essential part of their 'community'). Sorry to say this here, but I feel more concerned with the post-marxist Italian 'reception' (from Negri and on) or the French one (the journal *Multitudes*), because, on these matters, they understand the analysis of contemporary capitalism produced between *Anti-Oedipus* and *A Thousand Plateaus* as the exclusive reality condition of a biopolitical ontology of the present … And may I add, in parenthesis, that there is no 'Deleuzian politics' (or Deleuzian *dedefinition of politics*, in a sense quite close to the contemporary dedefinition of art insofar as it means problematisation, extension and intensification) without a denaturalisation of difference (to overcome the 'limit' of biophilosophical expressionism) which posits a biopolitical constructivism of 'resistance' as the ontological relationship between difference and social creativity. This is the hard political core of Deleuzian philosophy *after* 68 and *qua* 68 thought …

Peter: Well, in practical terms I don't really know what this amounts to, apart from a call to become experimental, more differential, more creative, etc. Can you say more about what you mean by this 'Deleuzian politics'?

Nick: Deleuze says that as well as becoming worthy of life, we have to try to become worthy of the intolerable, to face up to the intolerable. To be 'on the left' (this is Deleuze's characterisation, though it's not one I especially like) is to have an appreciation of the horrors of capitalist life, everyday life, the global situation: hence his essays on Palestine, on the occupied territories, which I think are crucial to Deleuze's body of work. So I don't see how he'd have any problems with what you're saying, Peter. I mean, I don't want to keep saying 'hence we should all agree': but this position would clearly not be in opposition to your analysis of the situation in Haiti.

Peter: Let's take the example of Palestine. I know Deleuze's essays on Palestine, and like many of his readers I happen to share his political opinion and priorities; but what does his *philosophy* contribute to an understanding of that situation, and to the formation of a political force or subject (or whatever you want to call it) that can actually intervene to change it? I mean, compare him to someone like Edward Said, for example. Said is partly inspired by Deleuze and Guattari - he appears to embrace a form of cultural 'nomadism', for instance - But when it comes to Palestine he says, roughly speaking: 'we need to get a *grip* on our territory, which is being bulldozed out of our hands; we need to have a strong state mechanism that can defend itself; we need to consolidate our collective sense of purpose; we need to ground it in our collective memory that is being erased.' If that's the position - which I think is broadly right, I think it's a good analysis of the situation - then what does Deleuze give you to help understand that process, if not actually a point-by-point rebuttal?

Nick: The first principle is that any politics based on the constitution of a people is highly problematic: hence the creation of Israel as a Jewish state is a problem from the start. The racialised fault line between Israeli Jews and Palestinians is more a *product* of this state formation than a cause. So Deleuze and Guattari make clear that we have to remove the notion of *a* people and *a* territory that are tied together; which I think is a profound intervention.

Then you have to appreciate the way in which a certain territory is treated as a kind of virgin land - so in this respect Israel's treatment of the Palestinians is consistent with the treatment of the indigenous Americans by the United States. Then you have to understand how a politics based solely on an emergent state formation in Palestine might itself be dangerous, because it may just re-play these problems - and I think that's Said's point as well: although I think that he supported the two-state solution at times ...

Peter: He's ambivalent about it - he doesn't know. As a matter of fact he went back and forth on it.

Nick: And I think Deleuze actually is ambivalent about it in these essays too.

Peter: Said talks about there being a 'Palestinian people', quite emphatically, just as most Palestinians seem to do, insisting that 'we *are* a people - that's not to say a uniform, unified people, but nonetheless *a* collective - and we constitute ourselves as such, and we demand a state of our own as a *first* position at least, from which we could maybe work towards what remains the utopian goal of a non-state solution or a single-state solution in which everyone is a citizen'.

That was the PLO's original position, of course: an undivided Palestine, ecumenical, in which everyone counts as a citizen. But there's a reason why the PLO eventually shifted on that, because this project hit a brick wall. It became an empty ideal. Yes it would be nice, it would be good, but how do you achieve it? In my opinion you get to it via a strong federal system in which the Palestinians have sovereignty over their territory. They can then, from a position of relative strength, press for a better future arrangement.

But I would still really like to hear more about what you concretely propose. I'm still not clear about what you mean by a politics of desire or engaging desire directly, or what you have in mind in terms of political experimentation or going further, or really breaking with capitalism, apart from general injunctions.

Éric: Dear Peter, you'll not be surprised that I feel the 'injunctions' on your side. Injunction to produce a political program *in abstracto*, and to concretise this abstraction in a generic decisionism working as a voluntarist *passage à l'acte politique* ... Coming back to Deleuze's 'Palestinian' interventions, it must be mentioned that the first one is an *interview* with Elias Sembar, Palestinian writer, important member of the PLO and director of the *Revue d'Etudes Palestiniennes*. Rather than insisting once more on a clichéd-reading of Deleuze limited to a spontaneist apology for 'deterritorialisation', I prefer to underline this matter of fact: Deleuze does not propose a model of interpretation, he does not formalise a kind of universal truth extracted from Sambar's experience, he does not think that Sambar needs him to sharpen any concrete political proposal - he tries to think with and from Sambar about why and how the Palestinian question is part of the political radicality of the collective agencies of enunciation which we were formulating in the early 1980s *because* the active 'solidarity' with the Palestinian cause (I was part of this activism) was *de facto* dependent on it ...

At a quite different level, I could refer at this point to the *joint-research* experience of *Recherches*, coordinated by Guattari; or I could insist on the importance of the *engaged* 'sociological' inquiries (or militant *co-research*) produced by the Italian autonomia to understand what was at stake in the passage from the fordist factory to the 'social worker' (and the mutations of the very notion of labour involved in a capitalism whose very first production becomes a production of subjectivity *qua* production of production) ... This point is quite important as far as it determines, on the one hand, the final 'Italian' pages of *A Thousand Plateaus* (and largely the Deleuzian project for a '*Grandeur de Marx*',[3] which echoes strangely the 'Grandeur of Arafat' published in the *Revue d'Etudes Palestiniennes* in 1983) *and* Negri's reappropriation of the Deleuzo-Guattarian politics of difference to define the multitude's problematics ... I should like to add that the social research produced with the Coordination des Intermittents *refuelled* my Deleuzo-Guattarian inspired criticism of Negri's teleological Franciscan-Workerism ...

Jeremy: I would like to draw attention to another potentially important example. I would say that what's happened in South America, what's happened in Venezuela, would not have happened under normal historical

3. Deleuze's planned, but never-written, book on Marx.

circumstances. Normally America would have stopped that happening. America has been prevented from stopping the massive swing to the left in Latin America by virtue of the extent to which America's global legitimacy has suffered, because of the lack of legitimacy of the war in Iraq.

Now, the global demonstrations against that war which took place five years ago, were key to that process whereby America's imperial legitimacy was undermined. Those demonstrations were not spontaneous: they were arranged at the first European Social Forum in Florence the previous November. Now, at no point in that process was anybody's conscious *intention* or *plan*: 'let's create conditions to make a constituent uprising in Venezuela or Bolivia possible'. But nonetheless that was part of the process, and to some extent it was a process that has worked at the level of a certain *affectivity*, in terms of creating a climate of illegitimacy for American imperialism, that the Deleuzian analysis is crucial for at least helping to *understand*, even if it doesn't generate a programme for it. It might not generate a programme, and I think that it's true that it's very difficult for any of us to answer the question which in effect Peter asks, which is: 'what is the programme generated by this analysis?'

Peter: It's not enough to describe it in terms of affectivity. It's a matter of justice and principle.

Éric: The principle is, at its best, a principle of equality, which is only a point of departure for a becoming-with which goes beyond 'solidarity', and which gives an autonomous creativity, a new differential empowerment to the logic of contradiction with the 'System'… Because there are not *real* political answers in the constituted political space! Because the equalitarian common as ontological presupposition remains *empty* without the expression and mobilisation of singularities which are hybridising a new practice of global and local-based democracy …

Jeremy: And justice and principle is not what motivated people! It's not going to motivate people to do anything about Haiti!

Peter: Well in that case the imperialists will have got away with what they wanted to do there.

Claire: The point is that you can have an argument and you can win the argument rationally, but then people can still not behave in such a way as to enact that rational conclusion, and so your political goals are still not realised. That's where the question of desire comes in, and the analysis of microfascism. Microfascism is a crucial issue here; it's about clinging on to things that consciously you recognise you ought to have abandoned, but you cling onto them nevertheless.

Peter: But we've also abandoned the argument, if you ask me, and that's a mistake.

Éric: Or we have tried to confront *your* argument in the real world, beyond the microfascist counterargument, if you ask *me*.

The roundtable was organised and chaired by Jeremy Gilbert. It was recorded in February 2008, and was subsequently collectively edited by all of the participants, for which the journal offers its sincere thanks.

Sexual temporalities

Katrina Schlunke

Susannah Radstone, *The Sexual Politics of Time: Confession, Nostalgia, Memory*, London and New York, Routledge, 2007; 256pp, £21.99

Time is extraordinarily labile and yet constantly called back to its ubiquitous task of inventing a now and a then, or a now and before. Even within a project of thinking about an order of sensation that exceeds or undermines teleological time, for example, scholars will deploy findings from biology that purport to measure the time between the moments of sensory memory and when memory proper (that, which can be recalled) is laid down. It is said to be two seconds. Two seconds of non-representational time? This slippage becomes even more overt when we begin to organise vast tracts of cultural phenomena through ideas like 'modern' and 'postmodern'. The brilliance of this book lies in its dogged capacity to keep showing the ways in which each conceptualisation of time, no matter how anti-teleological, becomes tied through its claim to a larger typology (e.g. modernity and postmodernity) to a politics of sexuality, and that those politics produce an often-overlooked variety in how temporality works in film, books, and museums, and as evocations of 'our' time.

Confession, understood as one aspect of the organising form of power within modernity through its assistance in the production of a 'subject in process', has its particular times. The most usual understanding of the time of the confession can be shown via Bruner and Weisser, who suggest 'this separation between the "telling" and "told about" self has a temporal aspect since the "I" that speaks or writes lives in the "instance of discourse" in which he attempts to impersonate a self created out of memory from the past'. This brings together versions of autobiography and aspects of religious confessions, and produces a subject caught up in the 'forward movement of becomingness'. But is this the only confessional temporality? Radstone suggests at least two complications to this now *de rigueur* account of the work of the confession. The first is to remind us that Foucault's confession was always a practice within which, or rather through which, a subject was made and unmade. That is, the subject self was recognised in the moment only to be unmade and made again by themselves and those who listened. The truthful effect of that institutional listening then had to be recognised by those who confessed. Although Radstone does not go this far, perhaps the 'agonism' of this process that is never complete and always ambiguous might also produce moments of such 'self exposure' that it may come closer to Bergson's notion of duration. In his idea of duration he puts forward the possibility of an immediate experience of intensity. In duration we can have

   DOI:10.3898/NEWF.68.REV 01.2009

direct access to the real 'if we could strike our senses or consciousness directly', which is surely what some versions of confession-cum-autobiography do or attempt to do? Bergsonian duration challenges the modern obsession with the regularly calibrated numerical time of the clock and the calendar, and with industrious production of the future, by facilitating a recollection, or rather a preservation, of the past within our current existence such as some acute and self consciously affective autobiographies attempt.

The second is a more social path that makes time in effect proliferate through connection rather than simply carry the individual bourgeois subject forward. This idea uses examples of feminist autobiographies via Rita Felski and Raymond Williams' critique of the urban dystopic ('all these alone people in the city might bump into one and other') to show that in many instances the 'confessional' also produced the means of connection to others. This involves not so much an individual becoming as a becoming with others. As a means of convening community, the confession's temporality becomes not so much a means of producing teleological individualism, as an order of radical connectivity. Perhaps that spill of contagious recognitions could best be described as presentism? Confession may still be producing the single representative subject of (modern) discourse as Foucault suggested, but an appreciation of the moments of 'in-betweenness' within confessional temporal modes and the social becomingness that might also emerge complicates the story. If it is precisely through these discursive acts that feminist sociality can be enacted and a single order of masculine certainty (but perhaps temporarily) undone, then exactly how 'individualistic' is it?

Radstone neatly identifies the two sins of nostalgia; 'nostalgia is criticized for its commodification of the past … [and] it is also conversely criticized for turning social change into private affect'. Nostalgia has routinely been blamed for the sentimentalising of the past, the destruction of history, the postmodern 'effect', and for its association with a conservative politics. Radstone mentions John Major's promulgation of an education system based on 'grammar, spelling, tables', but from Australia I could mention the more insidious call of our ex-Prime Minister John Howard for a return to 'Australian' values. It seems easy at first to see the problem with nostalgia. It 'tells it like it wasn't', and precisely because it often works through the mass media and governing institutions its effects are pervasive. The particular kind of time produced through nostalgia is seen as warm and bland, somehow blanking out a 'real' past which has more political and passionate effects. But what is unreal about nostalgic 'affect'? Is it the longing that Radstone tells us, via Hutcheon and Lerner, 'makes art possible', for example? The productiveness of nostalgia can be seen in the popular histories of the past and the heritage industries as well as in the 'feelings' of different populations that something profound and perhaps un-nameable has been lost.

The critique of Jameson's dismissal of nostalgia in part through a re-reading of Benjamin is very telling. The key insight is that Jameson's 'nostalgia' is 'lacking' and bound up with a phallocentric desire that was so much more possible when the reassurance of fetishism was also so much more possible. That is, when the phallic mother was so much more easily organised. This makes the appreciation of the Oedipal mother key not only to how we understand the politics of nostalgia but to the broader politics of temporality and its production through figurations of the masculine as well as the feminine. Are our inventions of different temporalities caught up with desires for ideal psychic states? This seems obvious within a particular cultural envelope, but also points to a sometime irritation with this book. Its style is to show one detailed argument after another within the same section, often from diverse areas, e.g. literature and psychoanalysis. Each argument is finely crafted and eventually evolves around a particular sexual politic, but it can be difficult to tell by chapter's end which of the many fine points was intended to be the major one. A complicated chapter which has given us many new insights and very rich re-readings will then end with a modest conclusion about 'the interweaving' of, say, the psychic and the historical, or the need to look at masculinity as well as the feminine. This is simply too modest and sometimes mildly confusing. But in the beautiful exposition of the film *Le temps qui reste*, something of the affective force of the film wends its way through the writing and the argument. This conclusion to a section concerned with nostalgia, masculinity and mourning shows us something of how memory and time can be done differently when both the material world, the idea of the elemental, and an imagining of circles rather than lines come into play.

The whole book is about the possibility that memory has surpassed nostalgia as the central temporal mode of our times. And in the last section, which concentrates on the rise and rise of the memoir, this is explicitly addressed. This involves both a return to psychoanalytic considerations about mythic pasts, and a reimagining of what masculine and feminine could become. We have already learnt from the previous chapters that both confession and nostalgia belong within modernity and postmodernity, and indeed complicate the temporalising of both, but what exactly does memory do? Radstone, after requoting Foucault's contention that confession has been established as one of the key rituals for the production of truth, writes: 'The contemporary rise of memory in general, and of the memoir in particular, might seem to suggest that Western culture may be witnessing confession's supersession by memory'. This is a bold claim in many ways. The published memoir arises out of a publishing industry often combined with a celebrity complex, and supported by various forms of advertising, merchandising and global sell. It is an event, a practice, but also a product. The body and mind (and soul) may be written of within its pages, but they are not actively called into being representative of the discourse of the discerned individual until that memoir is reviewed, read and scrutinised through what I would argue are the more confessional modes of Oprah Winfrey and other talk-back and live examinations of the text/author fusion. I am not disagreeing with Radstone (she's too convincing), but adding a rider that it is not memory alone that has superseded the confession but the rise of a memory/confessional complex that works through multiple (sometimes global) forms of memorising (e.g. memoir, autobiography) and the spectacle of their scrutiny by television audiences, film-goers, magazine readers, interactive network sites, reality TV and so on. In this way we have a circular re-joining of what Foucault saw as the pre-modern disciplining through the spectacle to the modern truth finding through confession. The disciplining public may no longer be actively tearing flesh from limb but we will, from the privacy of our homes, vote whether we 'believe' a story or hit the keyboards to express our outrage at our changing 'belief' in someone's memoir. This conditional truth produced in part by a dispersed public makes of time an affective event, an emotion perhaps.

But it is in Radstone's conclusions about masculinity and femininity that I found the most exciting reformulation of gender I have read for sometime. Through the examples of memoir, but recalling earlier psychoanalytic work in film and literature, Radstone suggests we may be witnessing a time when the myth both of the phallic mother and of primal phallic masculinity are being undone through a different order of remembrance. As she writes, 'what we are seeing here is a convergence of sorts, as feminine and masculine remembrance open masculinity as well as femininity to their unknowns'. This is to posit remembering in a very powerful and generative position, where it becomes a volatile, connective opening outwards rather than any order of nostalgic narration. And remembering is here understood as both corporeal and psychological, both affective and material - as a temporal figuring it literally transforms what masculine and feminine could be. The next step might be to see how this formulation works alongside the work on queer temporality and becoming that Halberstam and Horncastle, amongst others, are pursuing. But that is another story.

This is a dense but subtle book. And it is certainly an excellent book to teach with. Its approach takes us carefully through the intellectual context of each of its key themes; confession, nostalgia and memory - and these introductory sections are enough in and of themselves to constitute their own book. I have not read before such acute summations of the complex intellectual trajectories that have produced these three notions as foundational concepts to understanding our contemporary times. And so it is an added bonus at the end to find that it is not only time that has been re-written but also the possibilities for gender.

ORGANISING MODERN EMOTIONS

Katrina Schlunke

Gillian Swanson, *Drunk with the Glitter: Space, Consumption and Sexual Instability in Modern Urban Culture*, London and New York, Routledge, 2007; 212pp, £14.99 paperback.

The prediction in 1944 for what would happen to the untreated 'problem girl' was grim: 'the life of rich fantasy gives place to an increasing dementia until the patient glimmers dimly in a corner of the asylum, dull-witted as a cow'. This quote is not lightly emphasised by Swanson, for what was at stake in the national effort to save the 'problem girl' (and the good time girls and the prostitutes and the male homosexuals) was modernity itself. Each of these figures needed to be made to reach out from the possible effects of the Second World War, past any chaotic internal state, to a social, neighbourly and national future marked by progress and a new civilisation emerging from the damage and ruin of war. Swanson presents her extraordinary accounts, of what could be described as a national intervention into the emotions, within a very elegant analysis that lets the full weight of the primary material be felt. While she is obviously sympathetic to the ways in which Nikolas Rose's Foucauldian-inspired work sits easily with these produced 'problem subjects', we also gain a sense of the complexity of the national discourses that are trying to be established. And behind that, we sense the individuals living lives of great change in what came to be understood as modernity. That they would know themselves through their expressed emotions, their sexuality and the places they could take up in this unpredictable space is somehow simultaneously expected and yet extraordinary. We would now expect the processes of a national inquiry to be productive, in the end, of some order of constrained subject/citizen, but what is a surprise in this book is to be moved by the efforts of both the original inquirers as well as those who were subject to their gaze. This ambiguity results, I suspect, from seeing an idea of active government and public commitment to the emotional state of its citizens as both an order of care but also of intrusion, one no longer readily imagined in the national register.

The book begins with the new national focus on maternity and what were considered the effects of war upon it and women more generally. The imagined hysterical collapse on the home front did not occur, and so the establishment of constant familial routine (and so constant mothering) was to become one of the principles of maintaining wartime morale. But that principle of familial routine was caught up in other realities of the war period, such as the seventy per cent (and more) increase in venereal disease (1940-45) and the 'almost doubled' numbers of illegitimate babies in the same period. These

   DOI:10.3898/NEWF.68.REV 02.2009

same women, both constant and different, bedrock and threat to a national order, were not easily recognised by national programmes or amenable to the project of raising and maintaining national morale in wartime. But the situation of war meant that there were strong desires to mange the psychology of a group who may be 'disposed to mental breakdown' - a habit of scrutiny that continued after the war. That breakdown, as mentioned before, did not occur, and, as Swanson quoting Titmus (1950) writes: 'The most prevalent and the most marked symptom of psychological disturbance among the civilian population during the war was not panic or hysteria but bed-wetting'. Think of all those children removed for 'their own good' reacting to national threat and acute familial dispersal. Through this focus on nerves and marital relations and absent children and fathers, there arose an abiding concern, post-war, with the idea of the national character and its maintenance. Coming into the 1950s, this meant making a place for sexually satisfied mothers who, it was hoped, would fashion themselves through modes of acceptable consumption along acceptable paths through the growing cities.

This intimate management of women's lives extended to the 'problem girl', who was said to arise from a 'squalid' family situation that, in many different ways, was failing to keep its momentum progressively forward. At the same time, the psychological and the eugenic converged to create an individual as well as social explanation for existence. While her environment may partly explain her evolution, it was the girl herself, who 'lived for her own personal enjoyment' and was morally and emotionally unstable, that made it necessary that she should be managed by a society that was intent on moving forward. The girls could not be a part of a focused project of modernity if they were endlessly distracted by the new thrills of commercial entertainments, and became chronically inattentive. You begin to see how narrowly defined the 'right' behaviour of the working-class girl was. They were instructed to consume (but just so much), go out (but only some of the time) and agree to be scrutinised, as if as Bentham thought 'the more we are watched the better we behave'.

The Wolfenden Committee was established in the 1950s as a result of agitation to have the visible 'vice' of London's streets and parks stopped. Its more narrow focus became prostitution and male homosexuality. What Swanson so wonderfully portrays is the coming together of new modes of mobility (prostitutes' access to hire cars) and an imaginary of the independent worker (taking picked-up men to an apartment - perhaps in the suburbs) that spread the spatial network of the prostitute while undermining any sense of 'prostitute' being a simple and stable category recording sameness. The volatility of what 'prostitute' might mean emerged as her capacity to produce new social spaces expanded, and it appears that no national committee could bring itself to account for this changeableness, for something that could only be fleetingly seen. This relation between national concerns and what could be seen extended to homosexuality, although that was complicated by individuals seeking homosexual reform through a willingness to tell their story of their 'normal' and private lives.

But orders, and indeed ideologies, of male to male affections are complex and highly diverse, and Swanson counters the limited treatment of homosexual men in the Wolfenden report with a brilliant chapter on Lawrence of Arabia. This is a highly nuanced, historically rich work of imaginative scholarship. It reconstructs the figure of Lawrence (his writing as well as his simulations) with great insight. But does this engrossing work belong in this book? It seems by its content and cut-short conclusions to demand more space than a mere chapter. The arguments begun here deserve to be continued well beyond the modern, and with full rein, to call upon earlier traditions of men who did not like women and men who loved men in the many forms love takes. The material would make a book of its own, and an expanded version of this analysis would make it a highly original one.

The last case looked at is that of the 'perfect poppets' and satisfying male lovers of the Profumo affair. Here the sexual movements are international, as are the potential dangers to national security of bringing different orders and partners of sexual activity too closely together. With Swanson's help one cannot but begin to see the Profumo affair as some kind of harbinger of what postmodern sociality might bring. In it the assumptions of the ordering grand narratives of progress, and the discursive networks of knowledge and categorising, are broken down by multiple crossings as sixteen-year-old girls openly enjoy multiple sex partners with multiple nationalities, and sex as well as friendship with a man who is demonised and feminised. How could a desire for progressive order and the psychological health of the nation manage this order of spatial, political, class and sexual defiance? Particularly when one of the key explanations for the events is simply 'having a good time' - that is, engaging in the modern pleasures of consumption (travel, shopping, sex) that were, in a different order, so actively situated as the new post war aspirations for all.

I have a small quibble with the subtitle - Space, Consumption and Sexual Instability. I think that this is one of the best contextual works on Modern Emotions, and should have been marked as such. The leading emphasis on space is not, I would suggest, an adequate naming of the focus of the book. But the leading title, Drunk with the Glitter, is perfect. With its 'lure of urban cultures and the altered states that they were understood to stimulate', you see the sexed and embodied subject caught in all that was solid melting into air; a pulsing, confusing, and alluring modernity with its attendant psychological and emotional shifts that inspired new orders of national attention.

Ultimately this book enables us to think more carefully about our own contemporary moment of post or high modernity. We may now reach toward experience and affect, emotions and the senses, as a way out of a representational gridlock, but we might remember as we do just whose feelings and experiences have been a national problem for so long. The reports that form one of the key archives of this book saw the everyday modern as under attack from the unruly emotions of problem groups. And so they took steps through psychology and ideas of national character and fitness to ensure that an ordered emotionality was as much a sign of progressive modernity as constant and considered consumption. One of the many pleasures of this genuinely arresting book is noticing one's own changing sympathies with the past. Where a detailed examination of the measures and vocabularies deployed by national inquiries into the 'problem' of prostitutes or young women or male homosexuals, including discussions of their 'feelings', would once make us worry about the intrusion; now, after the affective turn, that consideration seems so very contemporary and important.

BOOKNOTES

Alain Badiou and Slavoj Žižek, *Philosophy in the Present*, Cambridge, Polity Press, 2009; 104pp, £9.99 paperback

Philosophy in the Present is a meeting of two of the most important philosophers of our time: Alain Badiou and Slavoj Žižek. The question posed by this book is: what role should the philosopher play in the world today? Badiou and Žižek each contribute an essay on this subject before the book closes with a discussion between the two.

Badiou: 'A genuine philosopher is someone who decides on his own account what the important problems are, someone who proposes new problems for everyone. Philosophy is first and foremost this: the invention of new problems' (p2). As such, the philosopher intervenes when and where it is necessary to invent a new problem. But in order to do this the philosopher requires some sort of sign, and here Badiou introduces the notion of the 'philosophical situation' to demonstrate how the philosopher comes to know to intervene. A philosophical situation occurs where there is an incommensurable conflict; where there is distance between power and truth; and where there is no common measure between event and law. How does the philosopher intervene? The task is 'to throw light on the fundamental choices of thought'; 'to throw light on the distance between thinking and power, between truths and the state. To measure this distance. To know whether or not it can be crossed'; and 'to throw light on the value of exception. The value of the event. The value of the break. And to do this against the continuity of life, against social conservatism' (p12). The philosophical concept is that which draws together the problem of choice, the problem of distance, and the problem of exception. 'The most profound philosophical concepts tell us something like this: "If you want your life to have some meaning, you must accept the event, you must remain at a distance from power, and you must be firm in your decision"' (p13). In all philosophical situations there is an incommensurable, a relation between heterogeneous terms, or, 'relations that are not relations' (p15). This is where philosophy takes place; incommensurability is the sign for the philosopher to create new problems.

Žižek: 'You're sitting in a café and someone challenges you: "Come on let's discuss that in depth!" The philosopher will immediately say, "I'm sorry, I must leave", and will make sure he disappears as quickly as possible' (p49). Why is this? 'Philosophy is not a dialogue. Name me a single example of a successful philosophical dialogue that wasn't a dreadful misunderstanding. This is true also for the most prominent cases: Aristotle didn't understand Plato correctly; Hegel - who might have been pleased by the fact - of course didn't understand Kant. And Heidegger fundamentally didn't understand anyone at all. So, no dialogue' (p50). For Žižek, the philosopher's task is not to debate but to change the concepts of the debate, of the problematic

                    DOI:10.3898/NEWF.68.BOOKNOTES.2009

situation; the philosopher rejects the concepts of the debate.

This book brims with vitality and the conversational style makes it a joy to read; I can almost picture these two contemporary thinkers sat together rejecting concepts and creating new problems. Žižek still manages to get a few laughs out of his short piece, and his contrasting style seems to complement Badiou's. This is an accessible introduction to the thought and style of both thinkers, as well as an important intervention into the problem of philosophy today.

David W. Hill

Ben Carrington and Ian McDonald (eds), *Marxism, Cultural Studies and Sport*, London and New York, Routledge, 2009; 250pp, £25.99

Capitalism is in crisis, and so, entirely un-coincidentally, is professional sport, a principal branch of what I'm afraid we have to call the military-industrial-financial-media-entertainment complex. Bankers and hedge-fund managers, after a decade manipulating digital simulacra of money, turn out to be conjurers rather than magicians, though we (not they) pay the price. Meanwhile a footballer dives to 'win' a penalty; a rugby player feigns injury using a joke-shop blood capsule to enable an otherwise illegal substitution; a Formula One driver is ordered to crash so that his team-mate can win. 'Punishment' is lenient at best. Cheats prosper.

In this moment, then, *Marxism, Cultural Studies and Sport* is particularly welcome. There can be no better time to examine the ways in which both Marxism and Cultural Studies have enabled an examination of sport that can go beyond the merely biomechanical, the simplistically psychological or sociological descriptions of most sports studies, and beyond the cynical world of sports journalism and the nerdish bloggery of contemporary fandom. In proposing a closer relationship between Marxism and Cultural Studies, the editors duly acknowledge that neither approach has taken sport seriously or consistently enough - paradoxically, the existing branch-line of the Marxist sociology of sport disappeared in the turn to culture which marked the adoption of Gramsci's ideas, while in that child of the turn, Cultural Studies, work in the past decade has finally begun to address sport.

So there's a lot to talk about, and the book does very valuable work, the first three editorial chapters laying the groundwork and exploring possible alliances between a revolutionary Marxism of reinvigorated political-economic critique, and the identity-oriented politics of resistance which still suffuses Cultural Studies. The following section establishes further a critical political economy of sport as alienated labour. Rob Beamish's essay on the failure of de Coubertin's attempt to establish a symbolically emancipatory Olympics against the desires of capital and nation match Anouk Bélanger's and Garry Whannel's explorations of the commodified sports spectacle.

The third section offers Brett St Louis and Jayne O. Ifekwinige's essays on race, masculinity and femininity, set mainly in the context of professional American sports, athletes, and celebrity culture; these are offset by Grant Farred's somewhat eccentric discourse on 'Scouse' identity in relation to two key Liverpool FC players. The final section (and this is probably the best way round) turns to key theorists. For Toby Miller, Foucault's work can genuinely illuminate Marx's - he insists on the value of reading sport as a technique of the self that, at the same time, literally embodies relations of power and domination. Alan Barner, on the other hand, attempts to rescue Gramscian hegemony from what he sees as the notion's dilution from its progenitor's assumption that power relations were class relations, and that their resolution was only possible through revolutionary politics. Finally, David Andrews somewhat bleakly knits present-day commercialised, corporatised and spectacularised professional sport into Jameson's 'late' capitalism.

The book is - as it should be - an uncomfortable read. Fore and Afterwords, by the slightly self-righteous Harry Cleaver and the more playful Michael Bérubé, might lead the reader to think that this is merely because the two approaches (Marxism and Cultural Studies) are not yet ready for productive alliance, but taken as a whole the book also represents a sense of unease shared among many on the left, as the present crisis unfolds without more than symbolic opposition (and even that is pretty thin on the ground). Perhaps, just perhaps, more work in this area might, in helping us more fully to appreciate the role of sport in the military-etc. complex, also help us to see more clearly the way out of late capital's constrictions. So let's do it.

Andrew Blake

Joanna Zylinska, *Bioethics in the Age of New Media*, Cambridge, MIT Press, 2009; 240pp, £19.95 paperback

Joanna Zylinska's book is a wide-reaching and rich text. It has much to offer, particularly to researchers and students in philosophy and bioethics. Its project is to re-imagine bioethics through a critical theorisation of the current conditions of the field and a series of contemporary case studies. These cases - popular science writing, makeover television and bioart - are designated as 'bioethics in action'. These are used to call for a condition 'of letting oneself be-together-with-difference' (pxv) for a new bioethics.

A central strand of Zylinska's bioethical formulation could be designated as a move towards a non-human relationality, and in this respect it joins a body of work signalling new forms of relation. These could be labelled as: feminist relationality in science studies; the turn to Levinas and the face of the other in socio-political and philosophical accounts of the subject; and the turn to interspecies encounter. These developments have references to Haraway's pronouncement that: 'the terms pass into each other; they are shifting sedimentations of the one fundamental thing about the world - relationality' (p37). However, Zylinska departs from Haraway, and she is intensely critical of Haraway's later work, arguing that in the case of companion species Haraway remains disappointingly humanist. Nevertheless, relationality underpins parts of Zylinska's thesis on being together with difference, and she uses this in conjunction with Levinas in an attempt to leverage her own work 'off the hook of humanism' (p118) on which she contends that Haraway's work remains. In her departure from relationality Zylinska instead develops her own formulation 'of letting oneself be-together-with-difference' (p173). She proposes that this formulation should be regarded as 'a hospitable - if not uncritical and unconditional - opening toward technology' (pxv). Although these are intriguing arguments, this reading misses many of the directions that Haraway develops in *When Species Meet*.

In Zylinska's pursuit of a being together with difference that is beyond humanism, she advocates a new 'nonnormative ethics of responsibility' (p163) through her case studies. Bioart operates as the most fruitful case of her 'bioethics in action' (p162), and she provides an insightful review of this area. Zylinska suggests that in the work of Stellarc, SymbioticA, Critical Art Ensemble, Eduardo Kac and Adam Zaretsky, bioart can enact a new ethics if the following conditions are met: 'It is only in the never receding obligation to address the question of the (other) human and nonhuman, and to come to terms with the human's "originary technicity", that these different projects will be truly ethical' (p160). Zylinksa draws on Bernard Steigler's work here by accepting his argument that technology is 'originary', or that it is what makes the human. This is, for Zylinska, one of the most central conditions for ethical possibility. Thus, a new bioethics requires both an acknowledgement of the already technical nature of the human, and an acceptance of openness to non-human others. The figure for this new bioethics is imaginative and striking, appearing as: 'a way of cutting through the flow of life with a double-edged sword of productive power and infinite responsibility' (p179). This formulation seems to echo Karen Barad's conceptualisation of the 'agential cut', although Zylinska never references Barad's philosophical work directly.

In sum, Zylinska argues that the realm of institutional bioethics needs radical revision to come to terms with the kind of 'being-in-difference' that she contends is the condition of the lives of 'humans, animals and machines in the age of new media' (p174). Zylinksa implies that, although biotechnologies pervade everyday life, the spaces for ethical engagement are limited, and with this I concur. In this context Zylinska's project is a rich, provocative and contentious intervention, and I have found many parts of this book helpful in my own thinking. I do not agree with the arguments about Haraway, or about makeover television, but they have offered stimulating challenges.

Kate O'Riordan

Jean-François Lyotard, *Enthusiasm: The Kantian Critique of History*, Stanford, Stanford University Press, 2009; 74pp, $18.95 paperback

Enthusiasm was first presented by Jean-François Lyotard as a paper in 1981 at a seminar hosted by Jean-Luc Nancy and Philippe Lacoue-Labarthe at the Ecole Normale Supérieure. Positioned between his Freudo-Marxist work (*Libidinal Economy*) and that on social justice and ethics (*The Differend*), *Enthusiasm* expresses the intellectual concern at the time about the limitation of politics for social change, that crisis of the left that came to be post-Marxism.

Here Lyotard takes a Wittgensteinian philosophy of phrases and maps it on to the Kantian faculties in order to think through issues of difference and justice, in so doing illuminating his own notions of dissensus and the differend. Kant's Third Critique, judgement, is read in the light of Lyotard's concern for respecting the heterogeneity of phrase families. Lyotard sketches a Fourth Critique, or 'Critique of Political Reason' (p11), whereby the judge judges the legitimacy of a phrase's claims to validity but also attests to the coexistence of heterogeneous phrase families. Judging is a matter of steering between these phrase families, like a navigator through an archipelago.

Kant's notion of the sublime is instructive for Lyotard; the sublime opens up a gap in judgement analogous to the incommensurability between phrase families. We glimpse this sublime gap in unpredictable events such as the French Revolution. Enthusiasm is this strong sense of the sublime experienced in revolutionary events, a 'painful joy' (p31) brought about by the unpresentable, 'almost pure disorder' of the revolution, 'devoid of figure' but 'really big however in historical nature' (p33). It is an expression of the desire for movement towards civil peace, or even international peace. For example, in the aftermath of Auschwitz, its visibility as a revolutionary event meant that 'an abyss opened up when an object capable of validating the phrase of the Idea of human rights must be presented'; or during May '68 'an abyss opened up before the phrase of "democratic" illusion, which hid the heterogeneity between power and sovereignty' (p63). These abysses are the gaps between an Idea and whatever presents itself in order to realise the idea, a sublime space evocative of enthusiasm that forces us to judge without criteria. When judging there is no rule to follow, says Lyotard, but we must critically judge nonetheless, whilst respecting the differend (or, the incommensurability of heterogeneous phrase families). This is a political manoeuvre.

This is a fine translation by Georges Van Den Abbeele, and his preface is far more vital than most translators' prefaces, concerned as they so often are with expressing the difficulty of their own task. None of this from Van Den Abbeele, as he contextualises and frames the text well, concluding by demonstrating the continuing relevance of the provocative thought contained in this slim and handsome book: the increasing importance of just manoeuvres in an information saturated society.

David W. Hill

Abstracts

DELEUZIAN POLITICS: A SURVEY AND SOME SUGGESTIONS

Jeremy Gilbert

This article surveys and evaluates the broad field of Deleuzian political theory with particular reference to its novel implications for anglophone cultural theory. It opens by discussing Mengue's and Hallward's recent critical studies of Deleuze and the wider problem of evaluating the normative and descriptive function of key Deleuzian concepts. It goes on to consider the specificity of Deleuzian approaches to the key notion of 'essentialism' with reference to a comparison between the ideas of Manuel Delanda and Ernesto Laclau and Chantal Mouffe, before moving into a consideration of recent appropriations of Deleuzian philosophy for the theorisation of gender and race. From there it goes on to consider various Marxist and post-Marxist uses of Deleuzian thought for the theorisation of capital, labour and the state in the work of writers such as Thoburn, Read and Lazaratto, following this with a consideration of recent debates over the status of democracy in Deleuze's political thought, arguing against any liberal interpretations thereof that would minimise the anti-individualism of this ideas or collapse its advocacy of 'rhizomatic' relations into an argument for the universal desirability of market logics. It moves on from here to argue for the relevance of Deleuze and Guattari's thought to green politics, and to the importance of understanding 'affect' as an irreducibly social, multi-directional and polyvalent phenomenon in recent cultural theory.

Keywords Deleuze; Guattari; anti-essentialism; democracy; Laclau; Delanda; Mengue; liberalism; rhizome; market; feminism

POLITICS AS THE ORIENTATION OF EVERY ASSEMBLAGE

Veronique Bergen

This essay is concerned with the question of where politics, as Deleuze understands it, resides. Vitalism dictates an understanding of politics as, in fact, the correlate of every assemblage (of thought or desire, individual or collective), and affiliates it to the ethical question of an affirmation of the powers of life. Every assemblage is *ipso facto* political in that it manifests a particular orientation to life, enriching it or mutilating it: it being understood that the consistency to be given to it is perpetually under construction, without any *a priori* guarantees. The article shows the ways in which the task of politics is cartographic, pragmatic - charting the composition of lines, and their consequences - and not hermeneutic. In the first section, we unpack the conceptual operators which Deleuze and Guattari make use of to develop their understanding of the political (the types of lines and the molar/molecular schema); in the second section we consider their triple impact (politics understood as an index of the bearing a body, situating itself in the paradox of a passive volition and shattering the distinction between the resignation of the beautiful soul and voluntaristic engagement). We conclude with an analysis of Bartleby as singular figure of an ethical-political orientation.

Keywords Deleuze; Guattari; vitalism; cartography; orientation; Bartleby

ON PUTTING THE ACTIVE BACK INTO ACTIVISM

Rosi Braidotti

This paper addresses a paradox: how to engage in affirmative politics, which entails the production of social horizons of hope, while at the same time doing critical theory, which means resisting the present. Drawing on the neo-vitalism of Deleuze, with reference to Nietzsche and Spinoza, the article argues in favour of an affirmative ethics: defined as a radical ethics of transformation. This new framework for re-thinking ethics moves away from the moral protocols of Kantian universalism, while also shifting its focus from unitary, rationality-driven consciousness to an understanding of subjectivity as processual in nature, propelled by affects and relations. Such a new framework disengages the emergence of the subject from the logic of negation and attaches subjectivity to affirmative otherness. Hence the self-other relation is reconceived in terms of reciprocity as creation and not as the recognition of Sameness. Taking critical distance from modern conceptions of self-centred individualism and the negative production of hierarchically inferior others which it assumes, an affirmative ethics for a non-unitary subject as proposed here aims at offering an enlarged sense of inter-connection between self and others, including the non-human or 'earth' others, following and enhancing the tradition of a bio-centred egalitarianism (Ansell-Pearson, 1999) that posits a nature-culture continuum (Haraway, 1997). Moreover by putting the emphasis on the positivity of affirmative ethics - conceived in a depsychologised sense similar to that of Nietzsche and Spinoza - the article suggests an ethics of sustainability: one that provides the subject with a frame for interaction and change, growth and movement; an ethics that affirms life as difference-at-work.

Key words affirmative ethics; vitalism; biopolitics; immanence; becoming; futurity; Deleuze; Nietzsche; Spinoza

A TRAGIC NOTE: ON NEGRI AND DELEUZE IN THE LIGHT OF THE 'ARGENTINAZO'

Jorge Camacho

In a conversation between Antonio Negri and Gilles Deleuze, translated under the title 'Control and Becoming', the former philosopher denounced the problematic status of the latter's work - specifically *A Thousand Plateaus*, co-authored with Félix Guattari - in the context of political philosophy. For Negri, as we gather from his comments, inasmuch as Deleuze's framework is essential for thinking about the contemporary world, it remains a catalogue of unresolved problems on the all-important topic of politics. One of the central points of divergence is related to Negri's optimistic and teleological philosophical orientation vis-à-vis Deleuze's decidedly non-teleological ontology and philosophy of history. Negri famously hears a 'tragic note' in Deleuze's open-ended account. This article explores and evaluates this divergence, philosophically and politically, in the light of the period of revolts and radical political experimentation that broke out in Argentina after 2001. Siding with Deleuze, philosophically and politically, it concludes that the positive outcome of such a 'tragic' perspective is a constant concern for launching and re-launching instances of concrete political experimentation with a regard for just this open-endedness of the historical horizon.

Keywords Deleuze; Negri; Argentina; politics; teleology; ontology; multitude; biopolitics; multiplicity; experience

BECOMING VULVA: FLESH, FOLD, INFINITY

Patricia MacCormack

The relation between morphology and becoming-woman is a contentious one. Deleuze and Guattari have been critiqued by Irigaray as fetishising woman. However Irigaray, Deleuze and Guattari each posit a challenge to phallologocentric paradigms through real life becomings via reconfigurations - beyond metaphor or alternate subjectifiation - of the subject as enfleshed. Subjectivity is manifold and folds with other subjects, so the subject is never entirely present to the self and never extricated from the connexions it makes. Such multiplicity, fluidity and connectivity negotiate the singularity, stability and dividuation inherent to phallologic. Deleuze and Guattari's understanding of 'Becoming', and Irigaray's model of the two lips, directly respond to the symbol of the phallus. As an experiment in extending and exploring these concepts, while simultaneously attempting to create a fold between the theories, this article offers the idea of 'becoming-vulva'. The vulva, with all its symbolic and psychoanalytic associations, is itself both the blind spot and rupture of the phallic. As a folding and folded organ the vulva is temporally metamorphic and apprehended through aspect rather than totality. It constitutes a schema of organ and pleasure which resonates with the folded and folding structure of desire itself. In this article both the vulva and desire are grounded in the political and ethical contexts of this feminist project while also being an abstract territory that opens out and potentialises ways of thinking the flesh.

Keywords Deleuze; Guattari; feminism; The Fold; morphology; Irigaray; vulva; corporeality

BECOMING-WOMAN BY BREAKING THE WAVES

Chrysanthi Nigianni

Begins from the argument that Deleuze's method of 'transcendental empiricism' requires a shift in the way we conceptualise both 'ethics' and 'politics'. This shift is examined in relation to the cinematic thinking of the film *Breaking the Waves*, since the latter problematises established ideas of what an ethics of (sexual) difference might be, as well as received political values tied to modern individualism such as freedom, autonomy, and reason. Moving through a filmosophical methodology, it is argued that the film manages to provide us with a post-theistic framework that resonates but also pushes further Deleuze's transcendentalism, opening new paths for a radicalisation of feminist materialist theories. *Breaking the Waves* provides us with a notion of (becoming-) woman in relation to Man that breaks away from the established discourses of difference, equality, reciprocity and respect that have traditionally informed the Self-Other relation, bringing in the themes of sacrifice, stupidity and belief. The latter constitute new political forces that actualise an-other politics: an affective activism and a vitalist pragmatism, that reinvent freedom on the level of non-representation.

Keywords transcendental empiricism; freedom; becoming-woman; ethics; post-theism; *Breaking the Waves*; Deleuze

QUEER VITALISM

Claire Colebrook

Starting from Deleuze's and Guattari's distinction between passive and active vitalism as set out in their last book, *What is Philosophy?*, this article posits the possibility of a new conceptualisation of political bodies outside notions of individual will, intent and agency: mobilising forces of change from within in the act of encountering. Moving away from the active vitalism of resisting and overcoming - acts that always imply new normative images/representations of 'being otherwise', being thus aligned to what Deleuze and Guattari would call majoritarian politics - passive vitalism mobilises forces of change from within the act of encountering, understood as the emanation and interaction of potentials always already found in the forces, percepts and affects that constitute actual bodies. Contrary to an active vitalism that strives to overcome the imposed norms that would reduce an individual's autonomy, but that also takes into account the vitality of traditions, cultures and practices that constitute bodies as individuals and agents in the first place, a passive vitalism is one of re-singularisation or counter-actualisation: this means that it takes bodies as they are, with their identifying and determining features, and then asks how the potentials that enabled those features might be expanded. It is within this new suggested framework that the article revisits gender and sexual politics: in terms of potentials and the virtual, and in radical distance from politics of recognition and theories of subjection. It thus suggests a new post-human articulation of the 'I' as a second, belated perceiving, understood not as a transcendent grasping but as one affectuation among others.

Keywords vitalism; Leibnitz; immanence; minor politics; schizoanalysis; queer; feminism; Deleuze

WEATHERMAN, THE MILITANT DIAGRAM, AND THE PROBLEM OF POLITICAL PASSION

Nicholas Thoburn

This paper is a critique of the political figure of the militant. In particular it seeks to understand the ways militancy effectuates processes of political passion and a certain unworking or deterritorialisation of the self in relation to political organisations and the wider social environment within which militants would enact change. To this end the paper traces a diagram or abstract machine of militancy, a diagram comprised of Guattari's cartography of Leninism and the model of struggle set out by the Russian nihilist Sergei Nechaev. Foregrounding specific techniques and affective and semiotic registers, the paper explores a particular animation of abstract militant functions in the Weatherman organisation in the United States at the turn of the 1970s. It then sketches the principle outlines of a counter figure - an 'a-militant diagram', or dispersive ecology of political composition - that draws together Marx's figure of the party, Jacques Camatte's critique of the political 'racket', and Deleuze and Guattari's approach to the problem of the group and its outside.

Keywords militant; Weather Underground; political semiotics; political affect; activism

DELEUZIAN POLITICS? A ROUNDTABLE

Éric Alliez, Claire Colebrook, Peter Hallward and Nicholas Thoburn

A discussion on Deleuze and politics with topics covered including: Deleuze's relationship to Marxism and capitalism; the political valency of the concept of deterritorialisation; the implications of Deleuzian thought for theorisations of collectivity and identity; its implications for thinking about revolution, universality and the party form; the problems of desire and the decision; issues of ecology and the implications of vitalism for them; problems of political strategy and organisation; the legacy of the invasion of Iraq.

Keywords Deleuze; Guattari; politics; Marxism; capitalism; deterritorialisation; collective will; passive vitalism; revolution; universality; desire

Why not Subscribe?

New Formations is published three times a year. Make sure of your copy by subscribing.

SUBSCRIPTION RATES FOR 2010 (3 ISSUES)

Individual Subscriptions
UK & Rest of World   **£40.00**

Institutional Subscriptions
UK & Rest of World   **£145.00**

Back issues: £14.99 plus £2 post and packing for individuals
                £45.00 plus £2 post and packing for institutions

Please send one year's subscription

starting with Issue Number   _____

I enclose payment of   _____

Please send me _____ copies of back issue no.   _____

I enclose total payment of   _____

Name   _____

Address   _____

_____ Postcode _____

Please return this form with cheque or money order (sterling only) payable to Lawrence & Wishart to: Lawrence and Wishart (Subs), PO Box 7701, Latchington, Chelmsford, CM3 6WL. Payments may also be made by credit/debit card (not American Express).